Beyond the Amur

Contemporary Chinese Studies

This series provides new scholarship and perspectives on modern and contemporary China, including China's contested borderlands and minority peoples; ongoing social, cultural, and political changes; and the varied histories that animate China today.

A list of titles in this series appears at the end of this book.

Beyond the Amur

Frontier Encounters between China and Russia, 1850–1930

VICTOR ZATSEPINE

UBC Press • Vancouver • Toronto

26 25 24 23 22 21 20 19 18 17 5 4 3 2

Printed in Canada on FSC-certified ancient-forest-free paper (100% post-consumer recycled) that is processed chlorine- and acid-free.

ISBN 9780774834094 (hardback)
ISBN 9780774834100 (pbk.)
ISBN 9780774834117 (pdf)
ISBN 9780774834124 (epub)
ISBN 9780774834131 (mobi)

Cataloguing-in-publication data for this book is available from Library and Archives Canada.

UBC Press gratefully acknowledges the financial support for our publishing program of the Government of Canada (through the Canada Book Fund) and the British Columbia Arts Council.

This book has been published with the help of the University of British Columbia through the K.D. Srivastava Fund.

Printed and bound in Canada by Friesens

Set in Garamond by Marquis Interscript
Copy editor: Matthew Kudelka
Indexer: Sergey Lobachev
Cover design: George Kirkpatrick

UBC Press
The University of British Columbia
2029 West Mall
Vancouver, BC V6T 1Z2
www.ubcpress.ca

To my parents, Margarita Viktorovna and Vladimir Ilyich

Contents

Figures and Tables

FIGURES

Tables

Preface

When the Soviet Union collapsed in 1991, vibrant cross-border trade between Russia and China emerged. In 1993, as a Russian exchange student living in China, I visited Heihe, a bordertown in Heilongjiang Province, where restless peddlers, Chinese and Russian, bargained in crowded markets and shipped cheap Chinese goods in oversized bags across the Amur River, an international border. People communicated with the help of electronic calculators and basic dictionaries. It was a chaotic place, where alcohol was cheap and trade negotiations were accompanied by drinking, shouting, and laughter. This grassroots border trade created an atmosphere of two overlapping cultures, united by economic interest and renewed curiosity about each other after several decades of ideological standoff between China and the Soviet Union. At the time, a local Chinese trader revealed to me that the Heihe municipal government hoped to turn this town into the Hong Kong of northeastern China. Returning a decade later, I did not see the same energy and optimism on the part of local traders. Cross-border trade continued, but in a more orderly fashion. Heihe had become a boom town, its best hotel complete with a revolving restaurant on the top, overlooking the underdeveloped Russian town of Blagoveshchensk across the Amur.

The Amur River – Амур in Russian, Heilongjiang (Black Dragon River) in Chinese – separates not only two cities but also two states and two distinct cultures, European and Asian. No international bridge has been built across this river, despite official plans to foster cross-border trade. The river flows from the mountains and plains of northeastern

China and Mongolia, marking the Chinese–Russian border along much of its course, before flowing through Siberia to the Sea of Okhotsk, beyond which lies the Pacific Ocean. In Heihe and Blagoveshchensk, local authorities use separate ferries for Chinese and Russians, and border guard vessels occasionally patrol the river. Winter crossings are less regulated, as people can simply walk from one shore to the other. The frozen river serves as a convenient highway.

The river is a silent witness to this region's past. The two countries disagree on the region's shared history: a visit to local museums in 2004 revealed contrasting official interpretations of the Amur frontier region's history. The Chinese Historical Museum in Aigun, an old Manchu outpost near Heihe, tells a story of Russian imperialist conquest of the lands north of the Amur. In 1858 and 1860, Russia annexed the Amur Basin and the Ussuri region under the terms of the Aigun and Peking Treaties. The Amur River became part of the world's longest border. The river acquired strategic significance: for Russia, as a route to the Pacific, and for the Qing state, as a key to the river system of Manchuria. The Chinese museum focuses on the military dimension of Russian expansionism, the seizure of Qing territory, and the destruction of Manchu settlements on the Amur. Another permanent exhibition in this museum is devoted to the tragic events of the Blagoveshchensk Massacre (1900), when Russian Cossacks killed several thousand Chinese civilians and invaded Manchuria. Life-size dioramas display in graphic detail the brutal methods used by the Russian forces to kill innocent Chinese civilians. The museum, as well as the town of Aigun, is closed to Russian visitors. Designed for the patriotic education of a domestic audience, this museum reminds the Chinese people of China's humiliations at the hands of Imperial Russia. Officially, China and Russia are now two friendly nations: Russian tourists and traders are welcome guests in Heihe. By allowing Russians into Heihe but blocking their access to Aigun, local Chinese authorities separate the past from the present and separate trade from potentially harmful historical narratives.

On the Russian side, the Blagoveshchensk Museum of Local History mentions the massacre of 1900 only briefly. Instead, it tells the story of Imperial Russia's centuries-old interest in geographic discoveries in the Russian Far East. It singles out 1689 as the year that Qing forces drove Russian Cossacks out of the Amur Basin, forcing Russia to sign the Treaty of Nerchinsk and preventing its further advance in this region. A panoramic oil painting captures an armed clash between Qing and Russian troops. It presents Manchu soldiers with evil faces, while Russian Cossacks look like heroic victims and carry Russian Orthodox icons. Local tour guides describe 1858 as the year that Count Nikolai Nikolaevich Murav'ev, governor of Eastern Siberia (1847–61), rightfully returned empty lands north of the Amur to Russia. The museum glorifies the Russian occupation of the region. An enormous portrait of a noble-looking Count Murav'ev hangs not far from the painting depicting Russian losses in the Amur in 1689, as a tribute to the man who gained new territories for Russia. All over the Russian Far East, Murav'ev is revered as a symbol of Russia's imperial glory, as a true patriot and a national hero. A peninsula in the Russian Far East is named after him.

These local museums reduce the past of the Amur frontier region to several episodes of rivalry between imperial states, minimizing the role played by the local people and by developments on the ground. Each empire presents the region as marginal, with no significant social history of its own. Official historical writings about this region in Russia and in the People's Republic of China are politically charged. Each country stands by its own interpretation of Sino-Russian cross-border relations during the late nineteenth century; both use the past to justify their present-day concerns about a shared border. Not content with official historical narratives, which tend to focus on provincial officials and the patriotism of the local people who sacrificed themselves in the face of foreign aggression, this study illuminates the shared local history of the Russian Far East and Manchuria, analyzing that history from social, economic, and cultural viewpoints. This book is the culmination of years of reassessing the history of the Amur River.

Acknowledgments

Writing one's first book is a journey along a bumpy road. I have been very fortunate to study, travel, and work in different places in Russia, Asia, and North America, where I met interesting people and many highly original minds. My teachers, colleagues, and friends greatly encouraged me during the torturous process of writing this book. I must express my gratitude first to Diana Lary, Steven Hugh Lee, and Alexander Woodside in the History Department at the University of British Columbia. Without their support, intellectual stimulation, and knowledge of Chinese, East Asian, and world history, I would never be able to cross the boundaries of traditional nation-centred historical narratives. Diana Lary's generosity and humanity continues to guide me in my work and daily life. At UBC and in the rest of Canada, I would also like to thank Olga Bakich, Blaine R. Chiasson, Anne Gorsuch, Colin Green, Ross King, Daniel Labbé, Glen Peterson, Leo Shin, Norman Smith, and Wang Ning for their interest in my research and friendship.

The late Neil Burton, Jennifer Clibbon, Virginia Hulme, Norman Smith, Ronald Suleski, Laura Victoir, and Jo Wilson read parts or all of the manuscript and offered valuable criticism. I am indebted to them.

In Beijing, I owe thanks to Kim Donggil, Niu Dayong, and Xu Ping in the History Department of Peking University as well as to Bu Ping and Xue Xiantian at the Institute of Modern Chinese History, Chinese Academy of Social Sciences. In northeastern China, the staff of the Heilongjiang Academy of Social Sciences' Institute of History, Harbin Municipal Library, and Jilin University Library helped me navigate

Chinese-language sources. In Hong Kong, the History Department and the Library of the University of Hong Kong provided an excellent research environment. Bert Becker, John Carrol, Ryan Crew, Peter Cunich, Mark Frost, Priscilla Roberts, Maureen Sabin, Laura Victoir, Victor Teo, Zhou Xun, and Xu Guoqi – among many others – were always generous with ideas and advice. Loretta Kim and Matthew Mosca, with whom I co-organized a conference on Qing borders at the University of Hong Kong, challenged my perceptions about frontier history. On Lamma Island in Hong Kong, where I lived, Jo Wilson taught me how to avoid running over poisonous snakes while riding a bicycle. In Sydney, special thanks to Catherine Armitage for making it possible for me to travel to both sides of the Amur River in 2004.

In Russia, I am grateful to the staff of the Oriental Collection of the Moscow Historical Library, the Khabarovsk Regional Museum and Archives, and the Russian State Archive of the Far East in Vladivostok. In San Francisco, the late Vladimir Shkurkin generously provided access to his private Far Eastern archive and photocopying machine. At the University of Hawaii Library, Patricia Polanski facilitated my access to historical sources about Russians in Asia. At the University of Connecticut, where I currently work and finished writing this book, I thank my colleagues at the History Department and at the Asian and Asian American Studies Institute for their support and a friendly working environment.

Parts of Chapter 4 and Chapter 7 appeared in articles in two edited volumes: "The Amur: As River, as Border," in *The Chinese State at the Borders*, edited by Diana Lary (Vancouver: UBC Press, 2007), 151–61; and "The Blagoveshchensk Massacre of 1900: The Sino-Russian War and Global Imperialism," in *Beyond Suffering: Recounting War in Modern China*, edited by James Flath and Norman Smith (Vancouver: UBC Press, 2011), 107–29. These chapters have been revised and updated for this book.

I thank UBC Press, especially Emily Andrew, who patiently guided me through the process of getting the manuscript approved for publication; Matthew Kudelka for his copy-editing; and Eric Leinberger for producing maps; as well as two anonymous reviewers for their useful criticisms and suggestions. I am grateful to the Asian and Asian American Studies Institute and the College of Liberal Arts and Sciences at the University of Connecticut and to the Chiang Ching-kuo Foundation for International Scholarly Exchange for providing financial support towards the publishing costs.

I will always remember with great affection my great-aunt, the late Maria Nikolaevna Sadchikova, who not only provided me with shelter in Moscow and the most delicious borsch, but also taught me a great deal about patience. My final thanks go to my parents, Margarita Viktorovna and Vladimir Ilyich, who are happily retired in Samara, the city from where my global journey started in the late 1980s. They worked very hard to achieve success in their highly scientific professions and always encouraged me to be passionate about work and life. This book is dedicated to them.

Note on Spelling

Transliteration of Russian words follows the US Library of Congress system, except for words and names that are popularly known by a different spelling – for example, "Tolstoy." In some cases, the Russian letters й and ий can be transliterated by the English letters *i, ii* or *y.* For example, I use Amursk*ii,* but other authors prefer Amursk*y*. Both are correct. The same rule applies to the Russian letter я, which in English can be either *ia* or *ya.* I use *Ia*ponska*ia,* which can also be *Ya*ponska*ya.* For Chinese words I follow the Pinyin system, with the exception of widely accepted names such as Chiang Kai-shek, Peking, or the names that European authors spelled differently. For example, I use Mukden, but it was also spelled Moukden. For Russian and Chinese words it is almost impossible to escape variations, as two different systems of romanization are applied to them.

Beyond the Amur

Introduction

The Amur frontier region's geographic features, cultural diversity, and long history make it truly unique. Its scenery changes dramatically, from steppe to mountains, from wetlands to coniferous forests, and its eastern edge borders a sea dotted with islands. For millennia, the lands of the Amur River and its tributaries have been home to numerous indigenous peoples and distinct cultures, including the Xianbei, Mohe, Khitan, Tungus, Jurchen, Mongol, Korean, and Chinese. Before the Mongol Conquest in the thirteenth century, this region was home at times to great ancient states and dynasties such as the Koguryo, Parhae (Bohai), Liao, and Jin, some of which ruled parts of China. The region was conquered by Chinese dynasties and finally claimed by the Great Qing Dynasty (1644–1911), whose Manchu rulers arose from the Jurchen tribes who lived in the forests between the Sungari (Songhua) and Yalu rivers. Beginning in the mid-nineteenth century, Imperial Russia expanded into the Amur frontier region, and this pressured the Qing government to open these lands to Chinese agricultural settlement. Since then, the region has seen unprecedented economic development, including burgeoning trade, new towns, railways, and commercial agriculture. It has also become a focus of domestic and international rivalries and even military conflicts that have changed the course of Russian and East Asian history.

I use the terms "Amur frontier region," "Amur frontier," "Amur River Basin," or simply "Amur" to describe the lands reached by the Amur River and its tributaries. This territory extends from the Manchurian Plain in the south to the Stanovoi Mountains in the north, and from the northeastern edge of the Mongolian Steppe to the shores of the Sea of Japan and the Sea of Okhotsk, covering an area larger than France, Germany, and Spain combined. Until 1858, this land was part of the Qing Empire, with the northern border loosely defined along the Stanovoi Mountains. Parts of this geographic area overlap with the political and administrative entities known as Manchuria,[1] Trans-Baikal, Eastern Siberia, and the Russian Far East.

"Manchuria" refers to the administrative region north of the Shanhai Guan, or the Shanhai Pass of the Great Wall, and south of the Qing-Russian border as defined by the Nerchinsk Treaty of 1689, from which the Qing claimed its authority in the region. Manchuria borders traditional eastern Mongolian land, which was partly incorporated by the Qing into the Manchu Banner administration. This region was ruled by the Qing military administration from garrison towns, of which Mukden and Qiqiha'er were the largest. In 1907, Manchuria became a fixed administrative region comprising three provinces (Dongsansheng), with provincial centres in Qiqiha'er, Jilin and Fengtian.

The Russian Far East (Dal'nii Vostok in Russian) did not have fixed boundaries and overlapped with different parts of eastern and northeastern Siberia, stretching to the North Pacific, until 1884, when the new Priamur Governor-Generalship was established. Since then, the Russian Far East has been a fixed territorial/administrative unit composed of several *oblast* and *krai*, or provinces. Two of these provinces, Amur and Maritime (Primorskii), have boundaries with China. Together, they are referred to as Priamur'e or Priamurskii region. The Russian Far East, under different names and internal territorial and administrative divisions, survived well in the 1930s. From the mid-1920s until the collapse of the Soviet Union, it was referred to as the Soviet Far East.

This book treats the Amur frontier region as a distinct place shaped by geography, climate, migration, and trade, where local interests and developments did not always align with state-sponsored expansion initiatives. It analyzes the Amur River Basin as a place, a local experience, and an imperial policy, all three bound in a complex triangular relationship that does not easily fit any preconceived formula, because each factor interacted with the others and changed over time. Geography and climate influenced human activities in the region, affecting local trade and expansion initiatives. The region's local societies emerged as a result of encounters between the indigenous people and the newcomers, encounters that were strongly shaped by the challenges of climate and geography. In particular, alliances and rivalries revolved around access to natural resources. When Imperial Russia and the Qing dynasty arrived in this region in their quest for resources, their efforts were often impeded by insufficient knowledge and overconfidence in their abilities.

The natural features of Amur frontier region greatly influenced human activities there. My identification of the Amur River system as a binding factor holding together this frontier region recognizes how the region's varied topography influenced human activity along this river. Settlement initiatives, railway building, economic expansion, urban development, and war all transformed the lives of local people, but that change was distributed unevenly, and many remote parts of this region remained untouched by modern civilization. In the twentieth century, the collapse of empires in China and Russia transformed the central and regional governments as well as the political regimes and social networks in this frontier region.

Geography and climate left a permanent mark on local society. Fertile land and rich natural resources, such as minerals and furs, made it an inviting place for private and state interests. But at the same time, the harsh climate, dense forests, mountainous terrain, long distances, and bad roads made access to this region difficult. As a result, most parts of this region remained isolated and sparsely settled. Nevertheless, the vast river system provided transportation routes connecting different parts of the region. That system had long served as a natural highway for the various indigenous groups, and newcomers learned to use it as well.

On a socio-economic level, indigenous tribes and newcomers encountered each other in the Amur region. Migrants, traders, and exiles came into contact with the indigenous people, and they interacted with each other through trade or the exchange of labour. Indigenous groups, such as the Goldi and the Orochen, served as intermediaries between the newcomers and nature, facilitating access to the region's natural riches, which included furs, ginseng, and gold. As they interacted, they borrowed from each other's cultures, establishing a hybrid society, different from that of southern Manchuria or eastern Siberia. Individual traders, whether Chinese or Russian, did not wait for government approval to extract rich natural resources, and they established trading networks in forest products long before the empires moved to regulate their activities. Chinese migrants and traders were the most entrepreneurial newcomers to this region. They dominated trade with the indigenous peoples and defied official restrictions on cross-border travel and trade imposed by the Qing and Russian states. This disregard for rules and authority characterized Amur frontier society; the imperial authorities could not effectively control the region.

On a political level, the Amur frontier region was the target of Russian imperial expansion and Qing internal colonization. After 1860, it became a border region between two empires. Russia claimed parts of it in 1858 by military occupation, forcing the Qing to sign the Treaty of Aigun, which gave Russia the northern bank of the Amur River. From the 1850s well into the twentieth century, Russia engaged in a variety of initiatives to expand its influence in the region, including geographic expeditions, production of maps, negotiation of borders, the introduction of settlers from European Russia, and railway construction. These initiatives were carried out with varying degrees of commitment. They were far from consistent until the 1890s, when Russia – like other European powers – began pursuing its imperial ambitions in China through concessions and spheres of influence. Instead of establishing firm control over the Amur frontier region, Imperial Russia moved into Manchuria (with an eye to the Korean Peninsula), launching two major colonization projects there: "peaceful economic penetration" by railway, and the military occupation of Manchuria in 1900, which lasted until Russia's war with Japan in 1904.

The Qing's efforts in Manchuria were more defensive in nature and led to the growing involvement of Chinese labour and trade beyond Manchuria into the Russian Far East, something that Russian and Qing officials had not anticipated. At first, Russia took advantage of Qing neglect of the Manchurian frontier. The Qing dynasty's fiscal and military weakness during the late nineteenth century limited its ability to contain Imperial Russia's economic and military expansion in Manchuria. Russia's lavish financing of the Trans-Siberian and Chinese Eastern Railways was part of a long-term plan to colonize the Russian Far East and Manchuria. Ha'erbin, Dalian, and Lüshun (known in Russian/English as Harbin, Dalny, and Port Arthur, respectively) were built on the foundations of existing Chinese settlements. At the same time, the Qing reorganization of Manchuria's frontier after 1905, part of empire-wide New Policy reforms, took advantage of Russia's perennial weaknesses in its eastern borderlands – specifically, its sparse population and undeveloped local agriculture. Qing rulers opened Manchuria for settlement and offered its land for sale and rent, counting on Chinese migrants to strengthen the Qing border with Russia. The arrival of Chinese and Korean agricultural settlers in Manchuria helped revive the region's agriculture, trade, and economy.

As a result, Manchuria acquired a strong regional identity, which the Russian Far East lacked.

This book focuses on the period from 1850 to 1930, when this region saw an explosion of economic and other activity. During this time, the two empires and their successor states failed to maintain a strong border. Because there was little control over the flow of people and goods across the border, existing informal cross-border trading networks and economic activities expanded, as did zones of interaction between the two empires' subjects. Facing a shortage of labour to exploit the region's rich natural resources, Russia relied on Chinese contract labour recruited from China Proper, especially Shandong and Zhili[2] provinces. Lacking its own agricultural base on the Amur and having failed to attract enough peasants from European Russia to feed the region, Russian provincial governments depended on agricultural products from Manchuria. Qing subjects dominated the region's labour force, replacing Russians in railway building, in construction, and in the service sector. They also displaced the indigenous people in extracting forest resources and delivering them to the growing towns on both sides of the border.

The tensions between formal imperial expansionist initiatives and local developments on the ground shaped this frontier region. These tensions were revealed every time grand plans were delayed or interrupted – for example, by the Boxer Rebellion, which spread to Manchuria in 1900. Often, state policies were ineffective because of poor management, sabotage, official corruption, and an inability to enforce the law. After the Russo-Japanese War, neither the Russian nor Qing governments were able to quickly re-establish control over this frontier. These two overextended empires almost simultaneously began introducing radical economic and administrative reforms to strengthen their authority and the local economy (Russia in the Amur and Maritime provinces, the Qing in northern Manchuria). These efforts were hindered, however, by a lack of resources in terms of competent administrators, settlers, funding, and stable institutions. Nevertheless, these efforts resulted in short periods of economic revival, which were interrupted by civil conflicts and international competition.

This study rethinks the concept of *historical frontier* as a place where individuals, social groups, and states interact. In what follows, *frontier* (or *frontier region*) refers to a large peripheral zone defined by geography and human activity. There is no single Chinese or Russian term that captures all the complexities of the different historical references to borders and frontiers in the long imperial histories of these countries. *Prigranichnyi raion* is the closest term in Russian: *prigranichnyi* is derived from *granitsa* (border). The Chinese terms *bianjiang* (border area, frontier), *bianjiang qu* (frontier region), and *jiangyu* (territory) best reflect this definition. The Chinese character *jiang* comprises three sub-components meaning *fields*, *territory*, and a *weapon*, which injects a "defensive" or "offensive" element into its meaning.[3] In contrast, the Chinese character *jie*, in words like *bianjie* (border) and *bianjiexian* (boundary line), means a clear division or dividing line.

This book re-evaluates long-established traditions of studying historical frontiers in the West. Historians have used the word "frontier" without properly defining it in relation to a particular temporal or spatial setting. "Frontier history" as a separate field in Western historiography carries the same ambiguity as the term "frontier" itself. In the twentieth century, it has been associated with Frederick Turner's pioneering work on the North American West.[4] Turner used the term "frontier" to trace the history of Anglo-Saxon westward expansion in the United States and Canada. Mixed into his loose definition of frontier were the open lands of the North American West, geographic expansion, human interaction with the landscape, and social evolution. Turner's Western frontier was more than a place; it was a migratory region, a stage of society, an imagined place.

Turner's frontier thesis linked regional history with the history of the United States. He demonstrated that the pioneer spirit of settlers shaped the national character of the United States. His work has inspired generations of scholars. One of them, Harold Innis, similarly explained the formation of Canadian frontiers as a result of human interaction with the landscape.[5] He focused on the extractive economy and on staple products such as fur, beaver, and cod. According to Innis, the fur trade stimulated Canada's westward expansion and shaped Canadian history. The main actors in his economic history were the Hudson's Bay Company and the North West Company, founded by Scottish and French traders.

Turner and Innis have both been criticized for making too many generalizations regarding frontier history and for presenting the frontier as a passive periphery waiting to be developed by a civilized core. By focusing on European agents of westward expansion, such scholarship has overlooked the role played by indigenous people in frontier trade and development and has failed to appreciate the diversity of the settlers, especially in the late nineteenth century. More recent frontier studies in North America have emphasized the dependence of white settlers on indigenous populations for the development of trade networks.[6] They also question the myth of the frontier spirit, or individualism, by demonstrating the role of the federal government, the British Crown, and trading monopolies in managing – or mismanaging – the North American frontiers.[7] David Weber in his work on the Mexican frontier suggests that "frontiers usually have two sides, both of them human," and argues that the agents of change came from both directions.[8] According to him, Mexican frontier society and the Mexican government's failure to manage its northern frontier should be taken into account when discussing the success of the American West.

Taking into account the approach of more recent frontier studies scholars such as Weber, this book looks at the Amur frontier region from different angles, examining local agents of change as well as state institutions. The Amur frontier region and the North American frontier were claimed by governments with different political systems, but their features were comparable: hostile climates, vast territories, rich indigenous cultures, and a history of state-sponsored expansion, railway construction, gold rushes, and urban development. Also, their indigenous populations were marginalized by the newcomers (although the North American frontier experienced more violence). This study analyzes the development of the Amur frontier region as a process in which local developments, such as trade and migration, interfered with state expansion efforts, such as agricultural settlement, railway construction, and military occupation. This study emphasizes the fluid and porous nature of this frontier, which was defined by natural conditions and human activities on local, national, and international levels.

Beyond the Amur is multidisciplinary in nature, informed by regional and national accounts of Northeast Asia. These accounts, originally published in Russian, Chinese, and English, cover history, geography, politics, economics, and culture. Three historiographic themes best explain this approach: the history of Sino-Russian relations, China's frontier studies, and regional and local histories.

In Western countries, until recently, the history of Sino-Russian cross-border contacts has been the domain of diplomatic historians, who focus on Russian imperial expansion and Qing reactions to it. They analyze the diplomacy behind a century-old Sino-Russian debate about territorial claims to the Amur Basin. Andrew Malozemoff has analyzed tsarist expansionist policies in Manchuria, playing down Russia's violations of previous treaties with the Qing as it formulated its policy in Manchuria.[9] Sarah C.M. Paine, by contrast, has demonstrated that pre-1917 Russian policies in the Far East had always been expansionist and continued to be so after 1917.[10] These studies tell a plain and well-documented story of Russian expansionism from the perspective of imperial court politics. But despite their merits, neither scholar explains how Russian policies towards China were formulated and carried out on the ground, nor do they analyze the reasons for Russian successes and failures.

More recent works have interpreted Russia's imperial policies with respect to its border with China. Mark Bassin, a geographer, explores the intellectual history of Russian geographic visions of the Amur River frontier. He demonstrates how the Russian imperial government, or a powerful lobby within it, came to imagine the Amur River as a Siberian Mississippi – an allusion to similar opportunities for settling new frontiers in the Russian Far East and the American West. After Russia occupied the region in 1858, this vision proved to be an illusion, for it would have required enormous financial and administrative commitments, which the government was not willing to provide.[11] David Schimmelpenninck van der Oye has discussed several concepts that shaped late tsarist policy in East Asia: conquistador imperialism, Asianism (the search for Asian roots among Russian intellectuals), peaceful (economic) penetration, and the propaganda of Yellow Peril that grew out of Japan's challenge to Russia in Manchuria. Of these four, only Asianism was a Russian-born ideology.[12] He maintains that the interplay of several confusing ideologies brought Russia to war with Japan in 1904. Bassin and Schimmelpenninck focus on the Russian elite and the intellectual history of Russia. They demonstrate that Russia's imperial visions of its East Asian frontier and its Asian identity had little to do with the political or geographic reality of this frontier. For the Russian court in St. Petersburg, Qing China and Imperial Japan were distant "others," exotic lands.[13] More than anything else, court politics determined Russia's imperial initiatives in the Amur region.

Historical writings focusing on Imperial Russia's role in China see Russia as the dominant imperial force, while treating Qing China as a passive player in the game of imperial conquest.[14] The focus on elite politics obscures regional and frontier developments. This book focuses on local developments as central to the understanding of imperial policies.

Government-sponsored historical writings about this region in Russia and in the People's Republic of China (PRC) remain politically charged. Historical writings in the PRC on Qing–Russian relations have strong patriotic overtones, as reflected clearly in the title of the monumental four-volume *Sha E Qin Hua Shi* (*History of the Tsarist Russia's Aggression against China*) by scholars of the Institute of Modern Chinese History at the Chinese Academy of Social Sciences. The premise of this work is that from "ancient times the ancestors of the Chinese people lived in the valleys of Heilongjiang and Ussuri rivers."[15] The unequal treaties of the nineteenth century, the loss of 1.5 million square kilometres of Chinese territory, and the subsequent Russian occupation had long-term negative consequences for the development of Manchuria. Even the term "Manchuria," referring to China's three northeastern provinces (Chinese: Dongbei or Dongsansheng), remains highly controversial, for in China it evokes imperial Russian and Japanese dominance. Similar Chinese studies argue that beginning with Vasilii Poyarkov's expeditions to the Amur in 1643, the Russian presence in Manchuria was for 260 years nothing less than a political, military, economic, and cultural occupation.[16]

After Sino-Russian relations improved in the 1990s, blatant criticism of Imperial Russian policies was replaced with an attitude of scientific inquiry among Chinese scholars. More recent works have moved away from a macro-narrative of confrontation towards more discrete aspects of Russia's presence in Manchuria, such as economic imperialism, railway construction, railway administration, and the activities of Russian troops in occupied Manchuria.[17] Corruption in the Qing court has become a separate theme in explaining the Qing's diplomatic failure and the penetration of foreigners into Manchuria. Yet such topics as border demarcation, the fate of indigenous people in Manchuria, the status of Harbin as a symbol of Russian imperial gains in Manchuria, and Qing–Russian tensions over control of Mongolia are still sensitive areas in Chinese official historiography. The history of the Mongols in the nineteenth and twentieth centuries is seen as a story of Russian, Chinese, and Japanese attempts to divide and absorb their territory and to dominate regional politics.

Soviet historical accounts of Qing–Russian relations were written in a spirit of partial criticism of Russian imperial policies towards China. Even so, these accounts supported the nineteenth-century official Russian view that the south bank of the Amur River historically was part of the Russian Empire. After signing the Nerchinsk Treaty in 1689, Russia "lost" those territories to the Qing, before regaining them in the nineteenth century. In Soviet official historiography, the key argument has been that the Russians did not find any traces of Chinese civilization beyond the Stanovoi Mountains, evidence that the region never belonged to the Qing. Russian Cossacks and peasants arrived at the banks of the Amur River in the mid-seventeenth century and were first to claim the land as part of the Russian Empire.[18]

Post-Soviet historical writings about the history of Sino-Russian relations are less ideologically driven and are open to new interpretations. For example, Aleksei Voskresenskii applies a Western political science model of *multi-factor balance* to analyze border formation between the two empires and argues that the two empires converged as a result of their natural simultaneous expansions, which created a "contact zone."[19] Other powers were also interested in Sino-Russian frontiers. The Amur Basin was an epicentre of geopolitical, military, and economic interests, not only between China and Russia, but also involving the United States, Great Britain, and Japan.[20] Russian historiography gradually abandoned the macro-narrative of diplomacy, favouring instead such topics as Russian institutions in Manchuria, border negotiations, railway politics, and socio-cultural aspects of Sino-Russian relations. However, these new histories still place a high value on the role of treaty negotiations and bilateral agreements in explaining frontier history.[21] A focus on diplomacy as an agent of historical development ignores the fact that border agreements were often ignored by indigenous people, migrants, and settlers. In the vast and sparsely populated Qing-Russian frontier region, these agreements were rarely enforced. Moreover, frontier authorities and the military rarely lived up to them.

In recent years, fewer scholars have been focusing on "Sino-Russian relations" as a separate field of study in history and international relations.[22] Since the Cold War ended, scholars have focused more on separate aspects of historical interactions between the two empires, blending diplomatic history with political science, geography, economic and cultural history, and anthropology.[23]

This study takes multiple approaches to the Amur frontier region; in doing so, it takes into account the well-established international scholarly field of Chinese and Inner Asian frontier studies. Owen Lattimore, who pioneered the study of China's historical frontiers, was one of the first Western scholars to demonstrate how nomadic peoples north of the Great Wall shaped Chinese history.[24] Taking Manchuria as an example, he viewed the frontier's history as a series of tribal inflows and as a meeting place of Mongol, Manchu, and Chinese cultures and political organizations.[25] Robert H.G. Lee developed Lattimore's thesis further by comparing the early Qing policy of treating the Manchurian frontier as an ancestral land with its later policy of treating this frontier as a buffer zone between China Proper and any hostile power coming from the north, be it Mongol tribes or Russians.[26] Both Lattimore and Lee see the Manchurian frontier as the homeland of the Tungusic people, from which the Manchus occupied China Proper.

Lattimore's work on the history of the Qing dynasty demonstrated the historical changes in relations between the Manchus in the political centre and frontier Manchus. In the process of governing China Proper, the Manchu elite in Beijing assimilated into Chinese society and became alienated from the frontier Manchu tribes. By the nineteenth century, the Qing political centre viewed its Manchurian frontier as a periphery in need of civilizing. Since Lattimore and Lee, scholars of Imperial China have tended to treat the evolving Qing policy towards the frontier as a process central to understanding the history of Inner Asia and China.[27]

China's rulers had a strong interest in studying its frontiers, but this interest always had a political tint. Late Qing literati like Wei Yuan (1794–1856) addressed Qing concerns about its Inner Asian frontier defences, while Qing official Cheng Enze (1785–1837) organized studies of frontier geography for the purpose of intelligence gathering.[28] During the last few decades of its rule, the Qing government became concerned about the weakness of its northeastern frontier and launched research on historical geography and contemporary frontier conditions for defence purposes. During the 1880s and 1890s, scholar-officials Cao Tingjie, Song Xiaolian, and Nie Shicheng produced historical works, surveys, and maps of Manchuria and its borders with Russia. During the last decade of Qing rule, Manchuria became a testing ground for imperial frontier reforms, reorganizations of the frontier administration, the development of frontier economies, and preparation against threats from foreign powers. In 1911, Xu Shichang, governor-general of Manchuria from 1907 to 1909, published a comprehensive study, "Political Outline of the Three Eastern Provinces," which described in detail the topography, frontiers, frontier settlements, and administrative and military structures of Manchuria.[29]

In the twentieth century, the study of China's frontiers in China was interrupted by war and revolution and remained highly ideological. In the 1980s, Deng Xiaoping's policies of openness inspired new interest in research on China's historical frontiers. In 1983, the Chinese Academy of Social Sciences established a centre to focus on this topic; it now publishes the journal *China's Frontier History and Geography Studies.* Research into China's historical frontiers has become more detailed and cross-disciplinary.[30] That said, the official goal of the new frontier studies in the PRC is to justify and preserve present Chinese borders and to protect China's sovereignty.[31]

Since the end of the Cold War, Chinese, Russian, and Western historians have become interested in the regional history of the Russian Far East and China's Northeast (Manchuria), paying attention to political, economic, social, and cultural links between them.[32] This shift reflects a growing interest in the history of local societies. These studies analyze how national policies, geography, migration, trade, economic development, culture, religion, and ethnicity have shaped regional history and regional identity.

Recent historical studies of Manchuria tend to focus on administration, urbanization, and socio-economic developments during the late Qing and early Republican period.[33] Kong Jingwei, for example, demonstrates the importance of state agricultural and economic policies to the establishment of commercial agriculture and modern industry in Manchuria, despite its economic dependence on imperial Russia and Japan.[34] James Reardon-Anderson has written about Han Chinese settlement in Manchuria and Inner Mongolia and on the incorporation of these territories into China. He argues that Chinese migrants and settlers to Manchuria reproduced and transplanted institutions and practices from China Proper, bringing with them Chinese society, economy, and culture.[35] With their emphasis on regional and provincial developments, and on relations between regions and the core, these studies analyze what happened within fixed state borders, describing the formation of regional politics, society, and culture. In these current regional histories of Russia and China, Manchuria does not overlap with the Russian Far East, and informal links between them are seen as occasional and treated as marginal. In contrast, *Beyond the Amur* analyzes the Amur frontier region as a meeting place for different cultures, despite the political and administrative divisions imposed by governments.

Japanese scholars have also studied Manchuria in detail, and their studies and accounts provide another perspective on this region. During the period of Japan's sphere of influence and consequent occupation of Manchuria (1905–45), meticulous Japanese studies of its history, geography, politics, and socio-economic development were completed. In much the same way as Russia viewed northern Manchuria, Japan saw southern Manchuria as in its sphere of interest. Government-sponsored research served the purpose of preparing and justifying Japanese occupation of Manchuria.[36] After defeating Russia in 1905, Japan acquired the South Manchuria Railway and received special rights in southern Manchuria. Afterwards, the Japanese conducted surveys and published volumes of statistical data. The Research Bureau of the South Manchuria Railway

Company funded and produced detailed studies of local conditions in Manchuria.[37] After 1906, many Japanese subjects living in Manchuria left first-hand accounts of their lives in Manchuria.[38] Imperial Japan also paid close attention to developments in the Russian Far East and considered expanding its influence there. Russo-Japanese rivalry over the island of Sakhalin, at the estuary of the Amur River, continued until the end of the Second World War.

This book incorporates frontier, regional, and international history. It analyzes the development of this frontier region as a complex process involving human interaction with nature, bilateral Qing–Russian relations, and a struggle between state and regional authorities and between official and unofficial forces. At times, the official regional forces prevailed over state decisions, and all the while, unofficial forces tended to ignore authority, be it central or regional. Indeed, in many areas, state supervision and law enforcement were limited or non-existent. As a result, internal and external migrations overlapped, and legal and illegal trade could barely be distinguished. Weak state authority in this region posed real challenges for the Qing/Republican Chinese and Imperial Russian/Soviet governments.

Beyond the Amur focuses on the interactions of the mostly Chinese and Russian subjects of the Qing and Russian empires with a hostile natural environment, indigenous peoples, and each other. The Mongol, Korean, and Japanese historical frontiers receive less attention, as they extend well beyond the Amur frontier region. Imperial Japan's territorial expansion in China and on the Korean Peninsula greatly affected Russian and Chinese policies in the Amur frontier region and has been subject of comprehensive studies.[39] The Manchu identity and its complex relationship with the Han Chinese, going back to the beginning of the Qing dynasty, has received detailed scholarly attention and is not analyzed here.[40] The maritime frontier is discussed briefly in relation to the Russo-Japanese War; the region's centuries-old connections to the Pacific Ocean deserve a separate study. Finally, several aspects of this history may never be fully understood, as indigenous people, seasonal laborers, peasants, and traders, most of whom were illiterate, did not leave their own written accounts. As a result, there are few historical sources documenting the forest economy from the perspective of seasonal hunters or indigenous families, for instance.

The period covered in this study, during which state-sponsored expansion occurred on both sides of the Amur River, has been chosen to demonstrate the dramatic changes in the Amur frontier's society. It encompasses Russia's expansion into Qing territory – the peak of which coincided with the peak of global imperialism in East Asia – from the 1890s to the end of the First World War. The arrival of multiple states to this frontier region brought new economic opportunities to the frontier people and the newcomers alike. At the same time, state authority depended on local labour and resources and on the willingness of local administrations to mediate among the various actors. The key features of this frontier during the period under investigation include its porousness, its volatility, and the tensions between the frontier society and the political centres, tensions that continued after both empires collapsed and become modern nation-states. Heavily influencing all of these features were the region's dramatic terrain and harsh climate, which made almost all human activity more difficult than in European Russia and China Proper and thus created unforeseen difficulties for expansionist initiatives.

Beyond the Amur's main objective – to describe and analyze the emergence of the Amur frontier society and how the region was claimed and divided by two states despite difficult natural conditions – is reflected in this book's structure. Each chapter demonstrates that imperial borders remained superficial despite state efforts and that the governments of China and Russia failed to keep their administrative regions of Manchuria and the Russian Far East separate from each other. Different chapters demonstrate the interplay of local, national, and international factors in shaping the frontier region and giving it a unique character. *Beyond the Amur* is organized thematically, with each chapter explaining the trends, events, or processes that contributed to the formation of Amur frontier society. It provides a panoramic or bird's eye view of this region, and then discusses particular moments in its history, or selected themes, that explain this region's transformation. Chapters 1, 2, 3, and 5 discuss local developments, while Chapters 4, 6, 7, and 8 analyze expansion processes and administrative reforms. Chapter 1, "A River Runs through It," describes the region's topography and climate and how they affected life and human activity prior to Russian and Chinese expansion into the region. Chapter 2, "They Came from Everywhere," shows that the Amur region was a place where indigenous people and migrants from different cultures met, a place where they engaged in trade and exchanged knowledge needed to live in the harsh environment.

Chapter 3, "Fur, Gold, and Local Trade," analyzes how local trade and the extraction of natural resources created unofficial networks and organizations among indigenous people and newcomers from European

Russia, Siberia, and China Proper. It shows that these associations helped supply labour in sparsely populated areas. The chapter also shows that China and Russia had little control over the region, which allowed trade to flourish unhindered by bureaucracy, much to the chagrin of the authorities. Chapter 4, "Imperial Russian Expansionism," analyzes how the Russian elite formulated their expansionist policies, resulting in stronger Russian influence on the Amur frontier region and in Manchuria. This chapter demonstrates that official policies did not consider the difficulties of transport and communication in the region, the difficulties of attracting settlers, and the populace's general disregard for authority. Chapter 5, "Chinese Migrants in Frontier Towns," argues that Chinese merchants, farmers, and labourers were the driving economic force behind the urban development of the Amur frontier region, despite occasional and largely ineffective Russian attempts to limit Chinese migration into the region. Chapter 6, "A Railway Runs through It," demonstrates the role of the Chinese Eastern Railway in the local economy and the weakness of Russian economic expansion into Manchuria.

Chapter 7, "Conflict and War," analyzes how two military conflicts – the Boxer Rebellion and the Russo-Japanese War – affected the frontier, cross-border relations, and the international balance of power in the region. Chapter 8, "Fading Frontiers" demonstrates the efforts by provincial governments on both sides of the Amur River to introduce reforms and modernize local economies, despite civil conflict and international rivalry. Finally, this book's conclusion emphasizes the primacy of regional developments in understanding empires and their interactions with one another and looks at the broader implications of this study for frontier, regional, and imperial history. Each chapter addresses the key findings of this book: that historical events on one side of the Sino-Russian border induced changes on the other side, and that the flow of people, goods, and ideas across this weakly enforced border and within this region flowed in more than one direction. A close look at Amur frontier society – with its diversity, trading networks, and disregard for authority – challenges imperial and national myths about predominance and about the effectiveness of state actions on these borderlands.

1
A River Runs through It

The Amur River has never drawn the sort of attention given to the world's great rivers and cradles of civilization, such as the Nile or the Yellow River. Until the nineteenth century, there were few comprehensive accounts of the Amur, for only occasional Russian or European explorers had navigated parts of it as they travelled between Siberia and the Pacific. These explorers did not stay long and did not understand what efforts would be necessary to adjust to and conquer the Amur's natural world. As a result, their observations were fragmented and misleading, and the Qing and Russian empires saw this region as distant and marginal. Even after Russia began colonizing the Amur region in the 1850s, and various, mostly Russian expeditions began surveying the Amur tributaries, lakes, and islands, and describing its flora and fauna, the river excited only a few – namely, devoted supporters of Imperial Russian eastward expansion. Most accounts of the Amur River were not encouraging to greater exploration and settlement.

As Mark Bassin has shown, the post-1850 high hopes for this river among Russians (and a few Europeans) were short-lived and were based on the expectation of geostrategic or commercial gains rather than on thorough geographic surveys. Several German and American entrepreneurs described the Amur optimistically as a convenient route for bringing the vast natural resources of Siberia and Manchuria to European and American markets. In 1860, Perry McDonough Collins (1813–1900), the first American explorer of the Amur region, wrote that navigation along the river would be less dangerous than along the Mississippi.[1] He believed that the river and its region had great potential for development, possibly with American participation. His dreams of "Siberian Mississippi" were shared by various social and political circles in Russia, even though few Russians had ever seen the river.

This chapter describes the topography and climate of the Amur frontier region, and argues that the harsh climate and rough terrain made access to its rich resources difficult and forced individuals and governments to adapt. Nature, that is, posed the main impediment to colonization, whether by Russia or China. Navigating its streams and living on its shores would not be easy. Storms, frequent floods, shallow waters, marshes, fallen trees, mosquitoes, and cold weather constantly hindered human activities. The Amur has an advantage over Siberian rivers in that it empties into the Sea of Okhotsk, whereas Siberian rivers run into the permanently frozen Arctic Ocean. However, entry to the Amur from the Pacific was blocked by Sakhalin Island, as if nature was protecting this region from human intrusion.

The social history of frontier encounters across the Amur River has also been a history of the human conquest of nature. Prior to colonization, the geography and climate were the key factors affecting the life of the indigenous populations. Long before the Qing–Russian border was drawn along the Amur in the mid-nineteenth century, mountain ranges, taiga (a swampy, coniferous subarctic forest extending south from the tundra), and marshes divided the landscape of present-day China's northeastern provinces and Russia's Amur and Maritime (Primorskii) provinces into multiple overlapping zones. In each zone, nature affected human activities differently. Harsh natural conditions left many parts of this frontier unsuitable for human settlement. Unstable rivers and capricious weather required that local people move from place to place and limit their economic activities to a few months of the year. In large part because of its punishing topography and harsh climate, the Amur's abundant natural resources remained intact until the early twentieth century.

From the air, the Amur River system resembles a vast tangle of ropes (see Figure 1.1). It crosses an enormous land mass stretching northeast from the Mongolian steppes to the shores of the Pacific. The Amur's complexity belies the twentieth-century view of it as a border between two empires (see Figure 1.2). The Amur Basin encompasses 1.85 million square kilometres, larger than those of the Volga or the Yangtze. With its two main tributaries, the Shilka and the Onon, it is more than 4,000 kilometres long, making it one of the longest rivers in the world. It has more than two hundred tributaries, which emerge from Mongolia, the Russian Far

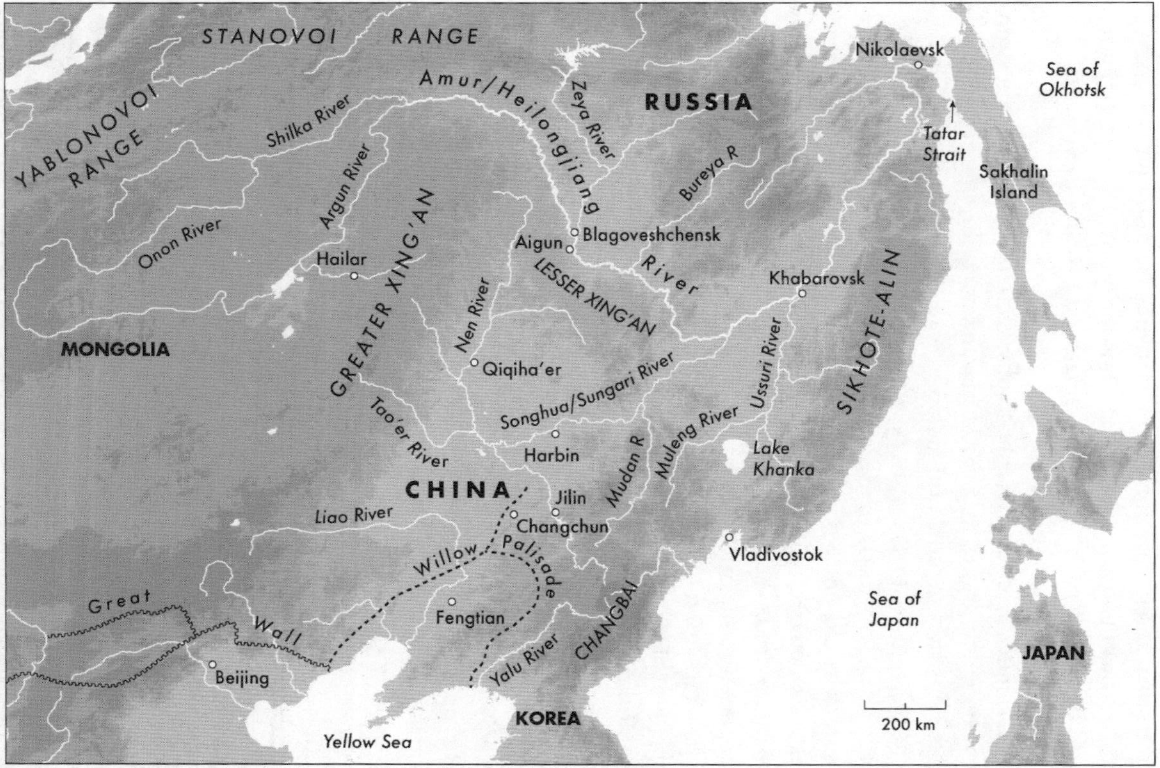

FIGURE 1.1 Amur River system in Northeast Asia

FIGURE 1.2 Sino-Russian border and northeastern Asia

East, and northeastern China. These tributaries are linked to 60,000 small lakes, of which the Khanka, or Xingkai Hu, is the biggest.[2]

For centuries, the Amur River system facilitated the movement of indigenous peoples along its tributaries: the Shilka arose inland in Siberia, the Argun in present-day Mongolia, and the Songhua in China. The lower and middle Amur connects its Siberian tributaries the Zeya, Bureya, and Amgun with the Ussuri (Wusuli) River, which arises in the present-day Maritime Province. The Amur's main channel enters the Sea of Okhotsk and the Sea of Japan through a broad estuary resembling the roots of a massive tree. Those roots link a rich array of cultures and ways of life, stretching from Mongolia to Korea and from China to Siberia.

The river's multiple names reflect the presence of different cultures. The main stream is known in Chinese as either Heilongjiang (Black Dragon River) or Heihe (Black River).[3] For the Chinese emperors, the dragon symbolized imperial power and the colour black referred to the river's black soil or dark, clean water. The Manchus called it Saghalian-Ula (Black River), and the Mongols Hara Muren' (Big Black River). The river's English name was adopted from the Russian Амур, although Амур is not a Russian word and there is little agreement about its origin. One popular theory attributes it to a small tributary, the Emuri/Emura, near the early Russian settlement of Albazin. Other theories link it either to the Mongolian name of the river's upper stream Hara-Muren' or to a Tungus greeting, meaning "kind peace." A late imperial Russian geographic dictionary explains it as a corruption of Mamu, the name used for the lower stream by the indigenous people known as the Goldi (Hezhe or Hezhen in Chinese). A Soviet encyclopedia traces its origin to the Gilyak (Nivkh) and Evenk words meaning "big river."[4] These names suggest a strong link between the Amur and its indigenous peoples, predating Qing or Russian claims to rights over the river.

What today is considered the main channel of the Amur River is a Russian colonial invention. Indigenous people such as the Goldi saw the Amur's main stream north of Boli (Khabarovsk) as a natural extension of the Songhua River. Both the Manchu and the Goldi considered the present-day middle section of the Amur River a tributary of the Songhua. The Manchu referred to the lower Amur as Sungari, meaning "the Milky Way." The Chinese adopted this Manchu practice and considered the Songhua to be the region's main river.[5] Similarly, the indigenous people living near the Amur's upper tributary the Zeya considered the Amur's main channel to be an extension of the Zeya.[6] Thus, the indigenous

FIGURE 1.3 Amur River | From photo album Khabarovsk (1901)

people considered the section of the river that was central to their lives to be the main channel.

The Amur River (see Figure 1.3) is navigable by boat all the way from its confluence with the Shilka to its estuary; along that stretch there are no major waterfalls or disruptions. Indigenous people navigated it in light canoes, while early Russian settlers used barges or rafts to transport people, animals, and goods. In winter, parts of the Amur and its tributaries functioned as the only available routes of transport, especially in the mountainous areas. In addition, minimal snowfall in the region between Lake Baikal and Khabarovsk turned the frozen Amur into a sledge-friendly highway in the winter.

The Amur varies in depth and width as it runs through different geographic zones. The shallow Shilka is a mountain river, while the Argun runs through a valley. Both rivers are narrow up to their confluence with the Amur. The river gathers strength and becomes wider after joining the waters of the major tributaries Zeya and Bureya. The middle sector of the Amur cuts deeply through the Lesser Xing'an Mountains. The lower section of the Amur, swelled by the waters of the Songhua and the Ussuri, is wide and flows slowly to the ocean through grassy valleys. In several places the river divides into multiple channels surrounded by lakes. At its estuary, the Amur is so wide that it is difficult to see one bank from the other.[7]

The waters of the Amur River and its tributaries flow relatively slowly. The Shilka is the fastest, flowing with a maximum speed of 15 kilometres per hour. Strong storms and winds made navigation of the river from the Shilka to the Ussuri a dangerous enterprise in the nineteenth century. In 1863 the Russian explorer Pëtr Alekseevich Kropotkin (1842–1921) travelled along it, accompanying a fleet of barges with provisions for new Russian settlers. He recalled:

> When the rainy season, due to monsoons, comes in July, the Sungari, the Ussuri and the Amur are swollen by unimaginable quantities of water; thousands of low islands, usually covered with willow thickets, are torn away, and the width of the river attains in places two, three or five miles; water rushes into hundreds of branches and lakes which spread in the lowlands along the main channel; and when a fresh wind blows from an eastern quarter, against the current, tremendous waves, higher than those which one sees in the estuary of the St. Lawrence, roll up the main channel as well as up its branches. Still worse is it when a typhoon blows from the Chinese Sea and spreads over the Amur region.[8]

The larger tributaries of the Amur are independent river systems and play more active economic roles than the main channel, both as transportation routes and as sources of irrigation. The Songhua is the Amur's largest southern tributary. It is more than 1,900 kilometres long and has a basin of 500,000 square kilometres. It wells up in the Changbai Mountains and runs northwest through Jilin Province, turning northeast in Heilongjiang Province to meet the Amur. The Songhua and its largest tributary, the Nen, provide irrigation for the rich soil of the Manchurian Plain. The basins of these rivers are favourable for human settlement and agricultural development. At 1,240 kilometres long, the Zeya is the Amur's largest northern tributary, with a basin of 250,000 square kilometres. The lands along the Zeya and another tributary, the Bureya, are mountainous and not favourable for human settlement. However, the headwaters of these rivers became the centres of a gold rush in the mid-nineteenth century and saw the arrival of gold-mining companies and fortune seekers.[9]

As noted earlier, Sakhalin Island blocks the entrance to the Amur River estuary from the Pacific. The shallow Tatar Strait between the estuary and Sakhalin makes it difficult for oceangoing vessels to enter the river, especially during low waters and the long winters when the water is frozen. Nevertheless, seagoing ships can navigate the lower Amur up to Khabarovsk when the water is high. The entry to the Tatar Strait from the Sea of Okhotsk is deeper than the entry from the Sea of Japan and is therefore more convenient for ships with a deep draft. Such limited access to the ocean prevents the Amur River from becoming a busy artery connecting this region to international sea trade. As a result, Khabarovsk and other river towns never became busy river ports like Hankou.[10]

The Amur River system runs through a varied landscape of mountains, plains, steppes, and forests. All of the Amur's major tributaries arise in the mountains. More than half of the Amur's basin is at medium or low elevation.[11] The river's middle and lower sections, from Blagoveshchensk to the estuary, are surrounded by at least six major mountain ranges. The upper and middle sections of the Amur River are locked between the Greater Xing'an and Lesser Xing'an in the south, and the Stanovoi and the Bureya mountain ranges in the north. The lower Amur and its tributary, the Ussuri, are separated from the ocean by the Sikhote-Alin Range. The Amur's main channel runs through the plains, with the exception of the upper Amur and its tributary the Shilka, where mountains come close to their banks.

These long mountain ranges break the region into various geographic zones. For example, the Greater Xing'an Range, whose peaks rise to 1,500 metres, separates the Manchurian Plain from the Mongolian Plateau. The Lesser Xing'an Range divides the Manchurian Plain from the Zeya-Bureya valley on the Russian side. The highest peak in the region, Mount Baotou, is 2,600 metres high.[12] The Manchurian Plain, the largest in China, is surrounded by a horseshoe of mid-height mountains. The American explorer Owen Lattimore referred to the topography of Manchuria as a "vast arc" of mountains, "running from the east round by north to the west," leaving the basin of the Amur outside this arc.[13] Similarly, the Zeya-Bureya valley is blocked by low and mid-height mountains from the northeast and southwest. Most mountain ranges in the region have natural passes, but these are covered with thick forests, making it difficult for travellers and provisions to cross them without donkeys or horses.

In other parts of the region, swamps pose an obstacle. Parts of the Manchurian Plain and the Zeya-Bureya valley have rich black soil but are swampy during the flood season. On the northern Sanjiang Plain are extensive swamps stretching to the confluence of the Amur and Ussuri rivers. Because of the mountains, the forests, and the swamps, little of the land along the Amur is suitable for settlement and cultivation. However, the southern part of the Manchurian Plain has access to the coast of the Bohai Sea through the Liaohe Plain. New settlements and modern means of transportation in the late nineteenth and early twentieth centuries did not eliminate the difficulties of travel in the region. Before the railway was built, the rivers remained the most reliable means of transportation.

Steppes are rare in the Amur Basin, except in the Barga region, which is located on the Hulun Buir (Hulun Bei'er) Plateau, extending northeast between the Argun River and the western part of the Greater Xing'an Range. This area, now part of Inner Mongolia, is geographically linked to the Mongolian steppe. According to Lattimore, the Russians adopted the name Barga from the old Mongol tribal name Bargo. The Chinese name for the Barga, Hulun Bei'er, is adopted from the Mongolian names for two lakes, Hulun and Buir Nur.[14] The Barga's Hulun Lake is the second-biggest lake in China after Khanka Lake. The many small lakes on the steppes of the Barga suggest that the plain is a dried-up prehistoric sea.[15] The Barga has a varied topography. The southern part is a steppe, while in the north it becomes part of the Greater Xing'an Mountains, which are covered by taiga. Despite its geographic isolation from Manchuria, the Barga has long been a meeting place of Tungus, Mongol, and Russian cultures. For centuries, the Orochen, Solon, and Daurs hunted here, the Mongol and Buryat nomads raised animals, and the Russians farmed.[16] This place was also a crossroads of trading routes.

Forests cover a significant part of the Amur River Basin. The flanks and foothills of the Greater and Lesser Xing'an, and the Changbai and Sikhote-Alin mountain ranges are covered with thick forests. The types of forests vary depending on the altitude of the terrain, the variations of climate from south to north, and the distance from the sea. Broad-leaved trees such as birch, poplar, willow and oak are widespread in the lowlands and on the lower slopes of the mountains, while larch, pine, spruce and juniper dominate in the mountains.[17] The larch forests of the Greater Xing'an Mountains are the southernmost extension of the Siberian taiga.

The Ussuri taiga is the densest forest in the region. Its trees reach a height of 30 to 35 metres and have a diameter of three to four metres. The taiga is the most difficult place to travel. Tall trees block the sunlight, making the days seem shorter and gloomy. Shrubs, fallen trees, rain and marshes crowd out man-made paths. Moving in the taiga with animals and provisions requires an axe to clear the way. It is easy to get lost and starve. Armies of mosquitoes, gnats, and wasps pose a constant challenge for people, horses and dogs.[18]

The Manchurian taiga is just as challenging. Its Chinese name, *shuhai*, or sea of forests, conveys a sense of endlessness. Covered with deep snow in winter and home to dangerous animals, the taiga proved to be difficult

FIGURE 1.4 Remains of a Russian hunter eaten by a tiger in Manchurian forest | From Nikolai A. Baikov, *V debriakh Manchzhurii: Ocherki i rasskazy iz byta obitatelei taigi* (1934)

to settle, let alone to explore for resources. The Russian explorer Nikolai Apollonovich Baikov (1872–1958) was one of the few to leave an account of his travels in the Manchurian taiga. He called it virgin, primitive and magical. Manchurian tigers occupy a central place in his accounts, for their attacks on hunters, their divine status and their ability to inspire awe among the indigenous people (see Figure 1.4). After many years of hunting and wandering, Baikov claimed that the people of the forests had their own language and a way of life that was foreign to the Russians in Manchuria and Siberia. But he viewed the lack of Russian interest in the indigenous hunting tribes who knew the taiga the best as the reason for this ignorance.[19]

Perceived as inhospitable by most Russians and Chinese, the dense forests had long provided shelter for undesirables, outlaws and bandits. With the arrival of Chinese and Russian migrants after the 1850s, the Amur's forests continued to hide those running from the law. The Russian explorer Vladimir Arsen'ev travelled to the Ussuri taiga in 1906 with a group of Cossacks. He wrote that meeting another person in the taiga was more dangerous than running into a wild animal. In the taiga, nearly everyone carried guns. Arsen'ev warned against a particular type of Russian "entrepreneurs" who did not mind hunting Chinese or Koreans, or stealing river boats or domestic animals.[20] The construction of railways, expansion of industries, clearing of land for agriculture began to open up the forests, but these economic activities did not eliminate the outlaws and bandits, who could easily hide in taiga.

The Amur River basin has rich and diverse fauna. The taiga, with its cold weather, is home in winter to animals with thick fur. Animals highly prized for their pelts, such as tigers, leopards, panthers, bears, fox, sable, squirrels, deer, weasels and wolves, live in the mountains and forests of the Greater and Lesser Xing'an and Sikhote-Alin. The temperate forests and grasslands of eastern Manchuria are home to deer, wild boar, and rabbits, while the temperate steppes of the Barga abound with rodents and gazelles. Animals of the Amur such as sable, badgers, wolves, foxes, raccoons, and beavers have beautiful dark fur, making them valuable to hunters and fur traders.[21]

For centuries, hunting was the main occupation of the region's Tungus and Manchu tribes. The Tungus hunted animals for both their pelts and their flesh. Sable was the most hunted animal because of the quality of its fur. Some animals were sacred, and thus taboo for hunters. The Tungus believed that they originated from bears and referred to them as brothers. Tigers and bears, widespread in the forests surrounding the Amur, Ussuri, and Songhua rivers, were believed to be the guardians of the forest and to play a central role in the migration of human souls.

The region's rivers are rich in sturgeon and salmon. For the Goldi people, fishing was central to their existence. They fished from the bank and from light boats, with nets or harpoons. They dried or froze fish, using the flesh for food and the skin for clothing. The Chinese referred to the indigenous tribes below the confluence of the Songhua and Amur as Yupi Dazi, or Fishskin Tatars.[22] The lower Amur is rich in sea fish, which enter it from the shallow Tatar Strait. The Sea of Japan and the Yellow Sea provide the people of the coast with rich maritime resources; from there, seal, otter, fish, crab, and seaweed find their way inland.

Domestic animals were part of the life of the indigenous people long before the arrival of the Russian and Chinese migrants. The reindeer was the most widespread domesticated animal among the Tungus. It can be found in the mountainous districts north of the Amur River and on Sakhalin Island. Some Tungus tribes are called Orochen, or Elunchun in Chinese, meaning "reindeer keepers."[23] The meat of the reindeer served as food, and the skin was used for making clothes, bedding, shoes, and bags. The horns were used for various utensils.[24]

The Goldi and the Manchu kept pigs and dogs. Pigs were used for food; dogs were used for hunting and transportation. In winter, dog teams pulled sledges across the frozen ground. The Manchus, Manegir, and Chinese used mules and horses for transportation. Sheep were introduced to Manchuria by Mongolian herdsmen, who occupied part of the Barga and the eastern Manchurian Plain. Sheepskins were popular for winter clothing and were exchanged for agricultural products at trade fairs in Hailar and Qiqiha'er. [25]

The fertile Amur soil produced rich vegetation. Its plains and forests produced precious herbs and plants, of which ginseng was the most valued among the Chinese. Arsen'ev reflected on the flora's unique variety: "The Amur river is home to three types of flora: Manchurian in the south, Dahur in the west, and Okhotsk in the north. The first is subtropical, the second is continental, and third is sub-arctic. The valleys accommodate the first type, hills – the second, and high mountain ranges and watersheds – the third."[26] The fields of the Manchurian Plain were favourable for agricultural development, especially for cultivating sorghum, ginseng, barley, wheat, maize, and different types of beans for producing bean cake and bean oil. In 1910, according to the British diplomat Alexander Hosie, opium poppies grew in southern Heilongjiang Province and north of the Songhua River, while tobacco was cultivated in all three provinces of Manchuria.[27]

The Amur Basin is rich in minerals, although mining emerged only in the late nineteenth century as a result of industrial development. Large-scale coal mining developed in the wake of railway construction.[28] Gold deposits are widespread in northern Heilongjiang, along the Songhua River, and on the upper reaches of the Zeya and Bureya rivers. In the 1860s the Qing government cautiously allowed the private mining of gold and silver in Manchuria.[29] Other natural resources, such as oil, were discovered and developed well after the collapse of the Russian and Qing empires. These empires did not explore the Amur's rich natural resources when they were at the height of their power. For the Qing, the main reason for paying little attention to Manchuria was the ban on Han Chinese settling beyond the boundary of China Proper. From the imperial Russian perspective, the Amur region was separated from European Russia by several thousand kilometres. The vast area between the Ural Mountains and eastern Siberia had its own untouched resources. When the Amur region became a new site for colonization in the nineteenth century, the topography and climate made it extremely difficult to access its natural resources.

The climate of the Amur Basin is determined by continental and maritime monsoons. In winter, the winds blow from the zone of high pressure in eastern Siberia towards the zone of low pressure in the North Pacific, creating continental northwestern monsoons. These monsoons bring cold, clear, dry winters with little snow. In summer, the hot surface of the Mongolian steppes and deserts creates low pressure that pulls southeastern monsoons from the sea. As a result, summer on the Manchurian Plain sees more intense precipitation than winter. Annual precipitation also varies with distance from the sea. As one approaches the sea from the northwest to the southeast, annual precipitation increases.[30] Table 1.1 shows the distribution of precipitation throughout the year in several cities along the Amur River in 1910. Heavy summer rains fall regularly in the Amur Basin, flooding the rivers, destroying villages and roads, and forcing people to move. Floods were a constant challenge for the early settlers. In the summer of 1896, the Amur River severely flooded Blagoveshchensk, forcing the townspeople people to use boats on the flooded streets. Harbin suffered similar floods in 1896 and 1914.[31] Indigenous people handled floods better than other ethnic groups in the region, because their mobility, their knowledge of the land, and their eye for the weather enabled them to avoid the worst flooding.

Spring and autumn floods created lakes and marshes on the plains and in the forests of the Amur Basin. The marshes between the lower Songhua and the Ussuri posed a major obstacle to human settlement and agricultural cultivation. They were also a breeding ground for mosquitoes. Jesuit priest M. de la Brunier wrote in the 1840s about his painful experience of travelling to the lower Songhua:

Table 1.1 Annual precipitation in the towns along the Amur River (mm)

	Blagoveshchensk	Ekaterin-Nikol'sk	Khabarovsk	Average
Summer	321.8	326.6	368.0	337.1
Autumn	105.4	101.0	102.5	102.9
Spring	76.0	76.8	111.3	88.3
Winter	3.8	1.9	25.0	10.2

Source: L.M. Bolkhovitinov, *Reka Amur ot Blagoveshchenska do Khabarovska* [Amur River from Blagoveshchensk to Khabarovsk] (St. Petersburg: Voennaia tipografiia, 1910).

> I have no words to express to you the multitude of mosquitos, gnats, wasps and gad-flies, which attacked us at every step. Each of us armed with a horse's tail fixed on an iron prong, endeavoured to strike them, and this weak defence only served to make the enemy more vicious in his attack. As for me, I was completely bitten, without strength either to advance to protect myself from the stinging of these insects; or if, at times, I raised my hand to my face, I crushed ten or twelve with one blow. Two wretched horses, which carried the baggage and occasionally our persons, lay down panting in the midst of the grass, refusing to eat or drink, and could by no means be induced to march. They were all covered with blood.[32]

Life-threatening diseases like pneumonia, scurvy, and bubonic plague were frequent in these wetlands, afflicting both people and domestic animals.

The cold winters posed another serious challenge to human activity in this region: the farther west from the sea, the colder the winter. In the twentieth century, the coldest winter temperature recorded in China, −52.3°C, was reported in Mohe on the upper Amur River.[33] The contrast between winter and summer temperatures in northeastern Manchuria is striking. In places like the Barga, the temperature in January can fall as low as −50°C, in July it can rise as high as +35°C.[34] And the winters are long – the cold weather can arrive on the Argun River as early as the end of August.[35] This climate is difficult to bear for people without adequate shelter, and only people familiar with cold weather, such as indigenous people and Russians from central Russia or colder parts of Siberia, knew how to protect themselves from it.

The long winters left their mark on economic activities. Along the middle reaches of the Amur River, permafrost limited agricultural land use. On the Manchurian Plain, the short growing season demanded intensive agriculture. Migrant workers from northern China supplied this labour during the warm seasons, returning to their homes for the winter.[36] Indigenous people survived the winters by hunting and fishing; peasants and merchants did so by exchanging goods, since winter provided the best opportunities for transportation, despite the cold temperatures. The frozen rivers served as highways, and frozen roads were good for long-distance travel. Sledges made winter transportation easy, but carts pulled by horses and mules were also popular. Peasants worked as carters in the winter. Before the railway was introduced in Manchuria, winter caravans of carts ran incessantly, connecting major agricultural centres with seaports.[37]

Settling in a region with such harsh winters required warm, solid housing as well as sufficient clothing and food. Only a few newcomers could afford to build a wooden or brick house. Few migrants stayed through the winter unless they were escaping from calamity or the authorities. Landless men in Manchuria during the late Qing era did not see themselves as permanent settlers and did not adapt to the cold winters as well as Russian peasants or indigenous people did. From the broad perspective of Han Chinese culture, most of the references to cold weather in Chinese have negative connotations, often associated with poverty and illness.[38] The sparse Chinese population of northern Manchuria even after the Qing government lifted the ban on migration there in the 1880s can be attributed partly to the cold weather. Chinese migrants from the warmer provinces of central China viewed Manchuria as a cold and hostile place. Also, the land along the Amur was not good for rice or cotton cultivation, and taiga, mountains, and marshes rendered vast areas useless for agriculture.

The impact of nature on Amur Basin societies has always been stronger than that of military and political conflicts, or of colonization. The river and its tributaries run through a landscape divided by mountains and forests. Vast distances and bad roads, many of them usable only during cold or dry seasons, made communication between villages and towns difficult. Settling near the river meant dealing with floods at least twice a year. No settlement along these rivers developed into a major commercial hub, except for Harbin on the Songhua River and a few older towns in southern Manchuria. And even Harbin and its area suffered at least one natural calamity every two years, be it a heavy thunderstorm, a flood, premature freezing, or an epidemic.[39] Diseases such as bubonic plague and scurvy were secondary effects of the harsh climate. Between 1905 and 1912, there were several outbreaks of the bubonic plague in eastern Siberia, and its earliest victims were Russians in the border town of Manzhouli.[40] An outbreak of pneumonic plague in northern Manchuria in the winter of 1910, carried mainly by the rodent *Arctomys sibirica,* spread from animals and lice to hunters and their relatives. It took around 44,000 Chinese lives.[41]

Vast areas of this frontier region remained scarcely populated until the mid-twentieth century. The history of human settlement along the Amur River and its tributaries is a story of human struggle against nature, which nature often won. For both the Russian and the Qing states, the Amur frontier region, whatever wealth of resources it possessed, was a cold, wet, and inaccessible place. For people living there, it was a world conditioned by nature – one that gave them food, clothing, housing, and means of transportation, but only after a hard struggle. The Amur River and its tributaries retained their significance by providing access to the most remote places, even after the arrival of the industrial age and modern transportation.

2
They Came from Everywhere

Despite the harshness of its geography and climate, the Amur frontier was a vibrant place with people on the move. The Amur River and its tributaries served as highways bringing together different cultures, including Tungus, Mongol, Manchu, Han-Chinese, Russian, Korean, and Japanese. Each culture had its own experience of arriving, adjusting to, or passing through this vast frontier region. Each claimed part of this frontier's land and resources through occupation of empty territory, negotiations, or force. Each exchanged its knowledge of geography and nature, and all cultures relied on one another's help to settle permanently or simply to survive.

The Amur frontier region was a land of enormous possibilities, with rich flora and fauna, and offered the resources to satisfy all human needs. Yet vast areas of this region were beyond human reach until the late nineteenth century and remained remote into the twentieth. Reaching the region from the outside was difficult, because the long distances and the lack of roads severely limited travel. Settling this frontier was even harder. Those who wanted to stay – or were forced to do so – had to make major adjustments. For the powers colonizing the Amur frontier, the major challenge was not just attracting settlers – it was also keeping them there.

This chapter argues that this frontier became a meeting place between indigenous people and different types of newcomers, whose interactions with nature and one another contributed to the formation of the unique frontier society and a strong regional identity, one that was shaped by new ideas, commercial opportunities, and disregard for authority. Their contacts were spontaneous, unrelated to imperial claims over the land and the local population. In tandem with the state-sponsored assimilation of the indigenous people into the Russian and Qing cultures, there was another, unofficial blending of the indigenous people and the new arrivals, driven by human responses to the common challenge of living in a harsh environment. Little is known about the daily lives of the indigenous people and the early migrants from European Russia or from China Proper. This chapter describes, to the extent possible, the people who lived on this frontier, focusing on their occupations, their relationships with the natural world, and their encounters with newcomers from Imperial Russia, Qing China, and Choson Korea.

The overlapping concepts of "migrants" and "settlers" need to be clarified here, as each culture and state had its own definitions, depending on the particular social, political, and historical context. Here, "migrants" refers to the broad category of people who arrived but did not necessarily stay for a long time. For example, Chinese seasonal labourers (*huagong* in Chinese), coolies (*kuli*), and refugees (*nanmin*) to Manchuria escaping famine in northern China (1876–79) belonged to this category.[1] "Settlers" came with the intention of staying permanently, either of their own will, sponsored by the state, or having been forced by circumstances. For example, state-sponsored agricultural colonization of the Russian Far East brought thousands of Russian Cossack and peasant families to the Amur frontier. The Cossack settlers formed hosts to defend the new Russian territorial possessions. Agricultural colonizers were farmers who came to cultivate land. They differentiated themselves between old-timers (*starozhily* in Russian) and new settlers (*novosely*).[2] On the Amur frontier, where state authority was often weak to non-existent, social categories were fluid and often overlapped.

Indigenous People: Goldi and Manchu

The Amur region was a meeting place for various indigenous groups long before the Chinese and Russians arrived, as the rivers facilitated their movements. According to Owen Lattimore, Siberian Tungus, Mongols, and Manchus and Central Asian Turks were historically linked by similar pastoral cultures and moved from the steppe into the forests, and from the forests into the river valleys of the Amur, in search of a better life.

The Manchus, originally a frontier tribe, built their power by force and expanded their territory and political influence in East Asia by recruiting Mongol, Tungus, and Chinese frontier groups.[3]

The languages spoken by the tribes of the Amur Basin belonged to three major linguistic families: Turkic, Mongolic, and Tungusic. It was common for indigenous people to be multilingual, and linguistic borrowing reflected cultural exchanges between various indigenous groups. The Manchu language, for example, adopted words from all three groups.[4] Moreover, colonization of the Amur Basin by the Qing and Russian empires spread Russian, Manchu, and, later, Chinese languages to the northeastern frontier. By speaking Manchu, Chinese, or Russian, the indigenous people often were able to act as intermediaries between settlers, traders, and frontier authorities.

After the Amur River became a political border, both empires intensified their efforts to classify the frontier people of the Amur Basin by their language, settlements, and ways of life. These studies were motivated by a desire to colonize, usually through a combination of force, trade, and profitable employment. However, it was several decades before the frontier tribes started to recognize the political border and to identify themselves with either Russia or China rather than with their fellow indigenous groups across the new border. In the mid-nineteenth century, the indigenous population along the Amur was sparse. For example, the population of the Gilyak, or Nivkh, on the lower Amur in the early 1860s was only 8,000, compared to 15,000 Manchu and Han Chinese in Aigun alone.[5]

Despite their diversity, the Amur frontier peoples shared several characteristics.[6] First, they were traditionally nomadic or semi-nomadic. They moved whenever and wherever they wanted, easily adapting to changing natural conditions. Their mobility was a constant concern for the colonial authorities. Territorial treaties between Russia and China during the late Qing and the early Republican period addressed illegal border crossing by their subjects. Unless forced to do so, indigenous people recognized neither the new Qing–Russian boundaries nor imperial authority. Unable to control the movement of tribes, political centres often extended their influence over them across the border. For example, Tungus Gilyaks living on both sides of the Amur travelled annually to the town of Sanxing to pay tribute in sables to the Qing authorities. In 1888, a Russian traveller saw about 230 of them in Sanxing, and reported how Chinese officials beat them with bamboo sticks for bringing them furs of poor quality. According to him, the Gilyak paid tribute in order to be able to trade for products such as wheat, oil, and tobacco.[7]

Second, among the indigenous peoples, nature dominated every aspect of everyday life. As they migrated from the river valleys into the forests, they fished and hunted. They depended on animals for transportation, food, and clothing. Fish skins served as their summer clothing; animal pelts and furs provided warm clothes in winter. Their culture was centred on nature. The oral traditions of the Tungus reflected their belief in the magical powers of animals, which were often perceived as either divine or equal to humans. Stories of women marrying bears, birds, fish, or tigers were common in Tungus folklore.[8] So were legends about people turning into animals, and vice versa. The decline of the forests and the growth of commercial fishing and hunting would eventually contribute to the decline of their population and weaken their tribal traditions.

Finally, most of the indigenous groups practised shamanism.[9] A *shaman* (the word is of Tungus origin) was a man or a woman who could enter into direct relations with the spirits. The Tungus believed that the world was inhabited by spirits that lived on and under the earth, in the sky, in the mountains, and in the rivers. Hunters often asked the spirits of the taiga, the sky, or the river for good luck and for protection from disease. The shaman served as an intermediary between the spirits and the people. Direct encounters with alien spirits caused maladies, and people relied on shamans to appeal to the forces of nature for a cure. The shaman was the guardian of the clan members' spirits, including the spirits of the deceased. But the shaman's most important social role was that of doctor, which here meant someone who could rescue the misplaced spirit of a diseased person and scare away the evil spirits. The shamans' knowledge of medicine and of hypnosis gained them the respect and trust of the tribe.[10] Thus, indigenous people saw shamans as crucial to the well-being of their communities. Shamanism regulated the spiritual life of the indigenous clans and unified them.

Scattered along the riverbanks and near forests, Amur Basin people exchanged goods and occasionally intermarried. By the late nineteenth century, Tungus tribes were involved in trade and were even intermarrying with Chinese and Russian newcomers.

The history of the Tungusic Goldi tribe exemplifies the role that indigenous people of the Amur River played as intermediaries in Qing–Russian frontier encounters. The Goldi, a Manchu-Tungus tribe, were among the first to witness the Russian and Qing cross-border encounters along the Amur River. Scattered along the lower Amur, they inhabited the marshy valleys between the Songhua and Ussuri rivers. Their early encounters with other tribes and with frontier settlers are reflected in their

FIGURE 2.1 Indigenous people of the Amur in canoes | From E.E. Ukhtomskii, *Puteshestivie gosudariia imperatora Nikolaia II na Vostok (v 1890–1891)* (1897)

multiple names. The Russians called them the Goldi or the Nanai (local people). Chinese records at various times referred to them as the Hezhe, or the Hezhen. The Manchu and the Chinese also referred to them as Yupi Dazi, or Fishskin Tatars, for their salmon skin clothing.[11] In Mongol their name means "near the river."

The life of the Goldi had always been associated with the river, which they navigated in birchbark canoes (see Figure 2.1). Their main occupations were fishing and hunting, and they paid tribute, usually in sable, to the Qing or Russian authorities, depending on which side of the new border they were on. The Goldi were related to the Manchu in several ways. Both were the descendants of similar tribes in the vicinity of the Changbai Mountains, both were clan-based tribal organizations, and their languages were closely related. However, the Manchu political conquest of China Proper reduced the power of other frontier tribes, including the Goldi. In 1880 the Manchu organized some of these tribes under a separate military banner. By serving as border patrols on the Qing frontier, they received land, hereditary benefits, and protection, thus earning the privileged status of the New Manchu.[12]

The Goldi were skilled fishers and hunters with deep knowledge of the taiga. They were indispensable forest guides for the Manchu and the Russians alike. The Russians relied on them until the early twentieth century. In Vladimir Arsen'ev's semi-fictional novel *Along the Ussuri* (1921), the author recounts how a Goldi guide saved him during a winter storm on the frontier at Lake Khanka.[13] This novel and *Dersu Uzala* (1923) were based on the author's friendship with a Goldi trapper during his expeditions to the Ussuri region between 1902 and 1908. *Dersu Uzala* became a Russian literary symbol of the Ussuri forest people facing the advance of Russian civilization.[14]

During the late Qing, some Goldi switched their loyalties between Russian or Chinese administration (both ways). Non-banner Goldi considered the Songhua River, not the Amur, the main channel, and they did not recognize the Qing–Russian international boundary along the Amur. Some Goldi families lived on islands in the Amur without knowing whether they belonged to Russia or China.[15] Emerging cross-border trade, the growth of Russian and Chinese settlements, and subsequent assimilation contributed to their decline. In 1930, Lattimore travelled to the lower Songhua River and met a Goldi shaman with blue eyes and a red beard, who could write Manchu and spoke Chinese and Russian.[16] By that time, most of the remaining Goldi had assimilated with the Russians or the Chinese. The Goldi became a marginal people in the Qing and Russian empires, and their population declined.

Descendants of the nomadic Tungus tribes who roamed the Changbai Mountains, the Manchus ruled China Proper from 1644 to 1911. By the late seventeenth century they had established military outposts along the Argun, Nen, and Songhua rivers to oversee the Qing dynasty's northeastern frontier. As the dynasty extended west and south and became more multiethnic and multicultural, the links between the Manchu nobility and the Manchu frontier groups in the northeast weakened. The Manchu banner system on this frontier employed Chinese, Tungus, and Mongols.[17] Intermarriage between Manchu and Mongolian nobles strengthened their ties, making it easier to manage the steppe Mongols on the empire's frontiers. The opening up of Manchuria for Chinese migration in the 1880s contributed to the assimilation of the Manchu with the Han Chinese.

Who were the Manchu in late Qing Manchuria? The Manchu identity itself remains a subject of debate. Edward J.M. Roads defines the

Manchu as a hereditary military caste, united by the banner system and transformed into an ethnic group.[18] David Farquhar writes that the Manchu elite were conquerors wearing different masks in order to rule a multiethnic empire, employing Chinese administrative institutions and practising Central Asian and Tibetan religions at the same time.[19] By the mid-nineteenth century the Manchu language and banner system had become weak markers of their identity in China Proper, and especially in Manchuria. During the late Qing, the Chinese language became the dominant language among the Manchu. However, the Manchu nobility maintained key hereditary positions in the banners until the administrative reforms in Manchuria in 1906–07 replaced most of them with a Chinese military and administrative elite.[20]

As the Qing dynasty approached its end, it was increasingly difficult to distinguish between Manchu and Chinese, despite the official Manchu insistence on a dress code and on hairstyle, and the lack of foot-binding for Manchu women. In 1903 the Russian observer Petr Rossov wrote that the Han Chinese in Manchuria distinguished the banner people from civilians, but they did not single out the Manchu as a separate group. He asserted that it was difficult to meet any people in Manchuria who considered Manchu their native language, suggesting that as an ethnic group "the Manchu were gone."[21]

Recent scholarship demonstrates that in the twentieth century, Manchuria's Manchu people did not disappear; rather, their identities constantly shifted with changing political regimes.[22] It was their culture, the political legacy of long Manchu dynastic rule, and their banner system of administration, that maintained their awareness of being different from the Han Chinese even after the Republican revolution of 1911. They were able to negotiate and reclaim their identity in the Peoples' Republic by becoming one of the largest minorities, despite losing their own language.

The Russians

Early attempts by the Russian Cossacks to explore the reaches of the Amur in the mid-seventeenth century met strong opposition from the Qing state. For more than 160 years after the Treaty of Nerchinsk (1689), they avoided encroaching on Qing territory; meanwhile, Russian trading interests in China were subject to bilateral trade agreements. After 1858, the Imperial Russian government launched a colonization drive to settle the newly occupied Amur Basin, even though for the first two decades St. Petersburg's support was minimal. Count Nikolai Murav'ev-Amurskii, governor-general of Eastern Siberia, played a major role in allocating settlers from Siberia to the Amur region; he drew the settlers from Cossacks, their families, peasants, and ex-convicts.[23] Early settlements were either sponsored or mandated by the provincial government, and spread along the middle and lower Amur. The three Far Eastern Provinces (*oblast'*), established in the 1850s – the Trans-Baikal (Zabaikal'skaia), the Maritime (Primorskaia), and the Amur (Amurskaia) – were united in 1884 into the Priamur Governorship (also referred to as Priamur Region, or Priamur'e) under a governor-general based in Khabarovsk.[24] Before the completion of the Trans-Siberian and Chinese Eastern railways, state-sponsored settlers from European Russia arrived in the Amur and Ussuri basins mostly by river and by sea. After 1900, railways replaced migration by sea as a quicker and more affordable means of transportation.

In the second half of the nineteenth century, Russian peasants from the Urals, Siberia, and the Trans-Baikal region settled along the valleys of the Amur. In the 1880s another wave of peasants, mostly Ukrainian, came to the Maritime Province by sea. Government ships linked Odessa with Vladivostok via the Suez Canal and the Indian Ocean. From Vladivostok, settlers proceeded north by cart and river.[25] The Russian advance into Manchuria after 1900 made it possible for Russians to settle on Qing territory in the cities along the Chinese Eastern Railway (CER). It is difficult to trace migration patterns, let alone the number of settlers, because of inter-regional migration between Siberia and the Amur and Maritime provinces. Overall, between 1860 and 1917, the population of the Russian Far East, including Amur and Maritime provinces, steadily increased more than tenfold, from 70,000 to 875,000.[26]

Initially, the Russian government limited its role to opening land for settlement, facilitating transportation, and providing settlers with land. The early agricultural settlers were usually relatively prosperous peasants who could afford to take the risk of moving to distant virgin lands. Later settlers were often poverty-stricken and relied on government subsidies. Many travelled to join relatives who had already settled there. Generational and class differences divided old and new settlers. Moreover, they arrived from different regions of Russia's multiethnic empire. Badly informed by the government and ill-prepared, they were disillusioned by what they found but did not have the financial means to go back. Among the major categories of Russians who came to the Amur frontier region were the Cossacks, members of religious sects, peasants, outlaws, traders, and industrialists.

The Cossacks, who were already well established in Siberia, were the first Russian settlers in the Amur region. Their military support in colonizing the Amur and Ussuri regions in the mid-eighteenth century had gained them special administrative and landowning rights. The Russian government offered them the best lands near the Qing–Russian border. In 1860 the government organized the Amurskoe Kazachestvo, a territorial Cossack entity, which in 1889 was divided into the Amur and Ussuri Cossack entities. By 1898 there were forty-five Cossack settlements in the Amur region, with more than 12,000 people overall.[27] In the 1890s, state-sponsored Cossacks arrived in the Ussuri region. Although they had their own land, the Cossacks did not focus on farming, as most of them were busy with military duties. Moreover, Cossack men between seventeen and fifty-six had to supervise and repair roads, organize transportation between villages, accommodate visiting troops, carry the mail, and provide security.[28] In the early twentieth century some of them became tenants or farmers, while others joined the regular army.

The movement of peasants from European Russia and Siberia into the Russian Far East was closely linked to several government initiatives: the emancipation of serfs in 1861, agricultural colonization policies in the Russian Far East from 1883 to 1885, and the Stolypin reforms (1906–16). The Russian state viewed peasants as food providers for the military forces on this new frontier. Accordingly, in the 1880s the Russian government intensified its support for agricultural migration to the Russian Far East. The state gave priority to the strategically important and sparsely settled coasts of the Sea of Okhotsk and the Sea of Japan. Table 2.1 indicates the number of peasants who came to the Amur and Maritime provinces between 1889 and 1908 (selective years, when the number of migrants exceeded several hundred).

As this table shows, peasant migrations intensified in 1899, fell during the Russo-Japanese War, and peaked in 1907 and 1908. The peak years saw the arrival of independent peasant migrants, who were fleeing the poverty of European and central Russia. Given the vastness of the region, the Russian peasant population before the 1917 Revolution in the Russian Far East and especially along the Qing–Russian frontier was inadequate to support government-sponsored agricultural colonization.

The early settlers in Amur Province came on their own initiative in the 1860s, bringing their families as well as animals and goods. Other groups

Table 2.1 Agricultural settlers in Amur and Maritime provinces, 1889–1908

Years	Amur Province	Maritime Province	Total
1889	3,027	2,308	5,335
1894	5,958	3,495	9,453
1898	540	5,102	5,642
1899	705	9,156	9,861
1900	3,493	11,542	15,035
1901	3,905	10,314	14,219
1902	6,399	6,643	13,042
1903	3,912	9,059	12,971
1904	770	362	1,132
1905	243	689	932
1906	3,112	8,169	11,281
1907	11,782	61,722	73,504
1908	8,490	21,856	30,346

Source: T.I. Polner, *Priamur'e: Fakty, tsyfry, nabliudeniia* [Priamur'e: Facts, numbers, observations] (Moscow: Gorodskaia tipografiia, 1909).

arrived two decades later and settled in Maritime Province, where they received higher state subsidies than did arrivals in the Amur region. Even so, the peasants of Amur Province turned out to be the more successful agriculturalists. As first-comers, they had the advantage of occupying virgin land and were free from government supervision. Another reason for their success was the presence of Old Believers among them (see below). Their organization and strong work ethic allowed them to survive the challenge of clearing the land of trees and coping with seasonal floods and long winters. Their strong sense of spiritual community helped them become more self-sufficient than the mainstream Orthodox agricultural settlers.[29]

The journeys of peasants to the Amur and Ussuri basins were not as well-funded as the journeys of Russian government officials and state-sponsored expeditions. The trip from European Russia was long, expensive, and dangerous. Even after the railways were built, it took settlers one to two months to reach their destination. Many new settlements were far from the railways and required an exhausting trip along rivers, across marshy valleys or through the taiga. For poor peasants, the journey to Maritime Province was especially difficult. During the migration boom of 1907, peasants from European Russia travelled in filthy conditions in overcrowded trains or boats. Diseases such as dysentery, scurvy, and typhus killed many children and elderly people. And not all peasants were able to adapt to the local conditions of the Amur and Ussuri regions. According to official Russian statistics, return migration from these regions during 1907–08 was between 15 and 20 percent of all arrivals that year.[30] Also, the new arrivals faced stiff competition from the earlier settlers and were easily exploited by wealthy and more established farmers.

The Amur region's sheer distance from European Russia, as well as its vastness, made it a perfect place to escape the central authorities. These lands attracted people who were at odds with the government or the Russian Orthodox Church. Members of Russian sects, such as the Old Believers, were one such group. The Old Believers included various Orthodox sects that had broken away from the Russian Orthodox Church in the seventeenth century and that had suffered varying degrees of persecution since. The opening of the Amur lands for settlement in 1861 attracted the Russian Old Believers, especially the Dukhobor (Spirit Wrestlers) and Molokan sects. The Dukhobors rejected the authority of the Russian Orthodox Church, believing in the authority of inner experience. They settled along the middle section of the Amur River, where they continued their religious practices undisturbed. The Old Believers relied on their own labour to support their communities. In 1890s, having succeeded as farmers, they began using imported machinery. Their entrepreneurial skills and strong work ethic gradually earned them (albeit temporary) recognition from the Russian government.[31] Until the Russian Revolution, they lived undisturbed in close-knit communities in the Amur villages. Dukhobor communities elsewhere in the Russian Empire were less fortunate. In 1895, members of their community in the Caucasus publicly burned arms as a demonstration of their pacifism. The Russian government persecuted them for refusing to be conscripted. Some Dukhobors were exiled to the northern Siberian province of Yakutsk. In 1899, the Russian writer Leo Tolstoy helped 7,400 of them migrate to the Canadian West, where they took up farming on the prairies of what is now Saskatchewan.[32] Farming skills, adaptability to hostile environments, and strong community spirit helped the Old Believers survive and prosper on the frontiers of the Russian Empire and, similarly, on the Canadian prairies.

Outlaws were another group of Russians who found themselves in the cold, distant parts of the empire. Siberia had long been a dumping ground for politically or socially dangerous elements of Russian society.

For more than three centuries it had been a final destination for criminals and revolutionaries. After the 1860s the Siberian exile system, established in the early seventeenth century, was extended into Amur and Maritime provinces. In 1869 the government of eastern Siberia sent eight hundred convicts from prisons in the Trans-Baikal region to a newly established penal colony on Sakhalin Island. The government operated a fleet of barges along the Amur River to carry convicts to Sakhalin.[33] Convict labour was widely used in mining, in building cart roads to connect major settlements along the Amur, and later in railway construction. Criminals were sentenced to hard labour; political exiles had more freedom to settle in emerging frontier towns, where they were prominent in the education, culture, and politics of the Russian Far East. Escape from Sakhalin Island was difficult but possible. Those who succeeded crossed the Tatar Channel separating the island from the mainland and moved along the lower Amur towards Gilyak and Cossack settlements. They stole animals, vegetables, and clothes, or begged, while seeking shelter on the Ussuri taiga. Those who stayed in the taiga depended on hunting and on the goodwill of the indigenous people. Others found jobs in gold mining or railway construction and lived in danger of being caught by the authorities. However, the strong demand for cheap labour often helped them to find temporary illegal jobs.

After the Ussuri railway and the CER were completed in 1903, Russian outlaws made their way to the forests of northern Manchuria. They moved in small groups, headed by veterans of the Sakhalin or Trans-Baikal prisons. The Russian writer Baikov encountered them in the taiga and found them more pitiful than dangerous:

> The cruel and reckless struggle for existence and severe discipline of the convict prison created its own law, bringing a crowd of very different people together ... These people, thrown overboard by society and the state, rejected and oppressed, were the members of a peculiar primitive social formation, created by nature itself, beyond any influence of culture or civilization. They had their own ethics and logic; their thinking was primitively original.[34]

Like the Old Believers, the outlaws found refuge on the frontier, where they sought new opportunities through hard work and by accepting a tough existence. The authorities found it easy to ignore them, for they provided cheap labour and were not as dangerous as rumours made them out to be. In effect, the Russian government was using the exile system to colonize barren lands. Most exiles to Southern Siberia and the Amur frontier region became free colonists. They turned to farming or found employment in the old and emerging towns and settlements.[35]

All of these groups often overlapped. Because of the shortage of labour and the seasonal nature of the work, people changed occupations frequently; Cossacks took up farming, while peasants became soldiers, and vice versa. Outlaws turned into gold miners or hunters. This social mobility was possible because of the lack of official supervision. Also, Amur frontier society lacked both an established gentry and a strong police force. After the Russo-Japanese War in 1905 the fabric of this frontier society changed again as many Russian ex-soldiers decided to stay. They turned to farming or became guards for the new CER. Russian colonial ventures in Manchuria brought traders and entrepreneurs (see Chapter 3).

Korean Settlers

At the end of the nineteenth century, Manchuria and the Russian Far East attracted poor Korean peasants escaping natural calamities and the crushing taxation policies of the Choson government. Korean peasants introduced wet rice cultivation to the cold climate of northern Manchuria, turning its fertile plains and hills into paddies.[36]

Korean migration coincided with the Qing government's opening of lands to Han Chinese settlement. Korean peasants settled mainly in present-day Jilin and Liaoning provinces. By the time of the Boxer Uprising of 1900, around 50,000 Korean peasants had formed agricultural communities in the Yalu and Tumen river basins.[37] The Japanese colonization of Korea in 1910 brought another wave of Korean migrants, who settled farther north and northeast of the Yalu, up to the main channel of the Amur River. By 1920, Heilongjiang alone had 44,000 Korean settlers.[38]

The Russian government tolerated Korean agricultural migrants, allowing them (after 1885) to acquire Russian citizenship and giving them land for cultivation. Koreans proved to be skilful farmers, supplying Russian and Chinese landlords with cheap labour and the frontier towns with fresh vegetables. They formed agricultural communities near major Russian frontier settlements, and their numbers in Russian territory grew quickly. In 1898 about 10,928 Korean settlers were registered in Maritime Province. By 1914 their numbers had reached 50,000.[39]

Unlike Chinese seasonal migrants in Manchuria, Koreans came with their families to settle permanently on this frontier. Korean peasants adjusted to their new life on the Russian side of the border by learning Russian, accepting Orthodox Christianity, and intermarrying with Russians. Despite this partial assimilation into the Russian way of life, Korean peasants preserved their language.[40] They enjoyed relative independence and the support of the Russian and Qing provincial administrations. The growing Japanese influence in Manchuria after 1905 inspired Korean nationalists to choose such cities as Harbin, Khabarovsk, and Vladivostok as bases for a movement against Japanese colonial rule in Korea.

The Chinese

The Han Chinese were relative newcomers to the Amur frontier and northern Manchuria. For them, the cold climate and tough natural conditions made northern Manchuria the Siberia of China. Yet Chinese had settled on the Liaodong plain in southern Manchuria even before the Qing dynasty. Loyal Chinese supporters of the Manchu conquest of China Proper intermarried with the Manchu and formed separate banners in Manchu armies.[41]

The Qing government maintained a few military settlements to oversee the Manchurian frontier and considered those lands to be a dumping ground for convicts. In the late seventeenth century, Chinese exiles formed military agricultural settlements, or *guantun.* They were sent to Aigun (Aihun), Mergen, and Qiqiha'er in northern Manchuria, where they worked on farms and in courier stations. Their descendants stayed in Manchuria.[42] After 1668, the Qing Imperial court banned most Han Chinese from settling beyond the Great Wall. However, peasants from China Proper settled in southern Manchuria long before the imperial ban was officially lifted in 1878. No doubt, the Russian seizure of the north bank of the Amur River in 1860 was one reason why the Qing government decided to allow the Chinese colonization of the empire's long-neglected northeastern frontier. The boundary separating Manchuria from China Proper was as porous and nominal as the Willow Palisade, which consisted of two lines of willow trees and random military checkpoints, marking the traditional edge of Chinese settlement in southern Manchuria.[43]

In 1880 the Qing government established the Colonization Bureau (*kenwu zongju*) with branches in Mukden (Fengtian), Kirin (Jilin), and Qiqiha'er. State-sponsored colonization of Manchuria took several forms:

military settlements, individual migration, labour battalions, and lease or sale of land to companies or trade associations. The Qing divided Manchuria into several colonization zones. Fertile lands in the river valleys sold quickly and often were resold at speculative prices. Lands along the Qing–Russian frontier, as a rule, did not attract Chinese settlers, as they usually ran through marshes, forests, or hills and were hard to cultivate. Nevertheless, that area's population gradually increased. In 1906 the population of Heilongjiang Province alone was around 1.5 million, similar to the population of the whole of Manchuria in the 1870s.[44]

The growing Chinese population on the Manchurian frontier was not simply the result of the government's strategic decision to fortify the border. Manchuria attracted Chinese peasants, seasonal labourers, and merchants, who moved there in search of economic opportunities and a better life. They became involved in agriculture, trade, and railway construction. After the Boxer Uprising and the Russo-Japanese War, the Chinese population began to dominate every aspect of life in Manchuria. In every year from 1902 to 1915, between 250,000 and 300,000 people entered Manchuria from China Proper as permanent settlers. However, considerable numbers of Chinese migrants moved back and forth between China Proper and Manchuria.[45] Between 1900 and 1909 the overall number of Chinese migrants heading to Manchuria was larger than the number returning to China Proper, except for 1901, when the Boxer Rebellion and the Russian military occupation of Manchuria forced them to move out. Most of the migrants came from Shandong, Hebei, and Shanxi. Disasters in China Proper, especially in years 1907 and 1908, encouraged them to move.

Unlike the Korean migrants, the Chinese came without families. Chinese economic migrants did not see themselves as permanent settlers in these cold and hostile lands. Chinese migration *within* Manchuria and return migration at that time makes it nearly impossible to establish accurate population statistics, which undercuts widely held assumptions about linear population growth in Manchuria during the Chinese colonization. Peasants often abandoned new settlements after collecting government subsidies. Many Chinese peasants were seasonal workers, who did not stay for more than two or three years, or who returned to their homes during the winter, when possible. They did construction work on the Ussuri, Amur and Chinese Eastern railways, then moved elsewhere when those lines were completed.

For most Chinese migrants, the Qing–Russian border did not exist. They crossed it by sea, rail, and land, and they could be found in all the major towns between Lake Baikal and Sakhalin Island. Arsen'ev distinguished several types of the Chinese in the Ussuri region: peasants, hunters and ginseng gatherers, small traders, and contract workers. Since the 1880s, the Chinese population has dominated this frontier region economically, not only in Manchuria but also on the Russian side of the Amur border (see Chapter 5). Many who did not find steady work turned to banditry.

Banditry had long been part of life in the Amur frontier region. Its remoteness and the weak political and military presence made it ideal for those who had little regard for the law and who were not afraid to use violence. In Manchuria and the Ussuri region, most of these bandits were Han Chinese from China Proper. Even though Manchuria was the ancestral homeland of the Qing rulers, Peking sent exiles and convicts there, where they contributed to the emergence of banditry. So did famine refugees and demoralized soldiers of the Qing army.[46] As the Qing government had banned Han Chinese migration to Manchuria, simply crossing the Willow Palisade northward without government approval made migrants illegal and subject to severe punishment.

In the 1850s, banditry emerged in and around communities of seasonal Han Chinese labourers, who were working in the gold mines and opium fields and as hunters. Qing official records described the bandits in various negative terms, most of which contained the Chinese characters *fei* (bandit), *zei* (thief), *dao* (robber), *ni* (traitorous, rebellious), or *pan* (rebel), referring to various bandit activities and their threat to society. Two popular terms for bandits, *hufei* (bearded bandit) and *hong huzi* (red beard), applied not only to the Chinese bandits but also to all male Russians, who intimidated Chinese communities in Manchuria. Chinese bandits usually appeared in groups, as reflected in the official terms combining the Chinese characters *gu* (gang), *qun* (group), or *bang* (gang, band) with *fei*.[47] Their groupings varied in size, from a dozen to several hundred, depending on the density of population and the government's control in a given area.

Historian Shi Fang describes several broad types of bandits: armed units who openly challenged the government, poor thieves who robbed the merchants or the rich, and ruthless bandits who would kill anyone for money or to intimidate others.[48] The bandits stole animals and goods and kidnapped people for ransom. They raided major trading routes and launched successful surprise attacks on merchant caravans. They disrupted economic activity in the forests, along the rivers, and in marketplaces, villages, and small towns. They moved freely between the mountains and river valleys and intimidated indigenous people, Manchu garrisons, and Russian and Chinese communities.

At the end of the nineteenth century, the growing economy and increased trade in the Amur frontier region brought new settlers, who were recruited by or forced to cooperate with the bandit groups. The bandits became better organized. Their own spies kept them well-informed about Russian and Qing commercial activities in the region. Bandit groups raided railway lines in Manchuria and Ussuri, looted and burned railway stations, and kidnapped railway officials and merchants, causing serious concern among Russian and Qing authorities.[49] Vladimir Arsen'ev described the cruelty of the Chinese bandits towards their Russian captives in the Ussuri region:

> The Russians caught by the bandits are subject to the most horrible torture. Their [bandits'] animal inclinations cannot be controlled, and their [animal] passion has no limits. The appearance of blood intoxicates them. They tie their prisoners to the tree, cut off nails, break fingers and toes, cut the mouth open, cut off the tongue, make holes in the ears, and pull out the eyes. This is done slowly, with intervals, to make sure that the victim suffers long enough before dying. Sometimes the torture lasts for days. This kind of torture is not rare. In 1900, a rifleman Ivan Tsarev had died from this suffocation. In 1905, my acquaintance Ivan Kitaev, an Old Believer and a hunter from the settlement Krasny Yar near Nikolsk-Ussuriisk, had been tortured to death on the Muren' River near the Lake Khanka. On June 10, 1908, a 9-year old son of Cossack Shilnikov was tortured, and in January 1910, two brothers peasants Kravtsov, were burned on a fire.[50]

Such cases of cruelty towards the Russians or Europeans were rare, for they often hired armed soldiers to accompany them in this lawless frontier region. Chinese farmers and merchants travelling with goods were more vulnerable to bandit attacks.

The fear of bandits generated long-term stereotypes regarding their ruthlessness and defiance of law. European and Russian travel accounts of Manchuria and the Ussuri or Amur regions reinforced these stereotypes, magnifying local rumours and legends about the bandits. Yet the reality was more complicated. The bandits had their own social organization, discipline, and code of behaviour. Despite their apparent disdain for authority, they followed certain moral rules and possessed spiritual values. For example, they did not target Buddhist monks and nuns or Daoist priests, women, children, the sick and dispossessed, street entertainers, or postal couriers. Nor did they rob wedding or funeral processions.[51] The bandits negotiated with frontier and provincial authorities, merchants, and foreigners. They offered armed protection against other bandit groups in exchange for money. In the absence of strong authority and fixed social norms, local governments hired bandit groups, which had experienced fighters, including soldiers and officers in their ranks. The tradition of frontier bandits continued after the collapse of the Qing dynasty and contributed to the emergence of warlords during the Republican period.

The indigenous people and the newcomers formed fluid, overlapping groups. Within such groups there were variations among members related to clan, generation, location, land claims, occupation, and social status. Within each culture, divisions between settlers became more pronounced, with the old settlers occupying the best lands and the more recent ones, often poor from the start, faced with a limited choice of land and dependent on the established settlers for work.

The absence of strong governmental authority, including legal authority, allowed people on the frontier to interact more freely than in China Proper or European Russia. The indigenous people traded or exchanged goods with one another and with the newcomers. In the taiga, unwritten rules demanded help and solidarity between strangers. The Cossacks employed Russian, Chinese, and Korean peasants to cultivate the land. Chinese and Russian traders depended on indigenous people to explore natural resources. Ex-convicts often found shelter among the indigenous people and offered cheap labour to settlers in remote areas.

These interactions resulted in widespread borrowing between different cultures. For example, other ethnic groups took up Russian-style housing suitable for the harsh winters, local modes of transportation such as canoe and dogsled, indigenous hunting and fishing techniques, and Chinese and Korean farming methods. Clothing patterns, decorative arts, and eating and drinking habits passed from one group to another, sometimes with far-reaching consequences. Chinese migrants introduced cheap alcohol and opium smoking to the indigenous people and the Russian peasants, often with disastrous results. The Russian Orthodox Church converted Korean settlers in the Amur Basin into devout Christians. And once they arrived in the region, people from different cultures faced similar challenges. For example, Chinese bandits roaming the forests of Manchuria and the Ussuri threatened peaceful hunters and peasants alike. Moreover, frontier officials, usually sent to the garrison settlements as punishment, were rarely of high caliber, and corruption and abuses of power were common.

The people of the frontier displayed a unique mix of pioneer spirit and tough character, shaped by the rough natural environment, a frugal existence, and frustrating social conditions. By the beginning of the twentieth century, there were several generations of Siberian Cossacks who had never seen European Russia, and Manchu and Chinese settlers who had never been to China Proper. In 1890, the Russian writer Anton Chekhov (1860–1904) visited the Amur Region on his way to the penal colony in Sakhalin. From Nikolaevsk, he wrote about the peculiar character of people there:

> If one listens carefully and long enough, then, my God, [one discovers] how far this life is from that of Russia! Be it cured back of salmon as a snack to go with vodka, or conversations, everything seems to be peculiar, not Russian. As I was sailing along the Amur, I had a feeling that I was not in Russia, but somewhere in Patagonia or Texas. Not to mention the original non-Russian nature, it seemed to me all the time that our Russian life-style was alien to the indigenous people of the Amur, that Pushkin and Gogol were beyond comprehension, and therefore useless, that our history was boring, and that we, coming from Russia, seemed to be foreigners.
>
> Here I noticed total indifference towards religion and politics. The priests I saw on the Amur eat meat during Lent, and, by the way, one of them, dressed in white silk cassock, was rumored to be a gold smuggler, competing with his spiritual charges. If you want to bore an Amurian, start speaking about politics, about the Russian government, or Russian art. Morality here is peculiar, not like ours. Noble treatment of women here has become a cult, but at the same time, there is nothing wrong in lending your wife to a friend for money, or an even better illustration: on one hand, there are no class prejudices – exiles are treated as equals, but, on the other hand, it is no sin to shoot a Chinese tramp in the forest, killing him like a dog.[52]

As an intellectual living in the European part of Russia, he found the local society along the Amur to be alien.

Socially and culturally, the Amur frontier was a world of its own, shaped by its unique environment and the blending of various indigenous groups, migrants, settlers and state agents. Indigenous people acted as intermediaries and facilitators in Qing–Russian frontier encounters. Agricultural settlers, seasonal workers, and traders brought their own regional cultures (from Siberia, Ukraine, Shandong, Korea, etc.), and also learned from one another. As they adjusted to the new environment, they acquired new skills, habits and beliefs. New settlements and frontier towns became venues where different cultures and social groups found new opportunities to interact with (and contest) one another and to exchange labour, services, money, goods, and ideas. This region's remoteness, harsh natural conditions, weak state authority, corruption, and violence contributed to the formation of a distinct regional identity. Another key element in the formation of regional identity was the drive to commercially exploit natural resources, especially furs and gold, which brought together people of different cultures and occupations and which defied the rules of trade and administrative control imposed by the Qing and Russian empires. This region's vastness and economic opportunities made it possible for different cultures and individuals to forge informal networks and alliances, intermarry, and learn from one another, while leaving enough room for cultural autonomy, economic competition, and political conquest.

3
Fur, Gold, and Local Trade

Commercial activities in the Amur frontier region existed long before the empires staked claims to its natural resources, but early trade across the Amur was sporadic and unregulated. Laws, diplomacy, and treaties exerted little control over this trade, individual traders, and their relationships with imperial agencies. Both Peking and St. Petersburg considered trade in the region insignificant and viewed the potential of the region with skepticism due to its harsh climate, sparse population, and poor communication and transportation networks.[1]

This chapter analyzes individual and state efforts to gain access to the rich natural resources of the Amur frontier region. It treats this frontier as a unified economic space where Qing Manchuria and the Russian Far East overlapped. On the Amur frontier, individuals and small companies competed with government agencies and enterprises to establish and operate trading networks. This chapter argues that the governments of Imperial Russia and Qing China were never able to exert sole control over this region's natural resources and that individual hunters, traders, and fortune seekers were as important as state-sponsored enterprises to the development of regional trade and commerce. After explaining the changing patterns of trade in this region, this chapter then uses the examples of gold mining and the fur trade, mainly in sable, to demonstrate how private and state economic interests clashed with each other, resulting in the emergence of official and unofficial trading practices. It concludes that difficult access to these resources and strong local initiatives combined with weak state control contributed to the unregulated cross-border movement of goods and people.

Before 1860, economic activity in this region was scarce. The indigenous people had direct access to rich natural resources and used them to satisfy their daily needs and to pay tribute to the state. The pioneering efforts of newcomers, individual traders, and entrepreneurs significantly expanded local trade, and the indigenous people introduced Russian and Chinese traders to the natural treasures of the Amur frontier. Through them, the traders gained access to animals valued for their fur as well as to rare animal parts and herbs, all of which were in demand in the markets of fast-growing towns from Irkutsk to Sanxing.

Since the seventeenth century, the Russian settlements in eastern Siberia and the Manchu settlements in Manchuria had been either garrison towns or centres of tribute collection from indigenous people, or both. Irkutsk, near Lake Baikal, was founded in 1652 and played a central role in the Siberian fur trade. In the late nineteenth century, Irkutsk became one of the administrative centres of Siberia, variously serving as a fort and a major trading centre. Early Qing settlements in Manchuria were built for defence. One example, the Sanxing garrison post, was established in 1715. The Qing incorporated the Hurka, the indigenous people of Sanxing, into a separate banner. The military government in Sanxing also extended its power over fishing villages in the Amur Delta. Even before the ban on Chinese migration to Manchuria was lifted, Chinese traders were coming into contact with indigenous people and gradually replacing the tributary system with commerce.[2]

In the late 1850s, Imperial Russia took advantage of Qing vulnerability on its northeastern borders by annexing a vast region north of the Amur River and east of the Ussuri River. Two treaties signed in Aigun (1858) and Peking (1860) established new eastern borders between the two empires, which put Russia in an advantageous position to explore the rich natural resources of the Ussuri forests and the valleys of the Amur and its tributaries. Besides achieving political objectives and demarcating the border, these treaties established rules for conducting cross-border trade. According to the Aigun Treaty, "the trade between the subjects of two states, residing along the Ussuri, Amur and Sungari rivers, was allowed for mutual friendship, and the authorities had to facilitate these trading activities."[3] Under the Peking Treaty, trade across this new border was to be tax-free, and barter trade was permitted.[4] Subsequent border trade regulations between Russia and China signed in February 1862 limited tax-free trade to the 100 *li* zone on both sides of the border. (One *li* equals 576 metres, or roughly half a kilometre.) Also, Russian merchants would be allowed to transport registered goods into Mongol lands under Qing jurisdiction.[5] Imperial Russia's intention with these treaties was to establish a dominant trading position in the Amur frontier region. The unequal nature of these treaties, which extended extraterritorial rights to Russian merchants on Qing territory, reflected Qing weakness in dealing with Imperial Russia, which, like other European powers, relied on superior military force to "open" China for trade.

Furs and gold were often absent from the list of officially traded goods, but high demand in both empires made them popular trade items between indigenous people, individual traders, and state agencies. State monopolies on gold mining, on hunting animals valued for their pelts, and on trade in fur and gold were difficult to maintain in this vast and sparsely populated region, and this allowed individual hunters, traders, mediators, and entrepreneurs to freely exploit these resources. State control was weak, and local trade was conducted along multiple routes that often ignored imperial regulations. In the Amur frontier region, local trade first developed in the forests and followed the rivers before moving into the towns. Hunters and dealers in furs met in the taiga to bargain and trade. River valleys, rich in alluvial gold, were ideal places for joint exploration by gold-seekers. The discovery of gold along the upper Amur River attracted fortune seekers from European Russia, Siberia, Manchuria, and China Proper.

Individual efforts to explore the riches of this frontier paid off, despite the challenges posed by nature and official bans on individual trade and mining. Local trade created informal networks among the indigenous people and newcomers from European Russia and China Proper, despite efforts by the empires to mobilize capital and people to create significant state investments in this bounty. These local-level connections facilitated the efficient use of labour in a harsh environment where it was scarce.

Sable and Fur

The Evenk, Orochen, Solon, Goldi, and other Tungusic-Mongol tribes had long lived by hunting and fishing in forests and river valleys. The thick forests covering the Sikhote-Alin and Xing'an mountain ranges were rich in animals valued for their fur, such as tigers, bears, foxes, sables, rabbits, and minks. The fur of these animals was used for winter

FIGURE 3.1 Amurian sable | Author's personal collection

clothing and bridal gifts. The animal world also provided food, transportation, and religious figures. Reindeer and dogs were used for transportation and hunting, while tigers and bears were cult animals. More important, some animal furs had long served as tribute paid by the locals to the imperial authorities. The Siberian tribal people paid *yasak* ("tribute" in Turkic) to the Imperial Russian administration; the indigenous people of Manchuria paid an annual *gongdiao* (tribute), usually in sable, to the Manchu court.[6]

In the nineteenth century, sable fur, long valued as a tributary offering, was one of the key trade items in eastern Siberia and China Proper. Sable was the most sought-after animal, valued for its dark, glossy fur (see Figure 3.1). It was a status symbol among both the Manchu nobility and indigenous tribal chiefs. Delivered to the imperial court from Manchurian tribes, it decorated the emperor's winter court robes and hats, emphasizing imperial grandeur and tribal connections to the Manchu ancestral lands. When British and French forces looted the Imperial Summer Palace in Beijing in October 1860, they found piles of precious furs, including sable, sea otter, and ermine, in the Emperor's private quarters.[7] Traditional centres of tribute payment were Qiqiha'er,

Ningguta, and, later, Sanxing. Once a year, the Qing administration sent envoys to collect furs. In the case of the Evenks living in the Buteha region in the valley of the Nen River, every adult male or family had to offer at least one pelt per year. In exchange, they received imperial protection.[8]

In the late Qing, sable tribute gradually declined; some indigenous groups joined imperial banners and were released from having to pay, while others simply did not show up at tribute collection centres, moving into the depths of the forests. Despite an imperial ban on Chinese settlement and trade in Manchuria, the high value of furs drew Chinese traders to the towns during the period of sable tribute collection. They obtained pelts from indigenous hunters in exchange for daily necessities.

In Russia, sables were abundant in the Siberian forests and had been hunted there for centuries. As the empire expanded eastward, large sable populations were found on the Kamchatka Peninsula and the Island of Sakhalin.[9] By the late nineteenth century, Russian traders had developed close contacts with the Gilyaks, Yakuts, Evenk, and other nomadic peoples of Siberia. They obtained furs from the local population in exchange for food, tobacco, alcohol, and metal products such as spears and pots. These furs were sold in major Siberian cities and delivered to trade fairs in European Russia such as the one at Nizhnii Novgorod. According to one Russian official report, a Chinese merchant from Sanxing in 1899 sent 10,000 sable pelts to the trade fair in Nizhnii Novogorod, Russia.[10] When the commercial quest for furs began to exhaust animal populations in Siberia and Kamchatka, Russian traders and hunters began looking for these animals in new locations. The forests of the Amur Basin became a new ground for commercial hunting. Sable populations varied with the climate and type of forest. They were scarce in the mountains of the Greater Xing'an but abundant along the main tributaries of the Amur River. These forests quickly became a magnet for hunters. Sable furs varied in quality, with the best ones found in mixed or coniferous forests and on the upper reaches of rivers away from human settlements.

The forests of the Sikhote-Alin mountains along the Ussuri and Amgun rivers were rich in high-quality sable. Less valuable was the grey-coloured sable in the thin forests along the middle section of the Amur River. Prices for sable furs ranged from several dozen to several hundred rubles.[11] Fur prices depended on where the animals had been caught, the time of year, the colour of the fur, and the size of the pelt.

Hunting for sable required patience as well as knowledge of the taiga and animal behaviour, for the sable is a small, fast animal. In winter the sable left misleading traces on the snow, or no traces at all, as the animal often jumped from tree to tree. Indigenous hunters would spend several months in the forests, following sable for days by scat left near water. Hunters often travelled alone or in pairs. Local hunters usually stayed within areas inherited from their parents. They had unspoken respect for other hunters and for the life of the forest, never killing more animals than they needed and avoiding hunting during the breeding seasons. Before rifles were introduced, they used traps and dogs to hunt. When the taiga was covered with snow and the rivers with ice, they used homemade skis to cover large distances quickly. Skis were crucial to their survival in cold weather, enabling them to return to their temporary huts by nightfall and avoid freezing to death.[12]

Indigenous hunters gradually learned about the growing commercial value of furs through their contacts with the Chinese and Russian traders, who bought furs directly from them, usually cheaply, and resold them to fur dealers in towns, thus developing a local fur trade on the Amur frontier. The hunters did not become rich, but the Chinese firms that resold furs in towns could make a fortune. Around this time, fur dealers started to move into the forests, spending several months each year in temporary huts and conducting trade with indigenous hunters near their settlements. The growing commercial demand for sables over the years led to their gradual decline. Another reason for the decline in sable was the increasing number of hunters. The indigenous population no longer had a monopoly on hunting. Chinese, Russian, and to a lesser extent Korean hunters appeared in the forests of the Amur frontier region. These new arrivals brought rifles and began hunting all year round. They also adopted hunting techniques from the indigenous people, using traps, nooses, homemade guns, and pitfalls. This variety of hunting techniques for sable reflected the need to reduce damage to the pelt, which was inevitable when rifles or dogs were used for hunting. Damaged furs were worth less. The indigenous people also taught these hunters how to make and use skis and how to survive in the taiga. Chinese hunters and fur dealers established a network among the Chinese in the Ussuri region and shared information about fur prices in Russian and Chinese towns. They established spheres of influence among the local population and maintained relationships with the same indigenous hunters over many years. The Russian government was concerned about the presence of Chinese hunters and fur dealers in the Ussuri forests, as fur from the Ussuri increasingly went to the Chinese – not the Russian – market. According to Arsen'ev, from 1899 to 1910 around 50,000 Chinese hunters or trappers visited the Ussuri region annually, spending the winter months in temporary cabins or indigenous villages. In the peak years, the Chinese hunters harvested between 100,000 and 150,000 sable per year.[13] When the sable population on the Ussuri taiga declined after 1910, the number of Chinese hunters there also started to fall.

In towns, the Chinese dealers sold furs to Chinese traders or firms, which provided them with equipment and provisions. As a rule, each Chinese dealer was tied to a particular firm and could not sell fur to anyone else. This left dealers with little negotiating power, for they had to accept the firm's price. These firms controlled the local fur market and sold furs nationwide and to foreign trading companies. In the first decade of the twentieth century, sable fur was in high demand. After the First World War, the price of sable tripled in East Asia and worldwide.[14]

Northern Manchuria had several major centres of fur distribution and trade. Furs from the Barga steppes and the Xing'an Mountains were delivered to the town of Hailar. Saghalian (later Heihe) was the main centre for furs from the northern part of Greater Xing'an, while furs from Lesser Xing'an went through the town of Sanxing and those from eastern Manchuria were sold in Ningguta and Kirin (Jilin). The furs of the Songhua Plain were delivered to Harbin, which became a major fur distribution centre in Manchuria and abroad. Furs from the Ussuri taiga passed through Sanxing and Ningguta on their way to the markets of Harbin and China Proper. The Sanxing trade fair became a popular annual gathering place for Chinese fur traders. The variety of animals available for commercial hunting on the Russian side of the Amur and Ussuri basins allowed new hunters to specialize in a particular species or switch to other animals when the market demand shifted. Because of its value, sable was a popular item for Chinese hunters, despite being rare and difficult to hunt. Instead of hunting, Russians often bought pelts from the indigenous people of Kamchatka, the lower Amur, and the Island of Sakhalin. According to Russian official estimates in 1916, Kamchatka alone provided 8,000 sable pelts per year, or half the sable hunted annually in the Russian Far East.[15] Kamchatka sable was famous for its thick fur.

Russian hunters tended to target larger animals such as deer, elk, and boar, more for their meat than for their skins. Furs from small animals such as sable and mink were used for making hats, collars, or coats. On both sides of the Qing-Russian border, the skins of tigers, bears, and leopards and other large, rare animals served as rugs and as prized gifts to officials. Chinese hunters on the Russian side of the border did not rely on sable alone; they would hunt other animals valued for their pelts, depending on availability, season, natural conditions, and market demand.

Chinese hunters also hunted animals whose parts had value in Chinese medicine. The tiger was hunted for its bones and claws; deer were hunted for their antlers and sinews. According to Alexander Hosie, the horns of a young deer in the customs returns of Newchwang (Yingkou) in 1896 were worth from $25 to $200 per pair.[16]

When the population of game animals was exhausted in the forests of eastern Manchuria, Chinese trappers moved into the Ussuri taiga, which played an important role as a supplier of sable pelts, animal parts, and ginseng for the emerging Manchurian markets. During his first trip into the Ussuri taiga in 1902, Vladimir Arsen'ev visited several Chinese winter huts. He was struck by the diversity of activities and products conducted:

> Animal skins were stretched for drying; the reindeer antlers were amassed in the storehouse. Hanging were bags of bear bile, deer fetus, furs of lynx, marten, sable and squirrel and the devices for traps: all this demonstrated that the local Chinese were involved primarily in hunting and trapping, and, to a lesser extent, in farming. Their huts were surrounded by cultivated land. They grew wheat, chumiza [a sort of millet] and corn.[17]

This forest economy was strictly seasonal. Sable was hunted in winter, deer in spring and summer. The antlers of young reindeer were harvested in the spring, when they were most valuable. Farming was conducted in summer. The combination of farming and hunting allowed Chinese hunters to be self-sufficient. It also enabled them to strengthen their influence over the indigenous people and other new hunters by selling food and daily supplies on credit. The forest cabins of the Chinese hunters were used for storing animal furs, skins, and parts waiting be sold to Chinese firms. Chinese hunters and fur dealers travelled long distances to Russian or Chinese towns to deliver their goods directly to those firms. The goods themselves travelled even farther. For example, reindeer antlers and sinews from the Ussuri taiga were sold once or twice a year in Vladivostok and then resold in Zhifu in Shandong Province.[18] Animal furs were in demand not only in China Proper but also in Korea, Japan, Europe, and North America. Along with other export items from Manchuria and the Ussuri taiga, such as animal skins, ginseng, soybeans, and grain, furs were shipped abroad from Vladivostok, Yingkou, Tianjin, and Shanghai. The appeal of the natural resources of the Ussuri taiga among Chinese hunters and ginseng gatherers grew due to the decline of Manchurian forests. The arrival of Russian settlers, as well as extensive fires between 1906 and 1910, destroyed large parts of the Ussuri forests, resulting in higher prices for fur-bearing animals and wild ginseng. The illegal hunting and trading in wild fur-bearing animals and ginseng would continue well into the 1920s.

Imperial Russian official statistics on cross-border trade between Manchuria and the Russian Far East between 1890 and 1910 do not mention fur as an export item. Precious furs were often traded or exchanged through private channels, avoiding bureaucracy and taxes. The Soviet historian Mikhail Sladkovskii suggests that contraband export of fur from Russia to Manchuria was worth 1.5 to 2 million rubles per year. Gold, alcohol, opium, and certain kinds of refined silk also followed unofficial trade routes, as their export from Manchuria was prohibited by mutual Qing-Russian agreements.[19] Official cross-border trade in the region was based on export products from Manchuria that were vital for the poorly developed economy of the Russian Far East. Manchuria exported to the Amur and Maritime districts livestock and food products such as flour, grain and vegetable oil, as well as silk produced in China Proper. Among export products from Russia to Manchuria were metals, cotton cloth, sugar, tea, and fish.[20] Yet the majority of goods crossing this frontier in both directions circumvented official trading channels, staying beyond the control of frontier authorities.

One reason for unregulated cross-border trade was the strong links the Chinese traders had established with indigenous hunters in the taiga, who had come to depend on Chinese fur dealers and who had even adopted their dress, language, and habits. Another reason was weak law enforcement. Due to the natural conditions, this border remained sparsely populated and poorly guarded. When nature allowed, people and goods moved across this border with relative ease. Finally, the abundance of furs on the Russian side of the new border and the demand for them in Qing China created incentives for this lucrative cross-border trade.

Gold

The river system of the upper and middle Amur was rich in alluvial gold. A 2,500- kilometre chain of untouched gold deposits ran along the Amur and its tributaries. In the late nineteenth century, the Russian and Qing governments recognized the potential of this land and began exploring the gold resources. Russia's century-old experience in gold mining in the Urals, eastern Siberia, and Trans-Baikal gave it an advantage over China in exploring the riches of the new frontier. Two prominent firms in

Table 3.1 Gold production in the Amur and Maritime provinces, 1869–1913

Years	Number of goldfields	Gold produced (poods)
1869	1	50
1874	4	150
1879	12	229
1884	22	323
1889	33	458
1899	214	550
1904	244	587
1909	338	556
1910	345	545
1911	360	501
1912	362	442
1913	380	406

Note: 1 pood = 16.38kg

Source: A. Kirillov, *Geograficheskо-statisticheskii slovar' Amurskoi i Primorskoi oblastei s vklyucheniem nekotorykh punktov sopredel'nykh s nimi stran* (1894), 33; A. Miagkov, *Ocherk zolotopromyshlennosti Sibiri* (1927).

gold-mining along the Amur River, the Upper Amur Company (established in 1868) and the Lower Amur Company (established in 1871), established multiple goldfields along the Amur, Zeya, Bureya, and Amgun rivers more than a decade before the Qing government developed its first official gold-mining enterprise in northern Manchuria, at Mohe in 1888.

Russian state-sponsored gold production from this frontier increased until the 1900s and thereafter remained stable until the First World War (see Table 3.1).

During its first three decades, the Upper Amur Company produced more than half of all the gold extracted in the Amur frontier region. Between 1868 and 1899, it produced 4,815 poods of gold, compared to 1,394 poods and 1,364 poods produced by the Soedinennaia Aktsionernaia (Joint Stock) and Nimanskaia companies, respectively.[21] However, towards the end of the century this situation started to change. These big companies had claimed more land for gold exploration than they could handle. Newly discovered goldfields in isolated locations were abandoned or were rented out to smaller companies. In 1903 in Amur Province, only 32 of 302 officially registered goldfields were active. In Maritime Province, only 5 of the 72 registered gold fields were in operation.[22] Weak state control of the gold-rich territories provided unlimited opportunities for unlicensed gold-seekers.

Individual gold-seekers of all kinds appeared in the Amur frontier region at roughly the same time as the state-sponsored companies. Small traders, ex-convicts, adventure seekers, poor peasants, and Cossacks panned gold independently or took seasonal jobs with gold-mining companies. These newly founded enterprises lured workers away from the government goldfields with promises of better pay, but once those workers arrived, they depended on hard work and good luck, for there was fierce competition and no guarantee of getting rich quickly. With a common dream of getting rich quick, they joined or built associations regardless of nationality.

An unusual example of such an association sprang up in the Zheltuga goldfields, where gold had been discovered in 1883 along the Zheltuga River, a tributary of the Albazikha, itself a tributary of the Amur. Known as the Zheltuga Republic, this self-governing organization was located on Qing territory, in the far north of the present Heilongjiang Province, close to the border with Russia. The Zheltuga Republic operated as a mini-state with its own laws, courts, and other administrative organs. Russians played a leading role in running this mini-state, but anyone could join. Zheltuga attracted Chinese, Korean, Jewish, German, French, and Polish people, as well as indigenous people from Siberia and northern Manchuria. In 1884 and 1885, Zheltuga's population reached 10,000.[23] The population of the goldfields was divided into five groups, each of which had two publicly elected supervisors. They reported to the head of the goldfields, who was also publicly elected. Free from state control, the Zheltuga Republic was governed by publicly accepted rules with which each newcomer had to comply. For example, petty crimes were punished by public beatings, while murder was punished by death. Remarkably, the Russian and Qing regional authorities tolerated Zheltuga's existence and unlicensed mining operations for several years. Its location near the border allowed the gold miners to escape and regroup when either Russian or Qing authorities appeared. Wary of a growing population that did not recognize its authority and anxious to reassert control over the goldfields, the Qing government established military control over the Zheltuga Republic in 1886.

Spontaneous cross-border cooperation among individual gold-seekers did not stop even after the Qing government quashed the Zheltuga Republic. It took the envoys of Li Hongzhang several years to secure authority over the area, known in Chinese as the Mohe goldfields, which were in the vicinity of the Zheltuga River. Qing and Russian provincial leaders also made efforts against banished gold-seekers, who sporadically appeared in various localities in the upper reaches of the Amur River long after the Zheltuga Republic ceased to exist.[24]

Under the leadership of Jilin official Li Jinyong (1835–90), the Mohe goldfield was established in 1887 as one of the first modern enterprises in Manchuria. It was government-supervised and commercially run, with mixed investment from the Heilongjiang government and various Chinese companies. Operations began in 1889 and lasted for a decade. Before 1900, Mohe produced nearly 237,000 *liang* (1 *liang* = 37.3 grams) of gold, hitting a peak of 50,000 *liang* in 1895.[25] In the 1890s, the provincial government of Heilongjiang established several gold-mining companies in Sanxing, Duluhe, and Kuanhe.[26] The Qing government's efforts to develop its own gold-mining industry in this region were interrupted by the Russian military invasion of Manchuria in 1900 (see Chapter 7). Except for the Mohe gold-mining company, which was relatively successful, government-supervised gold mines in Manchuria were short-lived and did not produce enough gold to compensate Qing fiscal expenditures in this region.

The upper reaches of the Amur River and its tributaries provided many opportunities for both official and private gold prospectors, and competition was fierce. As the search for gold in the upper Amur Basin became increasingly diversified, small Russian companies, short of Russian workers, looked across the border for labour and began to employ Chinese workers without notifying the local authorities. According to one observer, Chinese workers were more flexible, worked harder, and were less demanding compared to workers from European Russia.[27] Chinese workers helped small Russian companies meet their short-term goals of squatting on and exploiting gold-rich lands claimed by the Russian government. These groups of unregistered gold seekers and small businesses flourished. Government supervision was weak to non-existent due to the remoteness of these locations.

Russian official circles in the Amur region gradually recognized the role played by the Chinese workers in the Russian goldfields. In 1899 the Second Congress of the Gold Miners of the Amur Region obliged small companies, at least formally, to treat their employees equally regardless of nationality. This measure was aimed at attracting Chinese seasonal workers to Russian gold-mining companies, but many of these companies still paid Chinese and other non-Russian workers less. The congress also adopted a resolution to include Chinese and Korean workers in a proposed disability fund for Russian workers in Russian gold-mining companies.[28] However, this measure was short-lived. The Russian military occupation of Manchuria in 1900 heightened tensions between the Chinese and Russian populations on the frontier and scared away Chinese seasonal labourers.

The chaotic movement of gold prospectors across the Amur frontier made it difficult for Qing and Russian administrations to stem the flow of gold into private hands. Former and active local government or military officials joined the gold rush. Shady deals, official corruption, underreporting, and smuggling took place on all levels. In his report on gold mining in the Amur region in 1897, the Russian observer Bronislav Grombchevskii complained that nearly all Chinese companies in the city of Blagoveshchensk were buying smuggled gold. He noted that "in Saghalian and Aigun gold is sold openly as any other product."[29] The illegal flow of smuggled gold into China angered regional Russian authorities.

The flow of gold from Russian territory into northern Manchuria posed a challenge for the emerging Russian state gold-mining industry on this frontier. Instead of being sent to the Russian state reserve, the Amur gold went to China or was simply sold through private channels. Russian gold-seekers and small companies in the Amur frontier region found it more convenient and profitable to sell gold to the Chinese traders across the border than to the Russian state. Blagoveshchensk, as a centre of private (and often illegal) gold trade, had an advantage over Irkutsk, an official gold delivery centre. By selling gold to Chinese traders, small Russian companies avoided paying state tax on gold and saved on transportation, as Blagoveshchensk was closer to them than Irkutsk.[30] Some Russian companies made the contraband gold trade their major activity.

At the same time, illegal gold-mining became a major catalyst for the development of local trade in this region, reinforcing the position of this frontier as open territory. Official gold mining led to the development of such towns as Blagoveshchensk and Zeya; illegal goldfields created demand for a range of services, from transportation to food supply, which encouraged the development of these industries. Cheap Chinese alcohol was popular in the goldfields on both sides of the Amur River, becoming an important item in the contraband trade. Chinese traders supplied equipment, goods, and food to the goldfields across the border and often received payment in gold. While these transactions enriched individual traders, they irked the Russian administration, which could not collect tax on these transactions. In 1912, Priamur governor-general Pavel

Fyodorovich Unterberger (1905–10) wrote that the contraband trade not only threatened Russian trade interests but also had a demoralizing effect on the frontier population, especially on Cossacks, whose role was to guard and maintain order on the border.[31] The degree to which the frontier administration was involved in contraband trade was never established, but it is hard to imagine that underpaid frontier officials would not have taken advantage of such a lucrative trade.

The growing trade thus largely ignored the new Qing–Russian border and authorities on both sides of it. The rivers served as arteries for smuggled goods, and much of the taiga economy remained beyond the reach of state control. A tax-free trade zone on both sides of the Qing-Russian land border served as a cover for trade in contraband goods. Qing and Russian authorities were incapable of regulating the flow of furs, animal parts, ginseng, gold, and alcohol across their shared border. Although railway construction boosted the Russian presence in the Amur frontier region, unauthorized hunting and gold mining remained constant features of this frontier's local economy.

Until the First World War, the Amur frontier region operated as a unified economic space, despite the official international boundary that cut through its heart. Chinese gold-seekers, hunters, traders, and entrepreneurs expanded their activities beyond Qing's border, supplying the human capital needed for Imperial Russia's colonization of new territory and exploration of its abundant natural resources. The failure of Imperial Russia and Qing China to regulate cross-border flows of goods and people allowed trade networks to flourish and contributed greatly to this frontier region's development.

4
Imperial Russian Expansionism

Imperial Russia's expansion into the Amur frontier region was not driven by a single clear vision or strategy. The gradual colonization, described in this chapter, lasted from the 1850s to the collapse of the Romanov dynasty in 1917. Russian colonization took several loosely related forms: geographic expeditions, border-demarcation, and map-making. Grand narratives of Russian expansion beyond Siberia often overlook the role of these as independent agents of colonization, but they are examined in the following pages. Russian geographic expeditions collected the knowledge of the geography, natural conditions, and people that was necessary to conquer those regions. Border demarcation and new maps helped legitimize the territorial conquest and created new knowledge about these areas. A closer look at these colonization processes reveals the weakness of Imperial Russia's new frontiers in East Asia and the gap between the ideology of expansionism and developments on the ground.

Russian colonization was driven by several economic incentives, including the need to establish an agricultural base for the development of Siberia, to protect Russian economic and territorial gains in the North Pacific, and to find new trade routes to Asian markets. This colonization went through several stages: Russia's annexation of the area north of Amur River and east of Ussuri River (1850–60); a period of relative peace (1860–95); and Russia's advance into Manchuria (1895–1904). The first period was characterized by geographic exploration, land annexation, and border demarcation along the Amur River and went smoothly, despite insufficient government funding for bringing Russian settlers to the Amur frontier region and the subsequent lack of settlers. Then, for several decades, the new frontier was neglected. The Russian conquest of Central Asia from 1860 to the late 1880s diverted Russian attention from the Amur. Railway construction and the military occupation of Manchuria characterized the third period. Conflicting perceptions of Russia's destiny in Asia within the government resulted in Russia's military advance in Manchuria (1900) and drove Tsar Nicholas II to war with Japan (1904–05). Russia lost that war and subsequently lost influence in South Manchuria. Russia's colonization policies did not take into account the unsettled nature of the frontier. The formation of the eastern part of the Qing–Russian border along the Amur River demonstrated the lack of on-the-ground knowledge of natural conditions on the part of the Russian political centre. Russia lacked a strong economic and military base in the newly acquired Amur and Maritime provinces, and thus its plans for the colonization of Manchuria were overly optimistic. In addition, Japanese economic expansion northwestward limited Russia's opportunities in this region.

The Legacy of Nerchinsk and Kiakhta

Qing–Russian contacts in this region have a long history. The Amur River encounters of the mid-seventeenth century took place during the political and geographic expansion of Imperial Russia in Siberia and a dynastic change in Qing China; the Manchus took power in 1644. Both empires expanded by acquiring new lands and recruiting loyal supporters. Each had to accommodate indigenous populations along their new frontiers, either through force or by negotiation. After the Russian conquest of Siberia, Cossack groups from fortified Siberian settlements called *ostrogs* crossed the Amur River into the Amur Valley in search of furs and a new agricultural base. Far from the political centre, these detachments, led by Vasilii Poyarkov in 1643–46 and by Erofei Khabarov in 1650–51, acted on their own initiative and met armed resistance from the Manchus. After several years of military campaigns and negotiations, the Manchus regained their positions along the Amur.[1]

The Treaty of Nerchinsk (1689) limited Russia's influence in the Amur Basin and established regulations governing trade between Russia and China. While caravan trade and semi-diplomatic missions between Russia and China continued, Peter the Great's preoccupation with the Balkans, Qing expansion to the south and the west, and turmoil in

Central Asia distracted both countries from exploring the Amur River for several decades.[2] Yet the Qing court remained aware of the possible Russian threat, and for fifteen years after signing the Nerchinsk Treaty, it ran three lines of military patrol: one along the lower bank of the Amur, and two parallel ones from the Nen River to the Argun River. According to the Chinese scholar Liu Yuantu, the treaty only nominally marked the border along the Amur and was interpreted differently by each empire due to the linguistic and bureaucratic confusion it sowed (it had been ratified in five languages: Chinese, Russian, Manchu, Mongolian, and Latin).[3] Furthermore, the Qing government had transferred most of its Manchu troops to fight the Zunghars, leaving the Amur borderlands poorly protected.[4] The Treaty of Kiakhta (1727) maintained diplomatic parity between the two countries by establishing a clear border from the settlement in Kiakhta to the Amur's tributary the Argun, regulating on paper the status of the frontier tribes and encouraging caravan trade.

In both countries, integration of the new territories and border formation continued well into the nineteenth century, but the Russian and Qing governments still had limited knowledge of the vast lands and nomadic tribes separating their countries. For the Russian tsar, it was an empty land; the Qing court was better informed about the Amur Basin through its tribal and ancestral connections. Yet the Manchus had little control over the area from the upper Songhua River eastward to the coast of the Sea of Japan. Nor did they explore the estuary of the Amur River.[5] Having little or no direct knowledge about the Amur frontier, centres of political power relied on regional administrators in Siberia and Manchuria for information and control. After the seventeenth century, Siberian *ostrogs*, governed by military administrators called *voevodas*, were centres of diplomatic and commercial relations with the steppe nomads and frontier tribes, informing Moscow about developments in Manchuria. Because it could take months for news or couriers to reach the Russian capital, this reliance on regional administration continued well into the mid-nineteenth century.

Siberian Expansion and Advance into the Amur

The advance by Cossacks into the Amur Valley was part of the Russian state's colonization of Siberia. Russian eastward expansion from the mid-seventeenth to the mid-nineteenth century was driven by a quest for precious animal furs: sable in Siberia and sea otter in the North Pacific.

Fur was a major source of revenue for the Russian state. Cossacks and fur traders moved east of the Ural Mountains, either supported by the state or on their own initiative.[6] They established fortified settlements along the major Siberian rivers and obtained furs from the indigenous people by trade and by force. All major Cossack settlements in eastern Siberia were already established by the time the Russians appeared on the Amur. Yakutsk, on the Lena River, was founded in 1632; Okhotsk, the first Russian settlement on the Sea of Okhotsk, in 1647; Irkutsk, on Lake Baikal, in 1652.[7] Expelled from the Amur in 1689, Russian subjects moved northward. For the next 160 years, they continued to establish new settlements in eastern Siberia, as far east as the coast of the Sea of Okhotsk. Western Siberia had sparsely populated lands with rich soil and untamed natural resources; most of eastern Siberia was an unwelcoming place, due to the permafrost and long, severe winters. Siberia's major rivers, the Ob', Yenisei, and Lena, run from south to north, posing obstacles for long-distance travel by land from European Russia, especially during seasonal floods. European-focused Russian monarchs viewed the agricultural colonization of Siberia as costly and not worthwhile. After the late seventeenth century, the Russian state exiled dissidents and criminals to Siberia, in part to colonize it.[8]

In the eighteenth century, Russia's growing naval power and commercial interest in the sea otter drove expansion beyond Siberia to the North Pacific and on to Alaska. Under Peter the Great (r. 1696–1725) and Catherine II (r. 1762–96), several naval expeditions explored Kamchatka and the northwest coast of North America. These expeditions were followed by dozens of Russian merchant voyages to the Aleutians and Alaska.[9] After initial success in the sea otter trade, the Russians encountered growing competition from British and New England merchants. A century later, British and American merchants replaced Russians in controlling the Aleuts, their main suppliers of sea otter in Alaska.[10] But the Russian possessions in North America did not strengthen the Russian colonization of Siberia; on the contrary, they only exerted further pressure on the state budget. Not having a strong Pacific fleet, Russia found it increasingly difficult to maintain and defend its trade interests in the North Pacific, in part because the Siberian administration found it difficult to distribute agricultural products and provisions between different parts of landlocked Siberia and to support the weak Russian presence on the Pacific. For the Siberian administration based in Irkutsk, the Amur River was the only convenient water route potentially linking the agriculturally rich Trans-Baikal region with the Sea of Okhotsk.

In the First Opium War (1839–42), the British navy demonstrated its superiority over Qing fortifications on the coast of the East China Sea and the Yellow Sea and thus became the dominant European power in the Pacific. Count Murav'ev, governor-general of eastern Siberia from 1847 to 1861, suspected that the British, having rapidly expanded their trade with China, would eventually show interest in gaining access to the Amur River. In 1846, Tsar Nicolas I expressed his view that the Amur was a useless river and his belief that it could not carry oceangoing ships.[11] In May 1849, however, Count Murav'ev captured the Amur's economic and strategic significance when he wrote to the tsar:

> Whoever shall control the mouth of the Amur will control Siberia. At least up to Lake Baikal, and control it firmly, for it is enough to possess the mouth of this river and navigation on it as a key in order that Siberia, which is more populous and flourishing with agriculture and industry [than the Amur region], will become a permanent tributary and subject of whichever government shall possess that key.[12]

Being the main proponent and organizer of Russia's exploration and settlement of Siberia north of the Amur River, Count Murav'ev (see Figure 4.1) exercised even more power in the region than had been granted to him by the tsar. Within a decade, his bold initiatives had made Russian colonization of the Amur a reality.

The Opium Wars diverted the Qing government's attention from its northern frontier, and the westward expansion of the Qing Empire during the eighteenth and nineteenth centuries distracted its attention from the Amur frontier. The Qing emperors were familiar with the Amur frontier region, given that the dynasty's founders regarded the Songhua and Ussuri rivers, together with the Changbai Mountains, as their homeland. Moreover, the Qing emperors had isolated their ancestral lands from China Proper by imposing a ban on Han Chinese migration into Manchuria. They were not interested in the lands beyond the imperial hunting grounds in Jehol (present-day Chengde).[13] The northern edge of the Willow Palisade was separated from the main artery of the Amur River by hundreds of kilometres of forests, hills, and marshes. No emperor travelled there, and this frontier remained neglected and sparsely populated.

The isolation of the Amur Basin was soon broken. A series of explorations by Russian sailors, military officers, and scientists, known as the Nevelskoy Amur Expeditions (1849–55), meticulously studied the river system. These explorers came into contact with indigenous populations

FIGURE 4.1 Count Murav'ev-Amurskii | From F. Gruzdeva (Volgina), *Amur: Priroda i liudi Amurskogo kraia* (1900)

and, with the knowledge they gained from their expeditions, launched the Russian policy of colonizing the upper reaches of the Amur and the Island of Sakhalin. Most of the expeditions to the Amur estuary arrived from the ocean. They discovered that the river was accessible for ship navigation not only from the Sea of Okhotsk but also from the Sea of Japan. From the Amur estuary, Russian explorers penetrated the region in boats and canoes.[14] Their routes indicated Russia's new interest in establishing transportation links with a year-round port on the Pacific Ocean.

The Russian Geographical Society, founded in 1845 in St. Petersburg, was the main organizer of the Amur expeditions and promoter of Murav'ev's initiatives. Backed by a nationalist-minded group in the Russian government, the society's members were interested in the study of Russian boundaries in Asia not only for scientific purposes but also for determining what Russia's "civilizing" role in Asia would be. Petr

Petrovich Semenov (1827–1914), the vice-president of the society, was a prominent supporter of the expeditions.[15] His explorations in Central Asia in 1856–57, which earned him the title Semenov-Tianshansky (after the Tianshan Mountains), had goals similar to those of the Amur expedition: to gather geographic knowledge for possible imperial expansion.[16]

The Amur expeditions resulted in the Russian occupation of the sparsely populated west bank of the Amur River and the east bank of the Ussuri. Since the signing of the Aigun (1858) and Peking treaties (1860), the Amur River and its tributaries had acquired political significance in that they marked the eastern border between the two empires. Imperial Russia had joined the Western powers in a drive for territorial and commercial gains in China. The Qing ceded their northeastern lands to Russia without a fight, without even trying to establish military posts in Sanxing and Aigun.

The main negotiator on the Russian side was Count Murav'ev. He had an impressive record of achievement in state service before becoming governor-general of Siberia in 1848. Scion of a prominent family of politicians, diplomats, and explorers, he had participated in Russian military campaigns on the Polish border (1830–31) and in the Caucasus (1838–44), and briefly served as governor of Tula (1846–47). At the age of thirty-two, he was already a lieutenant general in the Russian army. He advocated the economic development of Siberia through agricultural colonization and by attracting foreign capital. He was an expansionist whose bold policies of territorial aggrandizement in Siberia, including acquisition of the Amur Basin, earned him both fame and enemies in St. Petersburg. One of his opponents, Russian foreign minister Count Karl Vasil'evich Nesselrode (1822–56), considered his policies in the Amur too expensive and diplomatically dangerous, for they had the potential to damage Qing–Russian relations.[17] For his role in adding vast territories surrounding the Amur River to the empire, Count Murav'ev later became a national hero in Russia, and the name of the river was added to his family name. The main negotiator on the Chinese side, Prince Yishan, enraged the Qing court by ceding a huge tract of land to Russia, and he was stripped of his rank.[18]

Expansion through Cartography

During the second half of the nineteenth century, the expanding Russian and Qing empires both used new maps to claim new territories – a long-established strategy for colonial expansion. Russian maps of Siberia and Qing maps of the Manchu ancestral lands already existed in the eighteenth century, and their quality was comparable to that of European maps at the time. During the reign of the Qing emperor Kangxi (1661–1722) and the Russian tsar Peter the Great, both empires employed Jesuit cartographers to display the extent of their empires domestically and abroad.[19] However, the two empires still had many gaps in their knowledge about each other's territory and shared borders. The presence of a Russian naval squadron in the Sea of Okhotsk since 1799 and the occupation of the lower section of the Amur River afforded Russia exclusive rights to survey there, whereas the Qing had better access to the middle and upper sections of the Amur from old military outposts along the Argun, Nen, and Songhua rivers.[20]

Japanese explorers produced detailed maps of the lower Amur and the Island of Sakhalin several decades earlier than their European counterparts. In 1809, Mamiya Rinzō (1780–1844), sent by the Tokugawa Shogunate, surveyed the estuary of the Amur and established that Sakhalin was an island. His map became available to the Europeans only in 1832, after it was smuggled from Japan by German botanist and explorer Philipp Franz von Sienbold (1796–1866). For decades, the Russians were either unaware of or skeptical about the Japanese map and the discovery of a possible sea route to the Amur estuary.[21]

The Treaty of Peking (1860) produced the first official map marking the eastern part of the Qing-Russian border, which established the Amur and its tributaries as a border. The treaty launched a new era of Russian scientific and military expeditions in this new borderland. The surveys and maps generated thereafter became a basis for negotiating territory with more precision. Over the following decade, more than forty Russian expeditions studied the topography, climate, and ethnology of the upper Amur River and the newly colonized lands. These expeditions also brought Russian settlers.[22]

A little later, the Qing government lifted the ban on Han Chinese settlements beyond the Willow Palisade and started its own surveys of this northeastern frontier. In 1885 the Chinese official and explorer Cao Tingjie (1849–1926) travelled the same route as the Russian Amur expeditions had thirty years earlier (see Figure 4.2). He departed from Sanxing, journeyed all the way to the mouth of the Amur, then followed the main artery and the Ussuri River, visiting Russian settlements along the way. He returned with detailed descriptions of the places he saw. His accounts of Manchuria and of the Russian territory are a mix of historical

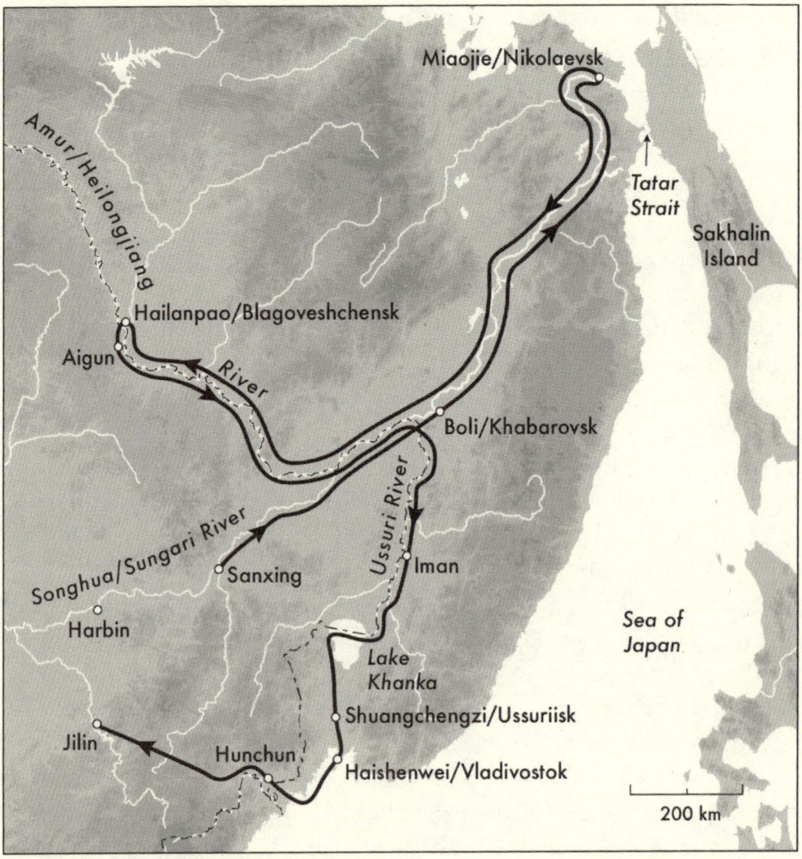

FIGURE 4.2 The Route of Cao Tingjie's travels in 1885 | From Cong Peiyuan and Zhao Mingqi, eds., *Cao Tingjie ji*, Vol. 2 (1985)

and geographic narrative. The maps and information he collected about the Russian and Chinese settlements along the eastern Qing-Russian border provided invaluable military intelligence to the Qing court.[23]

While Qing officials and military explorers studied the Qing-Russian frontiers on the ground, Qing diplomats stationed in Russia and Europe were able to access Russian maps of the borderlands. In 1887 the Qing scholar and diplomat Hong Jun (1840–93) was appointed an envoy to Russia, Germany, Austria, and Holland. While in Europe, he translated into Chinese Russian maps of the Qing-Russian border. His collection of thirty-five maps was published in 1890 under the title *Zhong-E Jiaojie Quantu* (Complete maps of the Sino-Russian border).[24] These maps were published just as Qing concerns over China's western boundary with Russia and over the Russian and British military presence there were increasing.[25] Hong Jun became a protagonist representing the Qing government's views in *Flowers in the Sea of Sin*, a popular novel by Zeng Pu written in the last years of the Qing dynasty. This widely read historical novel depicts the experiences of Qing diplomats in Europe. One of them, Jin Weiqing, buys a smuggled original Russian map of the Qing-Russian border in Germany in order to present it to the Qing court, hoping that a well-informed government would prevent foreigners from occupying China's borderlands.[26] This episode captures the concerns of the educated elite regarding the empire's uncertain borders with Russia, especially its western and northwestern sections.

Naming geographic places and settlements was another way of claiming territory and creating long-term perceptions about the state's historical legitimacy in colonized lands. This was a gradual process and involved the drawing of maps designed either for the general public or for political use at home and abroad. Russian maps of Manchuria reflected the collective efforts of the Russian Geographical Society, the Ministry of Finance, and the Russian military to map the increasing Russian presence in the Amur region. For example, the map of Manchuria produced by Leonid Ivanovich Borodovsky and published by the Russian Ministry of Finance in 1897 went through several editions, published in 1899 and 1901. In 1901, new Russian names of places and settlements were added, showing progress in colonizing the frontier. Royalty existed on Russian maps from the mid-nineteenth century: the Harbour of Nicholas I, or Imperial Harbour (facing the Tartary Strait), Nikolaevsk (in the estuary of the Amur River), Ekaterinovka (after Catherine the Great). Names of settlements along the north bank of the Amur River and the east bank of the Ussuri were predominantly Russian, celebrating distinguished regional administrators, explorers, and scientists. Thus, the military settlement Murav'evskii Post was named after the governor of eastern Siberia Nikolai Murav'ev; the village of Khabarovka (later Khabarovsk) after the seventeenth-century Russian explorer Erofei Khabarov (the Chinese called it Boli); the village Bussevo after the first governor of the Amur region Nikolai Busse (1858–66); and so on.[27] Next came the names of smaller Chinese, Mongolian, Korean, and indigenous settlements along the frontier rivers, reflecting the diversity and historical legacy of the non-Russian population there. Over time, many indigenous names were replaced by new Russian or Chinese names, marking the decline and, in some cases, the disappearance of indigenous populations.

River as Border

While the eastern boundary between Russia and China was fixed on the map, it proved difficult or nearly impossible to draw it along the river. The Peking Treaty (1860) formally established the eastern boundary between Russia and China. Article I states:

> The eastern frontier between two states, starting from the confluence of the rivers Shilka and Argun will follow the course of the Amur River to the confluence of the latter with the Ussuri River. The lands located on the left bank (to the north) of the Amur River, belong to the Russian state, and the lands located on the right bank (to the south), to the confluence of the Ussuri River, belong to the Chinese state. Furthermore, from the confluence of the Ussuri to Lake Khanka, the boundary goes along the rivers Ussuri and Sungacha. The lands located on the eastern (right) bank of these rivers belong to the Russian state, and on the west bank (left) to the Chinese state.[28]

The first official map of the Amur border accompanying this treaty was a result of mostly Russian surveys and efforts to define the border. The boundary on this map was marked by a red line with letters of the Russian alphabet, from A to U. The borderland of the upper Amur and the putative boundary south of Lake Khanka (Xingkai) were not yet properly surveyed, as parts of these ran through mountains and taiga. The treaty obliged both sides to establish a joint commission to further survey the border and install border markers along the river.[29]

The treaty did not specify whether the border followed the centre of the main channel. According to the treaty, Russia and China retained equal navigation rights along the border rivers, but the details of this navigation were not discussed. To complicate matters, the river is not a fixed border; its channel moves. The Amur changes shape at least twice each year during spring floods and summer drought. Demarcating and monitoring the Amur became a source of confusion for border authorities and political centres alike.

Numerous islands complicated the drawing of a precise line of division within the navigable stream. One of these islands, known in Chinese as Heixiazi Dao (literally, Black Bear Island), was located near the Russian town of Khabarovsk, at the convergence of the Amur and Ussuri rivers (see Figure 4.3). This island exemplifies what the Aigun and Peking treaties, as well as early maps, failed to resolve. The Qing government

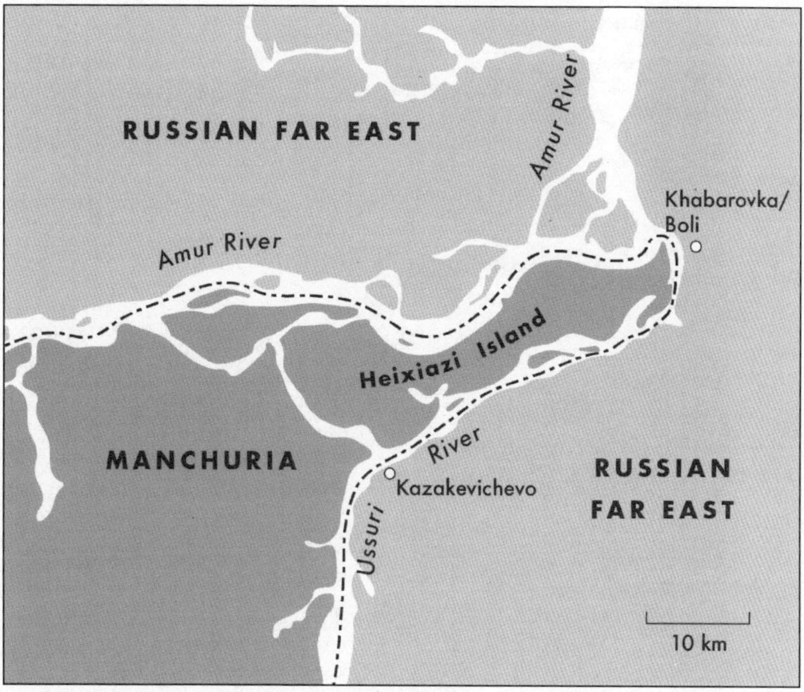

FIGURE 4.3 Disputed islands at the confluence of the Amur and Ussuri rivers | From Hong Jun, *Zhong-E jiaojie quantu* (1890)

considered the boundary to run through the meeting point of the main streams of the Amur and Ussuri rivers; in this way, it claimed Heixiazi as Qing territory. The Russians considered the state boundary to be drawn along the Chinese bank of the river, and claimed the island for Russia. The dispute over this and other islands was a constant source of friction in later Sino-Russian border negotiations.[30]

There was another reason why the Amur's islands could not serve as a border. Seasonal floods changed the number, location, and size of the islands, destroying settlements and fortifications along the river's banks. Summer drought made the upper Amur and Shilka rivers shallow. As a result, river islands increased in size and number, blocking navigation. The Russian merchant writer Dmitrii Stakheev, who lived in the border town of Blagoveshchensk and travelled the region in 1862 and 1863, recalled that during summer months chickens easily walked the waters of Shilka and people commuted from one bank to the other.[31] Over time, the channel of the Argun River moved west, became ever shallower, and created new islands. This caused territorial disputes over the eastern section of the northeastern border, where it was defined by the Argun River. Since the signing of the Nerchinsk Treaty in 1689, a 1,200 kilometre border had existed along the Argun River. In 1909–10, joint surveys by border commissions discovered that the Qing and Russian records of these islands did not match and that several islands were missing from contemporary maps. The Qiqiha'er Protocol, signed in October 1911, divided the islands along the Argun border between Russia and China, recognizing nature's effect on the border.[32]

Natural complications demanded constant supervision and the presence of substantial border patrols on the Amur River, which neither empire was ready to commission. British diplomat and explorer Alexander Hosie (1853–1925), travelling from Khabarovsk to Blagoveshchensk by boat in the summer of 1900, wrote:

> The Amur and the Shilka are marked, lighted, and in some places buoyed by the Russian government, and two vessels are constantly employed during the open season in surveying the river, and, as the channel changes, in altering marks. At all difficult crossings there are leading marks fixed on poles surmounted by oil lamps, red on the right bank, white on the left, which have to be kept in line to avoid grounding, for the shallowness of both rivers is remarkable and necessitates the employment of paddle or stern steamers only.[33]

The length of the Amur and the difficult access left most of its sectors unattended.

The process of demarcating and mapping this frontier allowed for human manipulation: the words and locations on the maps could be changed, omitted, renamed, or wrongly translated. With secrecy surrounding strategic maps of the border, maps could easily be destroyed or replaced. In times of peace, control over the Amur frontier river was lax. But even in times of Qing–Russian confrontation, this borderland was not as clearly drawn as Russia's borders with Europe.

Russian Colonial Experiments in Manchuria (1895–1904)

Russian colonial policy in the Amur Basin did not exclude the possibility of military and economic expansion into Qing territories. Russia's interest in northeastern China and the Korean Peninsula coincided with its desire to integrate the Siberian economy with the rest of the empire and to open it to East Asian markets. In 1891 the future Russian tsar Nicholas II passed through the Russian Far East, visiting Vladivostok, Khabarovsk, and Blagoveshchensk on his return from a grand tour of Asia, which included Egypt, India, Siam, China, and Japan. Nicholas was fascinated by Asia, despite an attempt on his life in Japan. Images of eastern Siberia and the Ussuri region stayed with him as powerful indicators of the greatness of the Russian eastern frontiers.[34] After witnessing the British colonies in India, Hong Kong, and Singapore, Nicholas II had the destiny of the Russian empire in Asia in mind when he ascended the throne in 1894 and supported Russia's colonial experiments in Manchuria several years later.

Early in Nicholas's reign, three major features of Russian expansion were the construction of the Chinese Eastern Railway (CER) through Manchuria, the CER's extension to the South Manchuria Railway, and the subsequent lease of Lüshun (Port Arthur) and Dalian (Dalny) on the Liaodong Peninsula.[35] The route of the Russian railway indicated Russia's strong interest in obtaining a shorter land corridor leading to an ice-free port on the Pacific, and Russia's firm grip over southern Manchuria offered a new sea outlet for the development of Siberia. Russian railways in Manchuria supported the Trans-Siberian line, built in 1893, and facilitated economic ties among European Russia, Siberia, and East Asia. Russia's railway and territorial concessions gained in southern Manchuria gave it new political and economic standing in coastal China and Korea.

Japan preceded Russia in gaining territory in southern Manchuria after it won the war with China in 1895, acquiring Taiwan and occupying, for a short time, the Liaodong Peninsula. The same year, Russia, Germany, and France launched the Tripartite Intervention in China to weaken Japanese influence on the Liaodong Peninsula. Russian expansion into Manchuria from 1895 to 1904 went hand in hand with territorial acquisitions and concession politics imposed on Qing China by Germany, Great Britain, France, and Japan. European imperialist powers, competing for spheres of influence in China and East Asia, recognized Russia's interests in the region: French bankers supplied money for the Russian railway concessions in Manchuria, and the British refrained from constructing railways or asking for territorial concessions north of the Great Wall.[36]

When Russian troops occupied major cities in Manchuria to protect its economic interests in Manchuria in 1900 (see Chapter 7), the Russian ruling elite became divided over its East Asian policy. Russian finance minister Sergei Witte, a proponent of peaceful economic penetration and the driving force behind the CER, objected to the military occupation of the Liaodong Peninsula and the rest of Manchuria. But Nicholas II backed the Russian military establishment by supporting the intervention. The Russian government's ventures in Manchuria worried some prominent Russian intellectuals. In 1902, Russian writer Leo Tolstoy wrote a letter criticizing the government's abuse of its own people and the policies of Nicholas II in China.[37] But for most Russians living east of the Urals, China was too far away to cause concern, and the policy did not change.

Rivalry between Japan and Russia

During the Meiji period (1868–1912), Japan's northwestward expansion brought it into contact with the Russian Far East. The early frontier that Japan and Russia shared at the Sea of Okhotsk was relatively peaceful. Russia and Japan protected their trading interests (sea otter, fish, and other maritime products) through negotiation, but their expansionist ambitions made conflicts unavoidable. The two expanding empires immensely influenced local life. Since the mid-nineteenth century, both Russia and Japan had claimed control over the indigenous people on the Island of Sakhalin and the Kurile Islands. For half a decade, Sakhalin had been a testing ground for the two states' territorial claims. Sakhalin switched in status from joint rule in the 1850s to Russian rule until 1875, and then back to Japanese rule in 1905, when Russia lost the Russo-Japanese War.[38] The Ainu and Aleuts were the major victims of Russian and Japanese imperial claims. Japanese colonization of Hokkaido, the Kurile Islands, and Sakhalin forced indigenous people to resettle and to assimilate into the dominant culture. In Siberia, indigenous people were converted to the Russian Orthodox faith, learned to speak Russian, and were forced to submit to Russian rule.[39]

The rivalry between Japan and Russia was resolved at Qing China's expense. Japan's imperialist ambitions in Korea resulted in the Sino-Japanese War (1894–95), which Japan won. In May 1895, Japan and Russia became long-term enemies as Russia and its allies, France and Germany, forced Japan to give up the Liaodong Peninsula, which Japan had claimed after victory in its war with China.[40] The northwestern expansion of Japan brought it into direct conflict with Russian imperialist ambitions in Manchuria. Japan had been interested in the fertile lands and agricultural products of southern Manchuria. Before the Sino-Japanese War, Japanese firms had slowly established trading links with the Manchurian ports of Yingkou and Dalian. Japan followed expansionist practices like those employed by the Western powers in East Asia, using force to leverage economic and political domination over weaker neighbours through concessions, treaty ports, indemnities, and special rights.[41] Japan and Russia settled their scores through war (1904–05), part of which was fought in Manchuria. After defeating Russia, Japan took over Russian possessions on the Liaodong Peninsula, including the railway rights, and started to play a dominant role in the foreign trade and economic development of southern Manchuria. By 1908, Japan accounted for 90 percent of Manchuria's foreign trade.[42]

The promise of economic reward and new opportunities on the shores of the Pacific drove the Russian government's decision to direct its imperial policy towards the Amur frontier region. State-sponsored expeditions prepared the ground for colonization. Border negotiations and the creation of new maps renewed Russia's claims over the river, surrounding lands, and indigenous people. Despite these explorations, imperial governments remained ill-informed about this region. Russian and European visitors to this frontier did not stay long enough to experience the challenges of daily life, and their accounts contributed to the Russian government's failure to grasp the geographic realities of the Amur frontier region. Compounding this lack of knowledge, the vast territories around the Amur River and its tributaries remained inadequately surveyed and sparsely populated. A misleading vision of Russia's "civilizing" role in Asia, successful early naval explorations along the northeastern cost of the Pacific Ocean, and the optimism of the Siberian regional administration headed by Murav'ev-Amurskii convinced St. Petersburg that it would be easy to take over the empty lands and "primitive natives" and turn the Amur region into another, warmer, Siberia. The second wave of Russian expansion in the late 1890s went beyond occupying sparsely populated lands and resulted in a railway line through the heart of Manchuria and new territorial concessions. But the Russian government paid dearly for redrawing the political map of its eastern border with China: expensive economic and military enterprises in Manchuria and on the Liaodong Peninsula drove it to war with Japan and weakened its position in Asia. As the next chapter demonstrates, Russia's inadequate colonization of this frontier made Russian frontier settlements and towns dependent on Chinese labour and trade, and on Manchurian agricultural resources.

5
Chinese Migrants in Frontier Towns

The Russian occupation of the Qing territory north of the Amur Eiver and east of the Ussuri in 1858 spurred bilateral agreements that allowed considerable flexibility in cross-border trade, migration, and settlement. These agreements recognized the rights of Qing subjects, who had long resided on both sides of the Amur, and allowed them to stay in their settlements. Frontier rivers were open to navigation and tax-free trading by Russians and Chinese equally, subject to government regulations.[1] The St. Petersburg Treaty of 1881 restricted the commercial activities of Russian and Chinese merchants to a 50-verst (53 km) zone of tax-free trading along the Amur.[2] Trade along the Amur grew in tandem with frontier settlements and towns. After the 1880s, the Chinese colonization of Manchuria and the Russian colonization of the Amur and Maritime regions brought more settlers, but Russian agricultural colonization progressed slowly. The new Russian frontier towns were sparsely populated and needed cheap labour and services. In contrast, Chinese migration to Manchuria progressed quickly and spilled over into the Russian Far East.[3]

Chinese migrants began to dominate local labour markets and cross-border trade.[4] Chinese contract workers, farmers, and merchants became a strong economic force not only in Manchuria but also in the Russian towns of the Amur frontier, where they established trading networks with ties to gold mining and forestry-related industries. Together with Korean and Japanese migrants, they provided cheap labour and supplied young Russian towns and settlements with food and other daily necessities. Their growing presence in these towns until the 1920s underscored the porous nature of the Amur frontier, which was open for multinational economic activities. This chapter further develops the argument in Chapter 3 that the Russian provincial administration had little control over its frontier with China, reflecting the weakness of Imperial Russia's colonization policies. Russian economic expansion to Manchuria went hand in hand with the increasing economic activities of Chinese migrants in the Russian frontier towns. This chapter examines Chinese activities in Khabarovsk and Vladivostok and the persistent Chinese economic influence in the Amur frontier region.

Frontier Towns

Established in 1858 as a Russian military settlement known as Khabarovka, Khabarovsk became the administrative centre of the Amur Province. It occupied a strategic position at the confluence of the Amur and Ussuri rivers, a point separating the Amur's lower section, which was Russian territory after 1858, from its middle section, which served as the Qing–Russian border. The two other major towns of the region were more than 600 kilometres from Khabarovsk: Blagoveshchensk to the east and Vladivostok to the south. Both had economic advantages over Khabarovsk. Blagoveshchensk was surrounded by rich reserves of gold, grew as a result of a gold rush, and soon became a thriving trading centre. Vladivostok, a military fort since 1860, eventually became an important seaport and remained so after the Russian Revolution. Khabarovsk was situated at the border of two Russian provinces, Amur and Maritime. When the newly established Priamur governor-generalship united Amur and Maritime provinces in 1884, Khabarovsk was named the new administrative centre, which gave it political clout.[5]

From early on, Khabarovsk had a Chinese population. In 1865 there were 1,294 Russians, mostly soldiers, and 20 Chinese. For the next two decades it remained a sleepy village, but after 1884 its population started to grow. In 1898, Khabarovsk District had 16,550 Russians, 5,761 Goldi, 4,555 Chinese, and 666 Koreans.[6] From the very start, the town faced a labour shortage. The Russian military and civil administration moved in quickly; Russian peasants and labourers were slow to arrive, in part because the town was unattractive to migrants in several respects. As a young administrative town, it suffered from inadequate housing and provided few economic opportunities. A few nearby settlements along the Amur and Ussuri rivers were established for defence and border control, but these settlements engaged in little trade with Khabarovsk. Food and daily necessities in Khabarovsk during its early days were expensive and limited. Nor did geography favour the town, which was located on several hills, at the confluence of three streams. Frequent rains and annual floods turned the land between the hills into a muddy breeding ground for mosquitoes and flies. The main streets were badly paved with cracked wooden boards that often caused leg injuries. At night the town sank into darkness, as only one main street was lit with oil lamps.[7] The winters were long and cold, lasting from October to March, with temperatures falling to –25°C.[8]

In 1893, Khabarovsk received the status of town. Faced with the task of building modern infrastructure, the town's administration turned to Chinese labourers, who were abundant in the Ussuri region (Primorskii Province) and in nearby Manchuria. Among them were people who originally came from Shandong Province and other parts of northern China. Early Chinese contract workers in Khabarovsk worked in eight brick factories and a booming construction industry (see Figure 5.1). The construction of the Ussuri Railway from Khabarovsk to Vladivostok, which started in 1894, brought in more Chinese labourers. Russian railway companies, like their counterparts in the United States and in Canada, turned to Chinese labour to address labour shortages in the Russian Far East. About 40 percent of all construction workers on the Ussuri Railway were Chinese or Korean. Chinese workers were recruited from Yantai and Tianjin in China Proper and shipped to Vladivostok.[9] After the railway was finished in 1897, these workers either stayed in Khabarovsk or Vladivostok, moved to other Russian railway projects, or returned to China.

Chinese Migration and Trade

Chinese labourers arrived in Khabarovsk by several overlapping routes. Before the railways, rivers remained the best way of reaching Khabarovsk (see Figures 5.2 and 5.3). Three major waterways – the Amur, the Songhua, and the Ussuri – converged in two locations in the vicinity of Khabarovsk. Chinese migrants from Manchuria could reach Khabarovsk by these rivers, travelling up and down them in fishing junks. With the development of commercial navigation along the Amur in the late 1890s, Russian and Qing subjects had a choice of travelling on Russian or foreign steamships. However, travel by river was seasonal and unreliable.

Figure 5.1 Russian Orthodox church and Chinese temple in Khabarovsk | From photo album *Khabarovsk* (n.d)

FIGURE 5.2 Chinese workers and Russian officials in Khabarovsk | From photo album *Khabarovsk* (1901)

Even during navigable periods, some sections of the Amur and the Ussuri became so shallow that travel could be delayed for weeks. Khabarovsk could also be reached by land, mainly by horse cart along roads from Maritime Province. However, marshy areas at the confluence of the Amur and Ussuri rivers complicated land travel from Manchuria. Deep forests and bad roads made a journey from Maritime Province by land slow and dangerous. Despite difficult travel conditions, however, burgeoning economic activity across the Ussuri River increased human traffic between northern Manchuria, Maritime Province, and the frontier towns along the Amur River in the first decade of the twentieth century.

After 1897 the Ussuri Railway connected Khabarovsk with Vladivostok, creating a convenient transportation route for Chinese contract workers hired in Zhili or Shandong and shipped to Vladivostok. Poor Chinese peasants could hardly afford to travel by train on their own and depended on the contractors who were sponsoring them to pay their fare to Khabarovsk. In 1903, the Chinese Eastern Railway (CER) was linked to the Ussuri Railway, making it possible to reach Khabarovsk by train from the major towns of Manchuria. Service was again reduced in 1905,

FIGURE 5.3 Chinese and Russian workers in Khabarovsk | From photo album *Khabarovsk* (1901)

however, when, after defeating Russia in 1905, Japan took over the management of the South Manchuria Railway and restricted railway travel from Port Arthur on the Liaodong Peninsula to Khabarovsk.

It is difficult to determine accurately how many Chinese migrants there were in the towns of this frontier region, because they were highly mobile and many of them were unregistered. Most of these workers were migrants attracted by seasonal jobs. When their work was finished, they moved to the next place. Contemporary observers took into account only officially registered Chinese labourers. The first serious population census of the Russian Far East was conducted in 1897; according to it, there were 3,652 registered Chinese residents in Khabarovsk (see Table 5.1 for the total population).[10] Before the Russian Revolution in 1917, Chinese comprised between 20 and 30 percent of the urban population of the Russian Far East.[11] The overall number of the Chinese migrants in the Russian Far East in the peak year of 1910 was between 200,000 and 250,000. In 1914, there were 11,408 registered Chinese in Khabarovsk.[12] In Blagoveshchensk and Vladivostok, the proportion of Chinese workers to the Russian population was even higher, at times reaching 50 percent

Table 5.1 Population of Khabarovsk

Year	Population
1891	5,000
1897	15,000
1906	19,000
1909	40,000
1913	52,000
1917	51,300

Source: A.A. Stepanov, "Nekotorye voprosy istorii Khabarovska" [Several questions about the history of Khabarovsk], *Voprosy geografii Dal'nego Vostoka* 4 (1963): 343.

of the overall population. These numbers should be used with caution; they do, however, reveal that there was a sizable Chinese migrant population in rural areas and that the population varied from season to season.

Border control posts near Khabarovsk were located in the Russian settlements of Kazakevichevo, Koslovskaia, and Grafskaia. However, the rest of the border along the Amur River was poorly guarded or did not have any customs stations, allowing for easy entry to Russian territory.[13] Border control was weak, for there were not enough personnel to staff this vast frontier. At official border posts, the Russian authorities issued temporary permits. Chinese contractors issued travel permits on behalf of Chinese contract labourers, who travelled in groups and were not individually checked at the official points of entry. Most of the Russian customs officers did not speak Chinese, and the lack of qualified translators made it difficult to regulate migration. On Russian territory, Chinese documents were often resold or exchanged, making it difficult for the authorities to distinguish between legal and illegal workers.[14] Once the Chinese migrants reached their destination, the Russian authorities did not bother to monitor their movements.

Chinese merchants followed the Chinese sojourners to establish their own trading networks in the Russian towns, offering a whole range of services to Chinese and Russian communities.[15] In 1882 the first Chinese merchant association was established in Khabarovsk. Its members helped build a Confucian temple and an administrative building. By 1891 the Chinese community in Khabarovsk had its own government and even its own court. Two years later, when the newly appointed Priamur governor-general Sergei Mikhailovich Dukhovskii (1893–98) arrived in Khabarovsk, Chinese and Korean communities sent delegations to greet him.[16]

In the early twentieth century, a local joke described Khabarovsk as a town of three hills, two chimneys, and ten thousand portfolios – a reference to the abundant Russian civil and military bureaucracy and lack of trade there. Russia's official efforts to encourage new settlers from European Russia foundered. Khabarovsk, far from other urban centres and with little economic activity around it, did not attract Russian merchants either. Further darkening the town's prospects, in 1903 the newly completed CER chose Harbin for its headquarters. Harbin soon overshadowed Khabarovsk as a new dynamic place for Russian trade; after 1905, large enterprises in Khabarovsk were concentrated in the branches of a few Russian companies based in Harbin, Vladivostok, or the old trading centres of Siberia. Russian traders were lured to Manchuria by new business opportunities, such as lavish contracts with the CER and its enterprises (see Chapter 6). But Chinese merchants quickly filled the gap, replacing Russian entrepreneurs in delivering products from Manchuria to the Russian towns of the Amur frontier region.

Chinese businesses, large and small, penetrated every aspect of life in Khabarovsk, dominating the construction business, food supply, and the service sector. Moreover, Chinese firms in Russian towns controlled the individual Chinese who supplied the towns with the products of the Ussuri taiga, such as ginseng, rare mushrooms, furs, and valuable animal parts (e.g., deer antlers and tiger paws). Chinese merchants also served as moneylenders to Chinese and Russians alike. A network of Chinese moneylenders existed in Russian towns and nearby indigenous settlements in the Ussuri region.[17] As noted in Chapter 3, the Chinese dominated the fur trade by establishing contacts with indigenous people throughout the Amur and Ussuri regions. Indigenous hunters exchanged pelts for daily necessities as well as for opium, alcohol, and tobacco and were often forced into debt. Chinese control over the indigenous economy infuriated Russian traders, who could do little to beat the competition.

Chinese merchants ran an extensive junk trade, using these iconic Chinese boats to trade with settlements along the Amur, Songhua, and Ussuri rivers. Before the railways, the Songhua River had been a major trade artery connecting Manchuria with the Amur region. Until 1900, Russian traders and administrators could not effectively control trade along the Songhua. One reason was the unwillingness of the Qing frontier authorities to let individual Russians trade there permanently. Another reason for weak trade was that Russian merchants did not understand trading conditions and local needs in Manchuria. Russian merchants who intended to trade along the Songhua on their own often could not sell their products. Compounding these difficulties, the language barrier forced Russian traders to rely on mediators, who were chosen from among the Chinese merchants, who often put their own interests first.

Geographic conditions gave another advantage to the Chinese merchants conducting the junk trade. The seasonal shallowness of the Songhua made navigation easy for junks and small boats. Moreover, the junk trade required a lifestyle to which only Chinese and indigenous fishermen and boat people were accustomed. Chinese merchants based in Sanxing, Bodune, and other settlements along the Songhua financed the junk trade by hiring boatmen and managing junks. These junks delivered agricultural products to Russian settlements along the Amur. Between 1893 and 1895, Chinese junks arriving from Manchuria along the Songhua brought to Khabarovsk wheat, barley, sorghum, millet, beans, noodles, oil, tobacco, and other basic supplies. Each year, the Songhua junk trade brought 500,000 poods of products to the Russian settlements along the Amur (1 pood = 16.38 kilograms). In 1894 they delivered 164,000 poods of agricultural products to Khabarovsk. The following year, they carried 194,000 poods, or 20 percent more. From Khabarovsk, these junks travelled to other settlements along the Amur and the Ussuri, carrying other goods for trade with local people. After these junks arrived in Khabarovsk, however, they had difficulty finding Russian cargo for the return trip. As a result, they were frequently sold or rented out to avoid financial loss.[18]

The Chinese junk trade was significant in Vladivostok, the southernmost extension of the Amur frontier. The harbour at Vladivostok hosted numerous Chinese seagoing junks carrying products such as fish, crab, seaweed, and trepang (sea cucumber). These products were popular in Chinese cuisine and medicine. Chinese firms hired individual Chinese traders to buy these products from fishermen, then processed them and sold them in Manchuria, China Proper, or the Chinese settlements in the Ussuri region. The Asian population of Vladivostok, which consisted of Chinese, Korean, and Japanese civilians, was another growing market for sea products.

Associations of Chinese traders in Vladivostok supervised the activities of nearly all the Chinese civilians there through regional associations (*huiguan* in Chinese), which were widespread in China Proper, frontier areas, and Chinese overseas communities. Most of the members of a given association were men from one region in China, residing or sojourning outside their home region.[19] Centred around a temple, these associations performed diverse functions for their members, including business, religious, social, and legal ones. They also established the rules of conduct that governed business and set standards of trade, which were observed across the Amur frontier region.[20] As a result of strong mutual support in the Chinese communities, these associations came to dominate small trade in the Amur frontier towns. This trade offered relative social mobility for Chinese migrants. According to the Russian observer P. Volnogorskii, any Chinese commoner in Vladivostok who saved several dozen rubles immediately turned to petty trade in virtually anything: oranges, nuts, threads, stockings, needles, and so on.[21] Between jobs, seasonal labourers often turned to different types of petty trade.

Chinese traders generally did not seek Russian citizenship; they came to the Russian towns to make money for their families, then returned to their homes. However, there were exceptions. One of these was Ji Fengtai, a Chinese merchant from Shandong Province, who became a naturalized Russian citizen in Khabarovsk, where he acquired a Russian name, Tifontai. Although he served as a mediator in the Sino-Russian border trade, little is known about his background. He first came to the Russian Far East in 1873. His company, Tifontai and Co., was based in Khabarovsk, but his commercial activities made him well known on both banks of the Amur. His firm was involved in a wide range of trading activities, including wheat and flour, tea and wine, furs, building materials, and railway construction. He built mills and brick factories and invested in land and real estate in Khabarovsk and Vladivostok. In 1895, Ji Fengtai and Khabarovsk merchant Dmitrii Bogdanov organized a trading expedition up the Songhua River on the steamer *Telegraph.* The aim of this expedition was to advance Russian trading interests in Manchuria. The steamer passed such trade centres as Sanxing, Hulan, and Bodune and returned with a barge and three Chinese junks carrying livestock, grain, wool, and tobacco. This trip inspired other Khabarovsk merchants, encouraged by the Priamur governor-general Sergei Dukhovsky, to begin trading along the Songhua.[22] Ji Fengtai became a pioneer in this trade, establishing ties with Chinese merchants in Sanxing and Bodune. In 1896 he represented Khabarovsk merchants at the Russian trade fair in Nizhnii Novgorod, where he displayed furs in the pavilion of the Priamur Governorship.[23]

As a naturalized Russian citizen, Ji Fengtai was a controversial figure during the period of Qing–Russian tensions around the turn of the twentieth century. His trade supported Russian colonization efforts in Manchuria. Before 1904, his company built military fortifications in Lüshun and Dalian, both on the Liaodoing Peninsula, under the jurisdiction of Imperial Russia. His loyalty to the Russian authorities made him a rich man. On the eve of the Russo-Japanese War, his personal wealth had grown to three million rubles. During the Russo-Japanese War, he supplied food to the Russian army stationed in Manchuria and on the Liaodong Peninsula.[24] According to Major General Mikhail Grulev (1858–1943), an officer of the General Staff who met Ji Fengtai in Fengtian during the war, Ji was trusted by the high command of the Russian army and offered to organize anti-Japanese intelligence gathering.[25] His company's operations in Manchuria could not possibly have gone unnoticed by the Qing provincial authorities, whose position during the war was threatened by the military presence of Russia and Japan.

Ji Fengtai's life provides a powerful example of a hybrid merchant identity that does not fit into official, nation-centred historical narratives in China or Russia. Because of his suspicious (from the Chinese point of view) dealings with Imperial Russia, historical studies about him are scarce in China. In Russia, he is remembered a loyal servant of the Imperial Russian state who was respected by the Chinese community in the Russian Far East and trusted by the Russian provincial authorities. As a first-guild merchant, he was entitled to conduct trade all over Russia and abroad. Navigating two cultural worlds, he spent most of his adult life in the Russian Far East but never fully gave up his Chinese identity. He petitioned Russian authorities to build a Confucian temple in Khabarovsk, and he took care of the Chinese community there. He also refused to cut his queue and continued to wear Chinese clothes. He became a natural go-between, able to relate to and negotiate between the Chinese merchants and the Russian authorities. As early as 1886, he offered his linguistic skills to the Russians during negotiations to demarcate the Qing–Russian border along the Ussuri.[26] Later, he was able to invest in businesses on both sides of the Qing–Russian frontier, thus spreading his trading network from Khabarovsk and Vladivostok to Harbin, Fengtian, Lüshun, and Dalian. He must have possessed a strong frontier spirit, for one had to be determined if one hoped to conduct cross-border trade while the relations between the two empires were deteriorating.

The facts of his personal life are scarce and fragmented, but they reflect the fact that his life and work straddled several different cultures. Like many wealthy Chinese merchants of his time, he had several wives and many children. He had several daughters by his first wife, who was Chinese, a son and a daughter by a Japanese wife, and a son from a Russian wife. He never adopted the Russian Orthodox faith, but several of his children converted to Christianity and remained in Russia. Despite supplying the Russian military during the Russo-Japanese War, his business suffered and never fully recovered. In 1907, his company ran into problems with contractors and creditors, and he moved to St. Petersburg, where he tried and failed to arrange government help in recovering his losses. Before he died there in 1910, he expressed his wish to be buried in China, but his final resting place is unknown.[27] Ji Fengtai's story is known because his public image as a prominent Chinese merchant in the Russian Far East attracted the attention of provincial newspapers. In contrast, the majority of Chinese migrants in the Russian Far East vanished without any record.

Sources of Confrontation

From an economic standpoint, the Russian authorities took a positive view of Chinese contract labour and trade. Chinese traders were considered to have superb organizational skills, and Chinese workers were seen as less demanding than Russian workers, but with an excellent work ethic. Chinese traders brought cheap products to the Russian population, especially food from Manchuria, while Chinese migrants provided labour. Economically, the Chinese contribution was a necessity, but with the development of Russian merchant trade on the Amur frontier, mixed feelings about the growing Chinese presence arose among Russian authorities and traders. During the first decade of the twentieth century, Russian concerns about the Chinese presence were manifold. One area of contention was the seasonal nature of Chinese labour. Chinese labourers saw themselves as temporary workers in an alien land; furthermore, they spent very little money in this same land, instead sending or taking their earnings back home. Also, Chinese migrants and traders refused to adapt to Russian cultural norms. Unlike Korean newcomers, Chinese migrants refused to convert to Christianity or become Russian subjects. Another area of contention was the Chinese merchants' economic domination of the indigenous population, which supplied them with furs and other animal products. According to Arsen'ev, indigenous hunters in the Ussuri taiga were reduced by Chinese fur dealers to the status of slaves.[28] Moreover, Chinese trading networks penetrated the Ussuri forests, nearly monopolizing the fur trade and seriously depleting Ussuri natural resources; all of this undermined prospects for Russian economic colonization and the development of Amur and Maritime provinces. Finally, Chinese traders were blamed for developing an illegal opium and *hanshin* (Chinese vodka) trade, not only among the Chinese and indigenous populations but also among the Russian peasants, the Cossacks, and the army. Thus they were seen as major contributors to opium addiction and alcoholism in the Russian frontier towns. Indeed, the Chinese quarter in Khabarovsk had a reputation for opium smoking, gambling, and prostitution.[29]

These Russian concerns were encompassed by ideological notions of the "yellow peril," which was the term typically resorted to by Russian officials when blaming the backwardness of Russian frontier towns on the growing presence of an "inferior race." Before 1900, the Russian authorities had started to introduce measures limiting Chinese migration to Russian towns. The Russian occupation of Manchuria in 1900 was accompanied by heavy restrictions on the Chinese population of the frontier towns (see Chapter 7). Between 1893 and 1902, Khabarovsk and Vladivostok passed laws that segregated all Asian migrants and that moved them to designated areas within the towns. In 1897 the Khabarovsk municipal Duma (an elected administrative body) moved all Chinese residents to the barracks formerly occupied by Russian troops near docks on the Amur River. A few wealthy Chinese were allowed to live outside the Chinese quarter. After the Russian defeat in the war with Japan, stricter measures were introduced across the region. Meanwhile, Russian official policy began to favour Russian settlers and to encourage more Russian labour. In the first decade of the twentieth century, new regulations to control the inflow of Asian migrants imposed the following restrictions:

1. Only naturalized Russian subjects could settle permanently in Russian towns.
2. The local population could not rent homes or land to foreigners.
3. Companies and individuals could not hire foreign labour.
4. Passports and migration documents were to be inspected at the borders and in the towns.[30]

These measures did not halt Chinese economic activity in these towns. By 1912, in Khabarovsk alone, there were 762 Chinese-owned trading and industrial enterprises and 1,160 enterprises owned by Russians. In other towns, small Chinese companies dominated the economic scene. In 1915, Kunst and Albers, a large firm headquartered in Vladivostok, made estimates of potential competitors among small Russian and Chinese companies in frontier towns. Khabarovsk had 223 Chinese and 220 Russian companies, while Vladivostok had 501 and 290, respectively.[31] Faced with an increasing Chinese and Korean population, and with growing economic competition, the Russian government introduced economic measures to curb Chinese economic influence. In 1914, Priamur governor-general Nikolai L'vovich Gondatti (1911–17) temporarily banned sable hunting in Amur and Maritime provinces. One year later, Russia reached an agreement with China to ban all alcohol trade in the 53 kilometre zone along the Amur border.[32] These laws were intended to destroy trading networks between Chinese communities in the towns and those in the taiga. During the same year, the Priamur provincial legislature passed the most radical measure to date: Asian citizens were to be removed from Russian towns. These measures were never effective and were relaxed as quickly as they were adopted. Law enforcement was inconsistent because of personnel shortages in the customs and police forces and because Russian police assigned to the migrant communities of Khabarovsk and Vladivostok were corrupt and inefficient. Then the First World War broke out, which led to the abandonment of any attempt to restrict Chinese migration to this frontier, for it was recognized that the Chinese were vital to the war effort in European Russia. In the Russian Far East, they became heavily involved in supplying labour and food for the army.

Who Runs Business Here?

While small Chinese businesses dominated local trade, big business was in the hands of Russian and Western companies. The Russian state did not invest large amounts of capital in civilian projects; nor was there a traditional landed gentry class typical of European Russia. Instead, all of the best lands were leased to Cossack settlers, who rarely prospered and who lived by renting their land to the poorer newcomers, usually impoverished Russian, Chinese, or Korean peasants. The construction of the Ussuri and Amur railways brought the first Russian industrialists and merchants from Siberia. Gold mining created wealth and an entrepreneurial spirit among Russian merchants in Blagoveshchensk, but nothing similar seemed to spur trade in Khabarovsk. On the contrary, Khabarovsk's bureaucrats had become the town's elite even though official salaries there were not very high. The towns along the Amur were built and governed much like towns in Siberia or European Russia. Despite a sporadic Asian and European presence, these towns remained Russian in character, with the highest building in each being either a Russian Orthodox Church or a provincial administration building. Real power was in the hands of the military and civil administration, whose personal interests overshadowed the power of merchants. In the first decade of the twentieth century, some local Russian merchants began joining the ranks of the municipal government. One of them, Aleksandr Vasil'evich Pliusnin (1864–1921), came from a local merchant family. In 1909 he inherited a local family business, which had been in existence since the founding of Khabarovka.[33] Pliusnin and Company ran lumber mills, flour mills, and retail shops and had offices in all nearby settlements. In 1914, Pliusnin, by then a millionaire, was elected head of the municipal Duma of Khabarovsk.[34]

The remoteness of the Amur frontier and its lack of development presented opportunities that attracted foreign entrepreneurs. Foreigners had a major share in paddlewheel and steam navigation along the Amur River. In 1895, one of them, the American entrepreneur Enoch Emery, established the Amur Navigation Company, organizing freight and passenger transport along the Amur on foreign steamers. His company purchased its equipment and ships in Europe and relied on local labour. Foreign capital was allowed with great caution; also, it had to be officially sanctioned, which opened numerous possibilities for bribery. Throughout Russia, foreigners secured their involvement in Russian commerce and industries by accepting Russian citizenship. Until the First World War, German merchants in the Russian Far East could become naturalized Russian citizens without losing their German citizenship. This was not surprising in a country where Tsar Nicholas II (1894 to 1917) had a German wife, a daughter of the Grand Duke Ludwig of Hessen and a granddaughter of Queen Victoria. The ethnic German background of two Russian governor-generals of the Priamur region – Andrei N. Korf (1884–93) and Pavel F. Unterberger (1906–10) – may partly explain their "tolerance" of German entrepreneurs in the region.

The dominant player in the commerce of the Amur frontier region, and the earliest European one, was a German firm, Kunst and Albers, founded in 1864 in Vladivostok by two Hamburg merchants, Gustav Kunst and Gustav Albers. The company was involved in general trade, shipping goods from Europe to Vladivostok and distributing them from there to the rest of the Russian Far East. Its commercial activities ranged from managing shipping and insurance businesses to running warehouses and major department stores built in German baroque style in Russian towns. The company even shipped seaweed supplied by Chinese junks on the coast of the Sea of Japan. By 1914, the company had forty branches worldwide and had became truly transnational, relying on smaller Russian and Chinese merchants and labour. Russian and Western entrepreneurs in this region looked more favourably on Chinese traders and labour than did Russian provincial officials, for they understood the importance of the Chinese to their own business empires.

The Chinese presence in Russian towns testified to the fluid nature of the Amur frontier region. Economic migration from China Proper northward went beyond Manchuria to Russian towns, by land and river, and circumvented Manchuria by sea from Yingkou to Vladivostok and the Ussuri Region. Half-hearted Russian efforts to limit Chinese immigration were ineffective, and Chinese migrants moved back to the lands lost by the Qing to the Russians.

Chinese migrants and traders travelled freely and established their own networks during the same period that Russian engineers, traders, and industrialists were moving into the heart of Manchuria. The Russian government, frustrated with the slow Russian colonization of the Russian Far East, recognized the importance of Chinese labour and trade and relied on it heavily. At the same time, Russian officials intended to restrict Chinese migrants to "coolie" labour. The growth of Khabarovsk and Vladivostok and the lack of a strong Russian merchant class allowed Chinese traders to participate in the local economy and to dominate cross-border trade. Official restrictions on Chinese activities had a limited impact. Despite measures to segregate Asian migrants, the Russian provincial government was confronted with an increasing Chinese population in "typical Russian towns." The Chinese themselves did not consider these towns entirely Russian and continued to use the century-old Chinese names Boli for Khabarovsk and Hailanpao for Blagoveshchensk, and the more recent Chinese name Haishenwei for Vladivostok.

The growing Chinese presence in Khabarovsk can explain why Russia never considered building a railway from Harbin to Khabarovsk. This line could have turned Khabarovsk into another thriving centre of Sino-Russian trade. However, Khabarovsk remained mainly an administrative and military town for geostrategic reasons. The Songhua River became a major trading route for Chinese goods to Russian towns. During the hostilities at the time of the Boxer Rebellion of 1900–01 and the Russo-Japanese War of 1904–05, Russian towns along the Amur became the backbone of the Russian army's presence and temporarily regained their status as pure Russian towns. Yet the importance of Chinese labour and small business for their development was tacitly recognized even by the most xenophobic Russian officials.

6
A Railway Runs through It

The arrival of railways transformed the Amur frontier region by creating new economic opportunities for the Qing and Imperial Russian subjects. The Chinese Eastern Railway (CER) (1898–1903) was the longest railway through Manchuria and the first built by the Russian government outside Russia. The CER symbolized the Russian state's efforts to stretch its political, economic, and cultural influence beyond its eastern borders. This railway's role in Russia's eastward expansion is well-known, but its influence on the Amur frontier region and on the local society and economy is less well understood. The railway strengthened the Russian presence in Manchuria and facilitated cross-border movement of people and goods; it invited international capital and brought industrial development and urban growth along its route. For the Russian government, it was also an enormous and expensive effort to expand its influence in China and in East Asia.

This chapter describes how the railway was built and how it transformed the economy and urban development of this region. It argues that despite Imperial Russia's ambitions and the promise of great profits in Manchuria, the CER's foray into this region was only partly successful, in part because the planners disregarded the region's natural conditions as well as the many costs of railway expansion in unfamiliar lands. In the long term, the railway was neither a successful tool of Russian expansionism nor solely responsible for the economic development of the Amur frontier region. As a transit line, backed up by Russian colonial interests and Russo-French capital, its benefits never reached the majority of the local, predominantly Chinese population; it served the commercial needs only of the settlements adjacent to it. As one of Russia's colonization projects in the Amur frontier region, it was only moderately successful and left a mixed legacy.

Railway and Imperial Expansion

The CER was part of the Russian state policy to link European Russia with its ice-free port on the Pacific, making it possible to travel and transport goods between St. Petersburg and Vladivostok. This railway extended the Trans-Siberian Railway, linking Siberia with Maritime Province and the Sea of Japan. Both the Trans-Siberian Railway and the CER were built under the guiding principles of the Russian finance minister, Sergei Witte, a firm believer in the state-guided industrialization of Siberia and Russia's peaceful expansion in the Pacific through trade and rail. He envisioned the construction of the CER not only as a strategic shortcut to the Pacific but also as a commercial enterprise potentially beneficial to Russia, China, and Japan.[1]

During the 1890s, the international situation along China's northern coast was tense as various powers competed for influence. The strategic location of the Liaodong Peninsula, on the Yellow Sea close to major ports and the capitals of China and Korea, turned it into a hotbed of imperial rivalries. After defeating China in a brief war in 1894–95, Japan gained control of the peninsula, weakening China and threatening Russian interests in southern Manchuria. Together with France and Germany, Russia demanded that Japan return the peninsula to China. By helping the Qing government negotiate with Japan for its return, Russia gained momentum in advancing its interests in China. At a meeting in Moscow on May 22, 1896, Witte, Russian foreign minister Aleksei Lobanov-Rostovsky (1824–96), and Qing senior official Li Hongzhang (1823–1901) signed an agreement of strategic partnership between the Qing and Russian empires against a possible Japanese attack. Under this agreement, the Qing government granted railway concession rights in Manchuria to the Russo-Chinese Bank, backed by the Russian government. On August 27, 1896, the Russo-Chinese Bank and the Qing government signed a contract for the construction of the railway. Through this contract, Russia obtained the right to build and use this railway to transport goods, civilians, and troops. The Chinese government retained its right to buy the railway back after thirty years of Russian ownership.[2]

FIGURE 6.1 Russian map of the CER and Manchuria, 1901 | From Evgenii Kh. Nilus, ed., *Istoricheskii obzor Kitaiskoi Vostochnoi Zheleznoi Dorogi, 1896–1923 gg.* [, Vol. 1 (1923)

Witte's policy of peaceful economic penetration was accompanied by territorial expansion. Two powerful lobbies within the ministries of finance and war convinced the young Tsar Nicholas II to move beyond Russia's agreements with China. In 1898, in violation of its promise not to seek territorial gains in China, the Russian navy occupied Port Arthur and Dalny[3] while the Russian government negotiated with the Qing court a twenty-five-year lease of a part of the Liaodong Peninsula. The same year, Russia obtained the right to build the South Manchuria Railway, which would link the future CER with an ice-free port in Dalny, on the southern tip of the Liaodong Peninsula (see Figure 6.1).[4] These agreements set the scene for Russian imperial expansion in Manchuria. Witte considered the Russian occupation of the Liaodong Peninsula a dangerous policy, one that would alienate China and Japan.[5]

The location of the CER (constructed 1898 to 1903) reveals Russia's geopolitical agenda, which was to strengthen its colonization of the Amur frontier region. This railway, together with the Ussuri Railway and the Amur Railway, form a semicircle around the northern territory of present-day Heilongjiang and Jilin provinces. The Ussuri Railway (constructed 1893 to 1913)[6] and the Amur Railway (1906 to 1916) were on the Russian side of the Qing–Russian border, parallel to the Amur and Ussuri rivers. The CER connected the Russian city of Chita with Vladivostok through Manchuria, crossing the Sino-Russian border twice. This railway network, when completed, would have connected landlocked Siberia to the Sea of Japan (via Vladivostok) and to the Yellow Sea (via Dalny and Port Arthur). However, the processes that put these three railways in place began at different times. Plans to build the Amur Railway were discussed in 1893, but actual construction started only after 1906.[7] The decision to build the CER as the shortest route to connect the Trans-Baikal and Ussuri railways delayed the construction of the Amur Railway. Completed in 1916, the Amur Railway connected Chita with Khabarovsk, creating a network of Russian railways surrounding northern Manchurian territory.

The route of the South Manchuria Railway suggests that Russia had designs on China Proper. Indeed, during the construction of the CER with its branch reaching into southern Manchuria, the proponents of Russian military expansion in Asia called for the annexation of Manchuria. The railways became a potential catalyst for military expansion. Ironically, by the time Russia completed its network of railways in the Amur Basin, its power in the region was exhausted. As Witte had predicted, Russia's military expansion beyond the Amur frontier brought it into war with Japan (1904–05). Ill-prepared, Russia lost this war and had to abandon its grand plans to absorb southern Manchuria; indeed, it surrendered Port Arthur and Dalny to Japan, as well as the Liaodong Peninsula and the South Manchuria Railway.

The Railway Company and Construction

Going back to the mid-1890s, the railway enterprise started with the establishment of the company. The Chinese Eastern Railway Company, established by the Russo-Chinese Bank and controlled by the Russian government, was responsible for building and operating the railway. It was a stock company operating under Russian law. Chinese involvement in this company was limited, even though the Chinese government appointed the president of the company and issued the corporate seal. It was the railway's general manager, appointed by Russia, who exercised real power; it was imperial Russian subjects who purchased most of the company's shares. Before 1924, the ownership and operations of the railway were in the hands of the Russian-controlled Chinese Eastern Railway Company, except for the southern Manchurian branch of the railway, which was ceded to Japan after the Russo-Japanese War.[8] This company administered the Russian colonization of Manchuria by managing concession zones and purchasing land. An agreement in 1896 granted the Chinese Eastern Railway Company a tax-free belt of land "necessary for the construction, operation and protection of the line, as well as the adjacent lands necessary for obtaining sand, rock and lime."[9] The original right of way (*polosa otchuzhdeniia*), a belt of land along the railway, was 220 feet wide. These favourable concessions turned the Chinese Eastern Railway Company into a major landowner.

The Chinese Eastern Railway Company also used its landowning rights to purchase land around railway stations to construct new towns.[10] For example, in 1900, the company purchased from local landowners 2,235 *desiatinas* (1 *desiatina* = 1.09 hectares) of land to build the new town of Harbin, an administrative centre to be located where the railway met the Songhua River. Expansion occurred rapidly; by 1902, the town had doubled in size. Within several years, Harbin had grown from a sleepy village into a thriving industrial and commercial town.[11] Several separate land concession agreements in 1904 and 1907 between the Chinese Eastern Railway Company and the Manchurian provincial administrations of Heilongjiang and Jilin provinces allowed the company to acquire more than 117,000 *desiatinas* of land, enabling it to play a major role in the economic colonization of Manchuria.[12] In addition, between 1898 and 1911 the company negotiated several coal and timber concessions with the provincial governments of Heilongjiang and Jilin. Initially used solely for the railway's needs, these concessions were later expanded for commercial purposes. In 1902 the CER had two coal mines in Fengtian – one in Jilin and one in Heilongjiang. After 1907 the railway administration negotiated free exploitation of coal mines within the 30 *li* (70 kilometres) railway mining zone.[13] The railway's forest concessions initially were limited to six areas along its route, three in Jilin and three in Heilongjiang, with access to the rich forests of Jilin. The railway's demand for timber grew quickly: according to several agreements with provincial authorities, signed in 1907 and 1908, the Chinese Eastern Railway Company annually needed 200,000 bundles of firewood, 800,000 railway ties, and 200,000 planks of timber. In Heilongjiang, the railway's needs were, respectively, 100,000, 300,000, and 100,000.[14] Enforcement of the agreements was loose enough that the company could purchase or sell land, timber, and coal well beyond the designated areas, either by paying bribes or by simply ignoring the agreements. These timber and coal concessions did not occupy a large portion of Manchuria, but the natural resources the Russians took over were among the region's best.

The CER accelerated Russian colonization by bringing Russian settlers to the stations along the railway. Harbin became a Russian town on Chinese territory, where the railway's administrators, engineers, and railway guards and their families came to live. In 1899, when the construction of the railway was in full swing, there were 30,000 Russians living within the railway zone; by 1911 their numbers had reached 200,000.[15] With growing Russian colonial enterprises in Manchuria, the Chinese Eastern Railway Company was similar to a colonial government, not only administering the railway zone and Russian settlements but also acting as a de facto diplomatic representative of the Russian government.[16] The Russian government saw this railway not just as an economic link between China and Russia but also as a means of bringing European civilization to Asia.

In 1923, Evgenii Nilus (1880–1945), an employee of the CER and the author of the first definitive history of this railway, compared it with the Suez and Panama canals. He wrote that this railway created a new opportunity for peaceful coexistence between West and East. He claimed that without the CER, Manchuria would remain an abandoned desert: "Here we can witness how the European West, armed with solid science and technology, has moved towards the East, and by this peaceful advance it gradually achieves a bright victory, joining in the new lands and people to the common creative work for the good of humanity."[17] Did the CER achieve this goal? Or was it an illusion, shared by the overconfident Russian administration in Manchuria?

The CER was built remarkably quickly – 2,500 kilometres of line in only five years. The T-shaped line ran from Manchzhuriia (Manzhouli) to Pogranichnaia (Suifenhe) and from Harbin to Port Arthur. In April 1897, the first group of engineers started surveying the land. Four months later, construction was officially launched.[18] In 1898, Harbin, conveniently located in the heart of northern Manchuria, was chosen as an administrative and industrial site, as well as the future meeting point of the railway's three sections. Construction was completed rapidly by building simultaneously from different directions. The construction was divided into thirteen sub-sections between the stations of Manchzhuria and Pogranichnaia, of which three sub-sections were around Harbin. The construction of the southern Manchurian line was divided into eight sections, of which three were based in Port Arthur.[19] Under the original plan, the section from Port Arthur to Harbin was to be completed first. An eastern section from Harbin to the border with the Ussuri region was second. A western section from Harbin to the border with the Trans-Baikal region was completed last. In 1901, all of the major segments of the CER were linked together, marking a soft opening, with temporary bridges, of the Trans-Siberian Railway.[20]

Overall, the CER's builders did not encounter any serious opposition from the local population, except for the disruptions caused by the Boxer Rebellion in 1900 (see the next chapter). From the very beginning, the railway's administrators upheld their agreement with the Qing government to bypass Chinese villages, graves, and sacred lands.[21] The railway's southern section ran through relatively populated areas of Shengjing (part of present-day Liaoning Province). However, its eastern and western parts ran through sparsely populated steppes and mountain ranges, home to scattered indigenous, Mongol, Manchu, and Chinese settlements.

Engineers, Workers, and Merchants

The railway's administrators and technical staff were predominantly Russian. The first president of the Chinese Eastern Railway Company was appointed by the Chinese government, but his power was nominal – the real head of the enterprise was the Russian-appointed chief engineer. From 1897 to 1900, Xu Jingcheng (1845–1900), a former Qing envoy to Russia and Germany, served as the railway's first president; from 1897 to 1903, Alexander Yugovich served as its first chief engineer. An ethnic Serb educated in England, he had supervised the construction of the Ryazan'–Ural Railway from 1892 to 1897.[22] In 1903, Dmitrii Leonidovich Khorvat succeeded Yugovich as chief engineer, holding the post until 1921. Russian finance minister Witte and the railway's chief engineer personally picked the best Russian engineers educated in St. Petersburg and Moscow, especially those who had experience in building the Ussuri and Trans-Baikal railways. Among such specialists were Nikolai Nikolaevich Bocharov and Nikolai Sergeevich Sviiagin, who supervised the construction of the eastern – most difficult – section of the railway. [23]

Railway workers with experience were especially welcome. The railway administration encouraged qualified Russian workers to come with their families, offering them financial incentives. Ex-soldiers and Cossacks were also welcome to join the workforce. They received training, temporary housing, and free transportation. During turbulent times, the Cossacks could protect the railway's interests and employees in Manchuria.[24] But despite these incentives, hiring qualified Russian workers proved to be difficult. Bringing workers from European Russia to Manchuria was expensive. Moreover, workers viewed it as risky to move with their families to unknown lands without the promise of a sizable and stable income. While Russia in 1900 did not have a shortage of qualified railway workers, the Russian side of the Amur frontier region was still sparsely populated, and labour was in short supply. When in 1901 a group of several thousand Russian workers arrived to build the railway from Irkutsk, Blagoveshchensk, and Chita, one railway official called them dregs, unwilling to work and constantly drinking and fighting. Dealing with them "seemed no easier than dealing with the Boxers."[25]

The CER would have been impossible to build without Chinese labour. The money and expertise might be Russian, but the labour was predominantly Chinese. Labour shortages in a sparsely populated area, and the high cost of bringing workers from European Russia, resulted in the mass employment of coolie labour from China Proper, especially after 1899. These workers were recruited from Zhili, Shanxi, and Shandong provinces, mainly through the ports of Tianjin and Zhifu (Yantai), with the approval of the Qing provincial governments. More than 100,000 skilled and unskilled Chinese labourers were involved in the railway construction and related projects.[26] Unskilled workers excavated land, laid tracks, cut lumber, worked in factories, and built tunnels, bridges, and buildings. Among the skilled Chinese workers who had previously worked on the Trans-Siberian and Ussuri railways were bricklayers, carpenters, and cabinetmakers. The Chinese labourers were paid less than Russians, had a better work ethic, and were available in larger numbers. Relations between the railway administration and the Chinese workers were relatively peaceful overall, exception during the Boxer Uprising, when Chinese workers fled in the face of growing hostilities. In 1903, when the railway was completed, it had nearly 40,000 employees, of whom half were Chinese.[27]

Railway construction depended not only on local labour but also on local merchants. With few Russian businesses operating in the region, at first the railway administration relied heavily on local Chinese merchants. Chinese compradors hired, transported, and accommodated Chinese railway workers, while Chinese traders provided food and other daily necessities. The railway administration paid its employees not only in Russian rubles but also in local currency, the value of which often changed and was determined by local merchants. In Heilongjiang, the merchants of Qiqiha'er controlled local exchange rates and sold commercial products to the railway administration according to the prices on the Qiqiha'er market. As mediators, the Chinese merchants also provided local transportation and rented out local storehouses. The railway administration also depended on the services of Chinese security companies, which provided armed guards to accompany cargoes carried by horse cart to their final destinations.[28] Before 1900, Chinese merchants had the upper hand in dealing with the Russian railway administration, which had no choice but to pay its mediators well to ensure smooth and fast construction.

Challenges

From the outset, the railway construction faced multiple challenges. In 1897, Manchuria did not have the industrial development necessary to satisfy the needs of the railway, so the company set about building its own industrial base. But before the Chinese Eastern Railway Company could build its own factories in Manchuria, it had to bring most of the materials from outside the region. Steel and iron came from Russia proper; the building materials, machinery, and equipment came from England. Buying and shipping Aragon pine from the United States turned out to be cheaper than building timber-processing enterprises in forest-rich Manchuria or bringing the timber from Maritime Province. Not satisfied with the quality of locally produced bricks, the railway administration built its own brickyards.[29]

Climate and topography posed constant challenges for construction. Manchuria was notorious for its rainy summers and cold winters. The land could be surveyed only in the dry season, and construction had to be done while the land was dry but not frozen. Late summer rains destroyed roads and slowed the supply of building materials, and Chinese labourers refused to work in the rain or the cold. Even after the railway was built, floods often damaged railway facilities. Manchuria's rivers and mountains required the construction of numerous bridges and tunnels. The lack of detailed maps showing the course of rivers and mountains, and scarce information about the composition of land, led to disagreements about the placement of the railway. The CER's initial southern route through Bodune and Ningguta, however significant it was geopolitically, proved to be infeasible due to the impassable mountain range that ran east of Bodune to the Ussuri border. In 1898, after a survey by the chief engineer Yugovich, this route was dropped in favour of the northern route through Qiqiha'er and Hulancheng.[30]

The Greater Xing'an mountain range posed the biggest topographic challenge for the builders. The route through these mountains was surveyed in 1898 and 1899. The construction of the three-mile-long tunnel slowed the completion of the western section of the CER. Headed by the Russian engineer Bocharov, the project employed Italian engineers and was a technological breakthrough in Russian railway construction.[31] The bridges across rivers had to meet the high standards of the railways built in European Russia, but to speed up construction, most of the major bridges initially had wooden bases, which later were rebuilt in stone. The CER's longest bridge was built across the Songhua River; at 900 metres long, it required the work of hundreds of craftsmen. The Xing'an Tunnel and six major bridges (two over the Songhua River, one each over the Nen, the Hong, the Taizi, and the Qing) were a separate final phase of the railway construction.[32] Because of the complexity of the task and the speed with which it was accomplished, the CER turned out to be one of Russia's most costly enterprises and the most expensive part of the Trans-Siberian Railway: the 2,400 versts (2,544 kilometres) of this segment cost 375 million rubles, equal to what the Russian government had initially planned to spend on building the entire Trans-Siberian Railway. Rough topography, imported materials, the construction of many bridges and tunnels, the development of supporting enterprises, and extensive maintenance had driven construction costs sky-high.

Adding to the already excessive costs, the CER's operations were constantly interrupted by poor-quality construction, floods, or man-made disruptions. For example, during the Boxer Rebellion, 580 kilometres of the railway were destroyed, delaying construction for one year. Repair work alone cost 71.2 million rubles.[33] Even after the CER was finally open for traffic, train delays were common. For example, in 1902, a train carrying the military governor of Jilin Province went off the rails between Jilin and Harbin, delaying his meeting with the visiting Russian finance minister Witte for half a day.

Trade along the Railway

After its completion in 1903, the CER contributed to the economic development of the areas adjacent to the railway in Manchuria by opening them to international markets. It played a positive role in Qing–Russian cross-border trade, bringing new vitality to what had been sparsely populated lands and adding two new cross-border routes. It ran across Manchuria's main rivers and thus offered important supply routes for building materials, equipment, and spare parts arriving from Vladivostok via the Ussuri, Amur, and Songhua rivers. The completion of the Ussuri Railway in 1896 facilitated the transportation of cargo from Vladivostok via rail to the Ussuri River. To further its reach, the Chinese Eastern Railway Company rented boats belonging to the local river shipping companies. In 1898 the company established its own Songhua River fleet, headquartered in Harbin. The first boats and barges were manufactured in England, Belgium, and France and arrived in Vladivostok by sea. By establishing the fleet, the Chinese Eastern Railway Company provided the basis for the development of local commerce along the Songhua River. In 1903 it created a department of river navigation, which supervised repair work, cargo supply, and the construction of river embankments and piers. After the Russo-Japanese War, the Songhua fleet played an increasing commercial role in transporting passengers, wheat, beans, and manufactured goods.[34]

The new trade route the railway provided connected traditional economic areas of Manchuria. Before the railway was built, Manchuria's economic activities were defined by geography: cattle raising in Mongol lands and Hulun Buir (part of the Mongolian Plateau overlapping with eastern Manchuria), agricultural production of beans and wheat on the Songhua Plain, and hunting in the forests and highlands of the upper reaches of the Nen River and in Jilin Province. These regions had long been linked by rough tracks, which could only be used during the dry and warm seasons. Domestic animals and two-wheel carts travelled along these tracks to annual trade fairs in the trading centres of Hailar, Qiqiha'er, and Sanxing.[35] The railway connected these regions and gradually brought northern Manchuria into contact with international markets. Having access to the seaports in Vladivostok, Yingkou, and Dalian and links with railways on Russian territory, the railway carried cereal and cattle to the Russian Far East, timber and flour to southern Manchuria, and beans and flour to Japan and Europe. Table 6.1 shows the CER's growing importance in the transportation of cereal.

Table 6.1 Transportation of cereal by the CER, 1903–17 (1,000 tons)

Year	1903	1904	1905	1906	1907	1908	1909	1910
Cereal	111.3	50	46.8	76.2	188.3	274.9	412.7	534.6
Year	1911	1912	1913	1914	1915	1916	1917	
Cereal	735.9	582	574.2	539	866	763.5	1002.1	

Source: North Manchuria and the Chinese Eastern Railway (Harbin: CER Printing Office, 1924), 86.

Besides becoming a major conduit for export products, such as beans and wheat, to international markets, the railway facilitated the flow of goods between Manchuria's sub-regions. However, the railway did not replace the old trade routes of Manchuria, as traditional carts proved to be a cheaper means of conducting local trade. Also, the railway bypassed the old urban commercial centres of Manchuria, and local trade was concentrated in rural areas and conducted along the old trade routes, far from the railway.[36] In 1907, 68 percent of the cargo carried by railway was for its own needs; only 32 percent was private shipments.[37]

The CER had moderately positive effects on Qing–Russian border trade, while never dominating it. Manchuria had been supplying meat, wheat, and other daily necessities to Amur and Maritime provinces even before the railway was completed in 1903. The railway crossed the Qing–Russian border at Manzhouli and Pogranichnaia stations, turning these places into vibrant cargo transit points. A dramatic increase in Qing–Russian trade along the eastern border after the Sino-Japanese War can be attributed to Russia's loss of the railway's southern branch to Japan. Table 6.2 demonstrates the share of Chinese exports to the Russian Far East in this trade. However, this railway did not reach the rest of the Qing–Russian border. While Vladivostok and Khabarovsk benefited from having a rail link to the CER, most of Amur Province, with its industrial and trade centre at Blagoveshchensk, did not have a railway connection and relied on cart routes for trade with Manchuria.

The railway brought Russian settlers and merchants to Manchuria. By 1903 there were 30,000 Russians in Heilongjiang Province. Compared to the local population of Manchuria, the number of Russian settlers was still small. From 1891 to 1908 the overall population of Manchuria increased from 8.1 to 15.8 million.[38] Russian influence was visible in the new railway stations and towns built along the lines in the Russian architectural style. Harbin, built as a Russian city on Chinese soil, became

Table 6.2 Imports and exports via the eastern section of the Qing–Russian border (1); and via Vladivostok and Nikolaevsk (2) (rubles)

Years	Chinese exports via (1)	Chinese exports via (2)	Russian exports via (1)	Russian exports via (2)
1901	12,353,324	6,470,536	212,265	789,300
1902	12,394,348	19,999,004	772,080	1,270,336
1903	22,927,226	15,869,313	13,711,022	1,512,619
1904	26,171,722	7,154,360	14,073,594	164,005
1905	11,616,614	19,822,410	24,676,406	4,850
1906	15,829,803	114,040,996	49,962,864	2,050,901
1907	23,159,039	86,660,162	15,401,784	5,409,250

Source: Statisticheskie svedeniia o torgovle Rossii s Kitaem i po otdel'nym vostochno-aziatskim granitsam za 1901–1907 gg. [Statistical data about the trade between China and Russia and along selected East Asian borders from 1901 to 1907] (Moscow: Moskovskii birzhevyi komitet, c. 1908).

the centre of CER economic activity. By 1911, Harbin had sixty-three factories owned either by the Chinese Eastern Railway Company or by Russian private capital. In 1913, it had more than one hundred Russian enterprises.[39]

Used mostly by the Russian state before the 1920s, the CER was too expensive to be used frequently by poor peasants or small merchants. For Chinese workers, a ticket for the express train cost the equivalent of several months' pay. The cost of freight and luggage for express and regular trains in general was higher than the price of a ticket, making the transportation of goods by train too expensive for small merchants. In 1910, British diplomat Alexander Hosie complained about the high cost of baggage while taking the CER. He advised others to travel light on Russian railways.[40] Table 6.3 shows the prices of tickets for different types of trains in 1912–13.

Harbin's Growth

The CER, despite its shortcomings, contributed to the economic modernization of Manchuria on terms favourable to Russia. One aspect of this modernization was the growth of towns along the railway. Several dozen stations along the railway developed into small towns, with Harbin

Table 6.3 Cost of travel and cost of transporting luggage along the CER, 1912–13 (rubles)

A. Express trains

From:	Manchuria			Harbin		
To:	1st class	2nd class	10 pounds of luggage	1st class	2nd class	10 pounds of luggage
Manchuria	–	–	–	54.00	33.75	45.35
Hailar	12.00	7.50	11. 85	43.50	27.75	37.35
Qiqiha'er	39.00	33.75	34.10	16.50	10.35	15.60
Harbin	54.00	33.75	45.35	–	–	–
Kuanchengzi	66.00	41.25	52.35	13.73	8.48	13.10
Pogranichnaia	84.00	52.50	59.85	31.50	19.73	28.10
Vladivostok	98.01	61.80	72.33	45.51	29.03	41.18

B. Regular trains

Stations:	1st class	2nd class	3d class	4th class	10 pounds of luggage
From Manchuria St. to Hailar:	8.40	5.00	3.00	2.00	11.85
To Qiqiha'er	26.00	16.25	9.75	6.50	34.10
To Harbin	36.00	22.50	13.50	9.00	45.35
To Kuanchengzi	44.00	27.50	16.50	11.00	52.35
To Pogranichnaia	56.00	35.00	21.00	14.00	59.85
To Vladivostok	63.43	39.46	23.97	15.49	72.83
From Harbin to Manchuria St.:	36.00	22.50	13.50	9.00	45.35
To Hailar	29.00	18.15	10.90	7.25	37.35
To Qiqiha'er	11.00	6.90	4.15	2.75	15.60
To Kuanchengzi	9.15	5.65	3.40	2.25	13.10
To Pogranichnaia	21.00	13.15	7.90	5.25	23.10
To Vladivostok	28.43	17.61	10.87	6.74	41.18

Source: Soobshchenie Evropy s Dal'nim Vostokom [Europe's transport connection with the Far East], Timetable (Winter 1912–13), 24.

FIGURE 6.2 St. Nicholas Cathedral in Harbin | Author's personal collection

and Dalny becoming major rail hubs. With the completion of the CER, Harbin, an administrative centre for the railway, took on a life of its own. Harbin was a Russian city on Chinese soil, and Russian extraterritorial rights protected Russian officials, railway employees, and residents both in Harbin and along the railway.[41]

Harbin itself was a boomtown. Long-time resident Simon Karlinsky compared the speed of its construction to that of the Imperial Russian capital St. Petersburg, built by Peter the Great as a "window to Europe," and to that of San Francisco during the California Gold Rush. During its first decade, Russian banks, schools, churches, and theatres were built there in the Classical Russian style. The town boasted a Russian stock exchange, grand administrative buildings, middle schools for Russian and Chinese children, chambers of commerce, a circus, cinemas, parks, and cafés.[42] By 1920, Harbin had institutions of higher education such as the Russian Law School and the Polytechnic Institute. The Russian Orthodox Church built a cathedral, named for St. Nicholas, in 1899 (see Figure 6.2). Over several decades, a seminary and twenty-two Russian Orthodox churches were built in Harbin, and the city became home to one hundred Orthodox priests.[43] Only a few of those Russian churches survive today.

Until the Russian Revolution of 1917, the Russians were a privileged group in a city with a rapidly growing Chinese population. In the first two decades of the twentieth century, the Russian population of Harbin grew steadily: 30,000 people in 1905; 43,000 in 1912; 60,200 in 1918, 131,000 in 1920.[44] Early Russian residents in Harbin represented most of the social groups in Tsarist Russia. The head of the railway administration from 1902 to 1920, Major General Dmitrii Khorvat, was from the nobility. The railway administrative departments were staffed by members of the Russian bourgeoisie, while Russian railway guards, stationed in Harbin, comprised 25,000 soldiers and 500 officers.[45] After Russia's defeat in the war with Japan, Harbin became a refuge for demobilized Russian soldiers and increasing numbers of merchants and entrepreneurs.

Urban society was organized along distinct class lines. According to Olga Bakich, most of the Russians in Harbin before 1917 were petite and middle bourgeoisie. Each group of Russians had its own neighbourhoods, clubs, and cultural and religious centres. For example, Novyi Gorod was a playground for the rich, and Pristan' was an enclave of traders. Russian workers lived in the Mostovoi and Koikovskii areas and poor Russians in Alekseevka, and the Chinese settlement was in Fujiadian.[46] During Harbin's early history, Chinese migrants could not achieve the living standards enjoyed even by poor Russians. With the development of international trade after 1906, Harbin became a cosmopolitan city, attracting people from other cultures of the vast Russian Empire (Poles, Jews, Georgians, Tatars, Armenians, etc.), as well as newcomers from China Proper, Japan, Korea, and Europe. The city's centre and its riverbank might be occupied by Imperial Russian subjects, but at least half the residents of Harbin were Chinese migrants, who worked in the railway facilities, helped build the city, and provided many services.[47] They were followed by Chinese entrepreneurs, who traded with the Chinese and Russian communities and supported the railway's operations and businesses (see Figure 6.3). Although Chinese Harbin lived and worked side by side with Russian Harbin, the Chinese population often resented the privileges enjoyed by Imperial Russian subjects, who rarely even bothered to learn Chinese.

Drawing on Chinese labour and on local natural resources, the CER brought new life to the existing Manchurian towns and created several dozen new towns along its route. But not all of its ninety-two stations became large settlements. Before the Russo-Japanese War, only thirteen railway stations grew into new towns with populations between 2,000 and 30,000.[48] While the creation of these towns gave a boost to the development of northern Manchuria, most Chinese migrants to Manchuria still lived in the countryside.

Figure 6.3 Board of Directors Building, Chinese Eastern Railway Company, Harbin | From Evgenii Kh. Nilus, ed., *Istoricheskii obzor Kitaiskoi Vostochnoi Zheleznoi Dorogi, 1896–1923 gg.*, Vol. 1 (1923)

The Limits of Railway Imperialism

The CER had a moderate influence on the local economy but was not an effective tool for the Russian colonization of Manchuria. Built rapidly and at great cost to the Russian government, it was perceived both as a commercial enterprise and as a strategic necessity to secure imperial gains in Manchuria. In these two roles, the railway was far from a success; it failed to make a profit until the 1920s, when it became a pure commercial enterprise. Before 1904, the Chinese Eastern Railway Company had done little to study trade conditions or transportation costs in Manchuria. According to British barrister Percy Horace Kent, who resided in China, the railway imposed "prohibitive rates, which left the native system of carriage by cart and river unimpaired ... The railway has thus far done nothing to foster trade, although the western and eastern sections pass through a line of country that promises at least reasonable returns on any well-managed line that serves it."[49] From 1905 to 1917, the net loss of the railway was about 450 million rubles.[50]

The CER enjoyed support from Tsar Nicholas II and the Finance Ministry, but it also invited criticism for severe mismanagement and corruption. General Evgenii Ivanovich Martynov (1864–1937), commander of the Amur border defences, criticized the railway company for granting lavish salaries to its managers and for having more employees than any

Russian ministry. Martynov's anger was directed at company's commercial agencies in Jilin, Qiqiha'er, Bodune, and Hailar, which consumed large amounts of money while being ineffective. He contended that the Finance Ministry was covering up the company's questionable commercial deals, besides stalling the efforts of the Russian Senate Committee to inspect it in 1910 and in 1913.[51] He was convinced that the CER did not serve Russian commercial or political interests.

Nor did it serve Russia's interests in indigenous communities. The company's hunger for natural resources brought its agents into the forests and river valleys. The Qing and Russian empires intensified their economic activities along the railway, depleting natural resources and creating new pressures on people involved in traditional hunting and fishing, thereby altering their ways of life.

The CER was Russia's easternmost line of imperial expansion, swallowing enormous quantities of state funding at the expense of the Amur and the Maritime regions, which remained economically weak.[52] Without a strong industrial base in the Russian Far East, Russia's position in Manchuria also remained weak. The railway ran through hostile territory and disrupted the lives of the local inhabitants. China's acquiescence to Russia's economic expansion hinged on Russia's promise not to turn Manchuria into a full-blown Russian colony like French Indochina or British Hong Kong. But expansion outside Russia's borders meant spending money for new possessions with an uncertain future. In 1909, Russian prime minister Count Vladimir Nikolaevich Kokovtsev (1853–1943) visited Harbin. Referring to the uncertain future of the railway and the towns along it, he lamented that after Russia had "poured gold into an alien field, we will have to leave it [the railway and the towns] to others ... for free."[53]

Kokovtsev's words were prophetic. The construction of the railway intensified international rivalries and conflicts in this region. After the revolution of 1917, Russia's influence in Manchuria declined, but the railway, its industries, and its new towns stayed on Chinese territory. Gradually, they became absorbed into the economic and cultural life of Manchuria. The CER brought economic modernization to parts of Manchuria and expanded Russian influence in the Amur frontier region, but maintaining these gains and further expanding by peaceful means was a daunting task. Eventually, Imperial Russia's railway expansion in Manchuria brought two major conflicts to this region, one with Qing China and the other with Imperial Japan. Witte's dream of peaceful railway expansion in Manchuria did not last long.

7
Conflict and War

Prior to Imperial Russia's expansion, war was a rare occurrence in the Amur frontier region. After the Qing lost its territory north of the Amur River and east of the Ussuri to Russia in 1860, both empires used peaceful means to strengthen their new border. State-sponsored agricultural settlers from China and European Russia established new villages and towns along the Amur River, but agricultural colonization was sporadic, owing to the lack of transportation, state funds, and knowledge about this region. Only limited Manchu frontier garrisons and Cossack contingents were stationed there. The conflicts that broke out on this frontier in 1900 and 1904 originated outside the region and were caused by the imperial ambitions of Russia and Japan on the Liaodong and Korean peninsulas. This chapter looks at the international and local dimensions of military conflict and examines how the military conflict related to the Boxer Rebellion (1899–1901) and the Russo-Japanese War of 1904 transformed the Amur frontier region. It argues that on an international level, these wars were the culmination of imperial rivalries among China, Russia, and Japan, which remained long after the collapse of the Qing and Russian empires. Domestically, these wars disrupted daily life and cross-border trade and created mistrust and anxiety in this frontier society. The local population adapted to war by either staying neutral or offering services to the occupying powers. This chapter also shows that military conflict in Manchuria drained Russian state resources, leaving the civilian and economic needs of the Amur frontier neglected.

Control over railways triggered military conflict in the Amur frontier region. Imperial Russia's railway expansion went hand in hand with territorial expansion and drove the Russian occupation of Manchuria (1900–03). Russian troops moved into Manchuria to protect the CER and its auxiliary enterprises; this was an unannounced war, part of the invasion of China by the forces of eight allied countries under the pretext of suppressing the Boxer Rebellion. The Boxer Rebellion was an anti-Christian and anti-foreign movement, originating in western Shandong and spreading north through Zhili Province.[1] In the summer of 1900, the Boxers briefly joined forces with official Qing militia in Shanxi, Inner Mongolia, and Manchuria. In Manchuria, the conflict involved Russian and Qing troops as well as Boxer rebels scattered among several major settlements along the CER. After suppressing the Boxers, Russia delayed the withdrawal of its troops from Manchuria. Russian territorial claims along the southern Manchurian branch of the CER and the presence of a Russian naval base at Port Arthur were the major reasons why Japan decided to launch a war against Russia several years later. The Russo-Japanese War (1904–05) was fought on a large scale in southern Manchuria and its surrounding sea. Its land battles involved larger armies than in 1900 and resulted in greater losses by the Russian and Japanese armies. These armies fought for influence on the Liaodong Peninsula and Korea in battles spreading from Lüshun (Port Arthur) to Fengtian (Mukden). This chapter discusses only those events of this war that were relevant to the transformation of the Amur frontier region. The Russo-Japanese War was a military conflict between Russia and Japan over control of Korea and the Sea of Japan and Yellow Sea. While the main battles were at sea, land battles on the Liaodong Peninsula, and especially the fall of Port Arthur, were equally crucial in determining the outcome of this war.[2] The Russian and Japanese military presence in Manchuria and in the surrounding seas turned the Amur frontier region into a hotbed of international rivalries, which not only alienated the governments and regional authorities, but also made the local frontier society more vulnerable to violence and displacement. Local populations and soldiers, drawn into these conflicts, became hostile to foreign enemies; they also grew to distrust their own governments.

Russia's Victory in Manchuria in 1900–01

A limited Russian military contingent appeared in Manchuria in the 1890s. Witte's "peaceful" economic colonization of Manchuria, backed by an agreement with Peking, did not guarantee Russian colonizers peaceful relations with the local authorities and population. In 1898 the Qing government leased part of the Liaodong Peninsula to Russia for a period of twenty-five years, and Russia treated it as a base for economic and military expansion in the region. Russia built an ice-free port at Dalny to facilitate international trade, as well as a new naval base at Port Arthur to protect and advance Russian strategic interests in southern Manchuria and Korea. In 1898, Port Arthur had fewer than 1,000 soldiers,[3] while the CER had several thousand armed soldiers to protect the railway and its property.[4] In the event of a military occupation of Manchuria, the future railway could serve as a major artery for moving troops from European Russia. By early 1900, there were around 11,300 Russian troops on the Liaodong Peninsula. Port Arthur had poor infrastructure – roads, housing, sewage systems, and drinking water were lacking – and much of what did exist would be destroyed during the Sino-Japanese War.[5]

The Boxer Rebellion, having started in Shandong and Zhili, spread to Manchuria.[6] The CER's armed defence proved insufficient and ineffective during the crisis. Qing government troops and Chinese rebels occupied all the major settlements along the CER, besides surrounding the railway guards in Harbin. For several months, railway construction was halted while the rebels damaged various sections of the line. The Boxers destroyed most of the railway's western and southern branches, burning railway stations and destroying telegraph lines.[7] Chinese contract workers either fled or were forced to abandon the railway. In June 1900, Russia started to mobilize troops from Amur and Maritime provinces to address the growing threat to its railway possessions in Manchuria.

The Blagoveshchensk Massacre (1900)

The first military clashes between Qing and Russian forces occurred at the Amur frontier. Indeed, the most violent events happened in the vicinity of the Russian town of Blagoveshchensk and spread to Qing fortifications in Saghalian and Aigun. Since 1858, Blagoveshchensk had served as an administrative centre of the newly founded Amur Province. In the 1890s a gold rush in the upper Amur transformed the town into a centre of Russian frontier trade with Manchuria.[8] Chinese traders, farmers, and contract workers supported the economy of Blagoveshchensk and surrounding areas. Dozens of Manchu villages on both sides of the Amur had stable trade relations with the Russian settlements, even though Qing and Russian subjects did not mix culturally.

In early June 1900, twenty miles east of Blagoveshchensk, Qing forces stopped and searched the Russian steamboat *Mikhail.* The steamboat was carrying arms and ammunition from Khabarovsk. When the Russian crew attempted to proceed, they were arrested. Qing soldiers occupied the south bank of the Amur, blocking river navigation for more than 160 kilometres between the Russian settlements of Ignat'evskaia and Poyarkova.[9] According to a later Russian official account, the Qing army repeatedly fired on Russian military boats travelling along the Amur between Blagoveshchensk and Aigun. A regiment of Amur Cossacks sailed from Blagoveshchensk and fired back at the Qing positions in Aigun. This led Qing forces to fire directly at Blagoveshchensk across the river, causing panic in the city. The presence of more than 4,000 Chinese traders and labourers in Blagoveshchensk added to the panic among the Russian population. Fearing that the Chinese residents of the town might help the Qing forces occupy the city, the military governor of the Amur region, Konstantin Nikolaevich Gribskii, ordered the police to deport them to Qing territory by forcing them to cross the Amur River.[10] The border crossing took place north of Blagoveshchensk.

Russian Cossacks divided the Chinese captives from around Blagoveshchensk into several groups and forced them to cross the river in at least four different shifts from July 17 to July 21. Those who refused to cross the river were beaten or killed. Since most of the victims could not swim, only a few reached the other shore. Many of the deportees were killed, and their homes destroyed.[11] Meanwhile, Qing soldiers intensified sporadic armed attacks on the Russians from Aigun. On July 21, Gribskii ordered Russian Cossacks to destroy all of the enemy fortifications on the Chinese side of the Amur.[12] Gribskii's orders could not be carried out immediately, as Blagoveshchensk did not have enough soldiers and arms to both defend itself and launch an attack. Earlier, in June, a small contingent of Blagoveshchensk Cossacks had been sent to Khabarovsk to join the expedition along the Songhua River to Harbin, which was besieged by the Boxers. For more than a month, Blagoveshchensk would remain poorly defended.[13]

The accounts of this massacre remain controversial, as there have been no serious investigations conducted in Russia since 1900. From the beginning, General Gribskii played a pivotal role in ordering the deportation of all the Chinese residents and allowing his subordinates to kill

Table 7.1 Details of the Blagoveshchensk Massacre, July 17–21, 1900

Crossing date	Chinese in each crossing	Russians in each convoy	Surviving Chinese
17 July	3,000–3,500	80–100	No more than 100
17 July	84	10	Almost none
19 July	170	50	No more than 20
21 July	66	36	More than half

Source: V., "Blagoveshchenskaia 'Utopiia,'" *Vestnik Evropy* 10 (1910): 232–35.

Qing subjects. The chairman of the Amur military government, Colonel V., whose full name was not disclosed, publicly told his staff that it would be no tragedy if all the Chinese were drowned and killed. He ordered the death of all the Chinese appearing on the Russian side of the Amur, without further instruction.[14]

Arrangements for the river crossings suggest that the killings were carefully planned. The organizers chose a quiet place near Verkhne-Blagoveshchensk, 10 kilometres up the Amur River from Blagoveshchensk, in order to avoid witnesses. Russian volunteers and the Cossacks, armed with guns and axes, accompanied the Chinese deportees, occasionally robbing and killing those who did not obey the orders. In Verkhne-Blagoveshchensk, no boats were waiting for the victims. Many Chinese were brutally killed before they were thrown into the water. Others either drowned or were shot while swimming. Table 7.1 provides details of the four documented "crossings." In the Blagoveshchensk massacre, around 3,500 Chinese died; only around 160 succeeded in crossing the river.

Similar methods were used against Qing subjects in other frontier settlements along the Amur River. Few living in Manchu villages near the Zeya River were able to escape the same fate as the Chinese in Blagoveshchensk. After forcing all the Chinese residents out of Blagoveshchensk, Cossacks burned all the Manchu villages around the Zeya, killing several thousand Chinese, Manchu, and Daurs, without distinguishing between civilians and the military. One survivor of these killings would recall that many corpses had been thrown into the Amur. Human blood covered the river's surface, contaminating the water.[15] Sporadic killings continued even after July 20, when General Gribskii issued an order to stop killing innocent Qing subjects and to aim only at armed Qing subjects who were attacking Russians.

The evidence suggests that the regional military command had organized the massacre as a tactic to frighten the Qing troops across the border. The killings carried a message that anyone attempting to challenge Russian power on the Amur would suffer a similarly brutal fate. On the eve of the Russian occupation of Manchuria, General Gribskii announced that "the name of the Amur Cossack will thunder through all of Manchuria and strike terror among the Chinese population."[16]

Russian writer Alexander Vereshchagin, who visited Blagoveshchensk three weeks after the massacre, naively believed that the massacre had been a tragic mistake resulting from fear and confusion over shootings from across the river. At the same time, he noted that local Russians were indifferent to the loss of life among the Qing subjects. He described the tragic scene he witnessed while travelling by steamer along the Amur River from Blagoveshchensk to Khabarovsk:

> "A Chinese!" – an old crew-member tells me in a low indifferent voice, as if talking about a snag … His face covered with a thin brown beard, he shows a disparaging smile, as if asking me not to pay attention to such a trivial matter …
>
> Our steamer passes a dead body. It is naked, of reddish and bronze colour, with hands hanging like whips, and widely open legs. It is floating, face down, as if thinking about something. The corpse was swollen, its legs and arms white as lime. Waves from the boat shake it, making it disappear in the water…More bodies of the Chinese appear, and now they float along the width of the Amur as if haunting us. The passengers come out of their cabins to see such a rare scene. It will stay in my memory forever. These are, possibly, those unfortunate who drowned near Blagoveshchensk …
>
> "Breakfast is served," – announces a waiter … The crowd goes inside. I do not feel like having breakfast. This horrible scene and poisoned air kill my appetite. I stay and continue to observe. The boat hits a corpse and the waves push it away. Its head is covered with a cloth. I think it must be a farmer. In Blagoveshchensk half of all farmers were Chinese.[17]

On reaching Khabarovsk, Vereshchagin met with the governor-general of the Priamur region, Nikolai Ivanovich Grodekov, who boasted about Russian military successes in Manchuria but remained silent about civilian casualties. Later, the author travelled south along the Ussuri Railway and found that news about the massacre was spreading only slowly in the Russian Far East. At a dinner party held by the governor of Maritime Province in Nikol'sk-Ussuriisk, attended by twenty Russian officers, he was "the first one to tell them about the Blagoveshchensk tragedy ... nearly one month after it happened."[18] The fact that his account of the massacre was published in 1903 in St. Petersburg is remarkable, for it exposed the ugly side of Russian expansionism to the Russian public in what was then a tightly censored imperial capital. But no further articles about this topic appeared, and no public discussion followed, for such things could undermine the news of Russian army's success in Manchuria.

Russian Troops in Manchuria

In late July 1900, in response to Boxer disruptions in Manchuria, Russian Cossack detachments crossed the Amur River and moved south towards major Manchu fortifications in Saghalian and Aigun. On August 2, with the help of artillery, the Russians took Saghalian. On August 5, they occupied Aigun and burnt it to ashes, forcing the remains of a 10,000-strong Qing army to retreat south.[19] The Russian army continued its advance in Manchuria and occupied all of the major settlements along the old trade route between Aigun and Qiqiha'er.

Another line of Russian attack followed the Songhua River. Alarmed by the news that Harbin was under siege, the Russians sent seventy-three boats there from Khabarovsk, burning Manchu settlements along their way. On July 28, they overran Sanxing and set it on fire. In August, the Russians seemed on the verge of achieving their goal, which was to conquer Manchuria, as the Russian horse cavalry commanded by General Paul von Rennenkampf (1854–1918) took Mergen and Qiqiha'er. The troops of General Vladimir Sakharov, commander of the Russian army in northern Manchuria, cleaned up all armed resistance along the main line of the badly damaged CER, from Qiqiha'er to Mudanjiang, and occupied Harbin.[20] Imperial Russia entered Manchuria from Manzhouli, Blagveshchensk, Khabarovsk and the Ussuri region (Figure 7.1). Russian troops converged on Harbin to celebrate the rapid conquest. With the fall of Qiqiha'er, the official seat of the Qing provincial government, the Qing army ended its organized resistance in northern Manchuria on August 28. It took the Russian army two months to restore control over major settlements along the CER's northern line.

In northern Manchuria, the Russians fought mostly with Qing troops, as Boxer influence did not spread to the north and west of Harbin. In southern Manchuria and along CER lines, Boxer influence was strong due to connections between the Boxers and migrants from Shandong, who worked as contract labourers along the railway and travelled all over Manchuria in search of seasonal work. But while anti-Russian resistance was limited to the destruction of railways and Russian property, the Boxer threat provided the Russian army with an excuse to move freely and wield power in occupied Manchuria. Sparse population and insufficient Qing defences allowed Russian troops to advance quickly and conquer major Manchurian settlements (see Figure 7.1).

Domestic Tensions

After the Manchu defeat in the north, the war in Manchuria was not over. Southern Manchuria, especially the area along the southern branch of the CER from Harbin to Dalny, was destroyed and persistently raided by the Boxers. By early autumn 1900, the Russian government had sent an additional 100,000 troops to Manchuria by rail and sea. Most of them arrived from Siberia and Amur and Maritime provinces, with smaller numbers coming from European Russia.[21] These troops were not enough to cover the vast territory of Manchuria, so after occupying major settlements from Aigun to Qiqiha'er, the Russian army concentrated its efforts in the south. For the purpose of conducting military operations, the Russian army divided Manchuria into northern and southern sectors, conveniently separated by the CER main line.

Domestic tensions in Manchuria facilitated the Russian military victory. First, there was no unified response to the presence of the Russian military; the Chinese population of Manchuria was divided. Local bandits had ravaged urban and rural areas of Manchuria before the Boxer Rebellion. But while the lines between bandits and Boxers may have been blurred, these groups were far from being a unified force wholeheartedly supported by the local population. The leaders of Manchuria were divided in their attitude towards the Boxers. Shou Shan, the military governor of Heilongjiang Province, and Jin Chang, the *fudutong* (lieutenant general) of Shengjing, sympathized with the Boxers' anti-Christian and anti-foreign objectives. Zeng Qi, the military governor of Fengtian, on the contrary, advocated suppression of the Boxers.[22] These leaders responded differently to the Russian military occupation of Manchuria. Shou Shan opposed Russians by fighting to the end; surrounded by the Russian troops in Qiqiha'er, he committed suicide to avoid being taken prisoner. After the fall of Qiqiha'er, Chinese official Cheng Dequan, Shou Shan's former aid, declined the Russian offer to become the next military

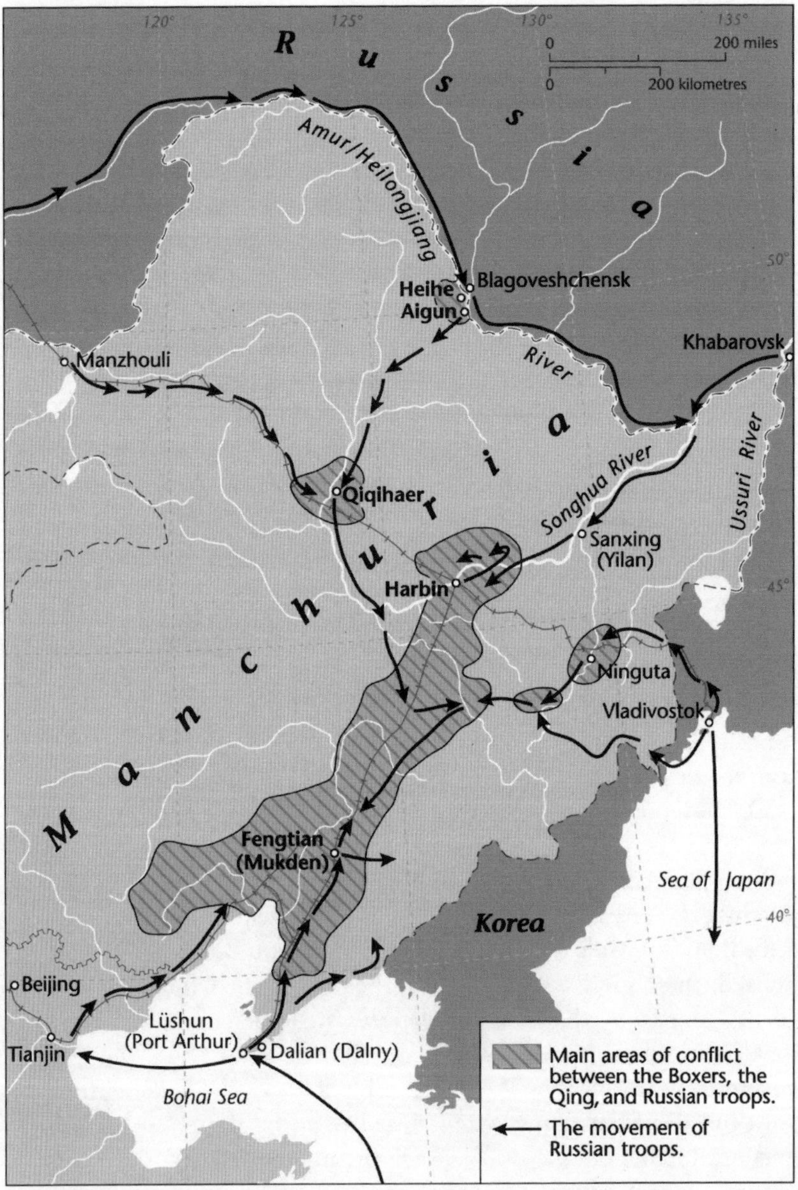

FIGURE 7.1 Boxer Rebellion in Manchuria and the movement of Russian troops, 1900 | From *Zhongguo Jindai shigao Dituji* (1984)

FIGURE 7.2 Russian soldiers in Qiqiha'er, Manchuria, 1900–01 | From photo album *Manchuria* (1900), Provincial Library of the Khabarovsk Region

governor of Heilongjiang and was briefly imprisoned by the Russians.[23] For his part, Chang Shun, the military governor of Jilin Province, chose to compromise with the Russians while secretly siding with the Boxers.

Facing a military threat from a foreign power, Qing troops stationed in Fengtian and Jilin provinces were ordered to side with the Boxers in armed opposition to the Russian military. However, Russian Cossacks and artillery, in a series of battles during August and September 1900, defeated them and took major cities along the southern branch of the CER (see Figure 7.2). Russian troops moving from Harbin to the south occupied Kuanchengzi, Jilin, and Kaiyuan. Those moving from Dalny to the north took the towns of Anshan, Shahe, Haicheng, Liaoyang, and, finally, on October 1, Mukden. In most of the battles, Qing troops outnumbered the Cossack and Russian troops.

So within several months, the Russian troops had been able to gain control over an area densely populated by Chinese and home to the two provincial Qing armies. How was it possible? One reason was the gradual demoralization of Qing troops after humiliating defeats in northern Manchuria that resulted in desertions. Also, the Qing troops lacked popular support, in part because the peasants found it difficult to distinguish between Boxer rebels, bandits, and fleeing soldiers. Devastated by marauders and intruders of all kinds, the local people hid food from their own troops. Russian generals then used tensions between the Qing military and civilians to their advantage. In an effort to gain the trust of the local population after their harsh treatment of the Chinese civilian population on the Amur, the Russian troops were instructed, on pain of death, not to abuse the local population of Southern Manchuria.

The Qing court's changing policy towards the Boxers, from opposition to support and back to opposition, led to changing attitudes towards cooperation with the Russians among the Manchurian administration. This may explain why, in September 1900, a group of Cossacks headed by General von Rennenkampf was able to take Jilin, a fortified city of 120,000, without a battle. A day before the planned siege, the confused military governor of Jilin had received an order from Peking to suspend hostilities against the Russian troops.[24] Nor did the occupying Russian forces meet unified opposition from local civilian leaders. For example, the administration, gentry, and merchants of Jilin were not interested in supporting armed opposition against the Russian presence, as protracted war would have jeopardized mutually beneficial contracts in railway construction and commerce.[25]

The Russian military occupation of Manchuria had several long-term consequences for the development of the Amur frontier. For the Chinese, the violent expulsion of Qing subjects from their settlements along the Amur River and the destruction of these settlements served as a painful reminder of the Aigun Treaty of 1858, which they had been forced to sign. Chinese traders, merchants, and seasonal labourers were well aware of their vulnerable position on this frontier, where it seemed no law could guarantee their safety, even though the Aigun Treaty supposedly recognized and protected all existing Manchu settlements on the Russian side of the Amur River under Russian law.[26] The Russian looting and burning of sixty-four Manchu villages along the Zeya River, a tributary of the Amur River on the Russian side of the border, had violated this treaty. Surviving Chinese victims and witnesses of forced repatriations from the Amur carried the news of slaughter, destruction, and looting to northern Manchuria, discouraging other peasants from going north of the river.

The Qing–Russian war in Manchuria fed anti-Russian sentiment among students and merchants in China's treaty ports, especially when Russian troops were slow to withdraw from Manchuria.[27] Admiral Evgenii Alekseev, head of the Pacific fleet and Russian army on the Liaodong Peninsula, advocated keeping Russian troops in Manchuria. On November 13, 1900, an agreement signed by Alekseev and Fengtian's governor, Zengqi, established the position of Russian military commissar, who was to supervise military affairs in Fengtian Province. This undermined the power of the local military administration.[28] When the Allied forces withdrew from Peking in September 1901, a reduced contingent of Russian troops stayed in Manchuria. They were stationed in the main towns along the CER and continued to suppress bandit attacks on the railway and nearby settlements. Only after the Qing–Russian agreement of March 26, 1902, did Russia start a gradual withdrawal of its troops from Manchuria. At the end of September 1903, the last contingent of its troops officially "left" Heilongjiang Province, although some of these stayed, disguised as railway guards.[29]

Economic life in the towns returned to normal. Chinese workers were rehired to rebuild the damaged CER and continued to work for the Russians in different capacities after the railway was finished in 1903. But Russia's destruction of the Chinese settlements along the Amur, occupation of Manchu ancestral lands, and disruption of local governance sharply contradicted Witte's policy of peaceful economic penetration in Manchuria. Among the Qing subjects on this frontier, military conflicts along the Amur frontier in 1900 brought an end to Russia's image as a peaceful ally.

Russian–Japanese Tensions

Russian troops had been gone from Manchuria for only a year, and the wounds from the Russo-Chinese War had not yet healed, when fresh hostilities started between Japan and Russia in 1904. One war led to another; indeed, the Russo-Japanese War was a natural outcome of Japanese and Russian imperial expansion. In the decade preceding this war, both Japan and Russia had demonstrated their might to Imperial China: Japan had defeated a Qing fleet in the war of 1894–95, and Russia had defeated Qing armies during its occupation of Manchuria in 1900. In 1904, Manchuria became a testing ground for Russian and Japanese imperial ambitions. The war that year was a military conflict between two foreign powers for influence in Manchuria, on the Korean Peninsula, and in the surrounding Yellow Sea and the Sea of Japan.[30]

From the perspective of the long-term colonization of Manchuria, this war was predictable. As early as 1898, Russian war minister Aleksei

Nikolaevich Kuropatkin was concerned about a possible Japanese attack on the new Russian naval base at Port Arthur. After 1900, several anti-Russian societies emerged in Japan. One of them, Kokuryūkai, or the Amur River Society, called for the expulsion of Russia from the East and for the incorporation of Manchuria, Mongolia, and Siberia into one region under Japanese rule.[31] Eventually, Japan's desire to colonize Korea and the threat it perceived from Russia's forest concessions on the Qing–Korean border along the Yalu River made war inevitable.[32] Russia and Japan were two expanding empires headed for collision. During the five years preceding their military clash in 1904, both had pursued policies of "peaceful" economic penetration – Russia in Manchuria and Japan in Korea – by building railways, purchasing land, and investing in business and industrial enterprises. Russia reached beyond its gains in southern Manchuria, using economic and political tactics to acquire influence in the Korean Imperial court.[33] In their efforts to expand their spheres of influence, each empire found it convenient to paint the other as a threat to Qing or Korean sovereignty.

In 1902, Japan signed a treaty of alliance with Britain, Russia's long-time rival in Asia. This treaty recognized Japan's special interests in Korea. Having established diplomatic ties with a leading naval power, Japan continued to build its economic power on the Korean Peninsula, while strengthening its army and navy at home. Japan insisted on linking Korean sovereignty with Manchurian sovereignty. Russia considered the fate of Manchuria to have already been decided by Qing–Russian bilateral agreements and wanted to expand its economic interests on the Korean Peninsula. Accordingly, Russia suggested to Japan that they split the Korean Peninsula into separate spheres of influence – an offer Japan declined.[34] When the two countries failed to negotiate a neutral zone between Manchuria and Korea through peaceful means, Japan launched the war against Russia, confident of victory, having defeated Qing naval power in the same region in 1894–95.

Russia's Defeat in Manchuria, 1904–05

Southern Manchuria and the Qing–Korean frontier became contested ground for Japan and Russia. The Qing and Korean governments were too weak to offer resistance. The war between Russia and Japan broke out on January 24, 1904, when the Japanese government cancelled earlier bilateral negotiations over spheres of influence in Korea, severed diplomatic ties with Russia, and, three days later, launched a surprise attack on its naval base at Port Arthur, damaging two Russian battleships and a cruiser.[35] The Russo-Japanese war involved significant military campaigns at sea and on land, as well as large armies and modern military technology; it was the first modern military conflict in this region. Both countries suffered heavy casualties and material destruction and were exhausted by this war. The ease with which Russia had defeated Qing forces in Manchuria and its lack of intelligence about Japan's meticulous war preparations help explain the determination and confidence with which Russia entered this disastrous war.

In 1904, Japan threatened Russian possessions in Manchuria from both land and sea. It enjoyed several advantages over Russia. First, Japan's strong new fleet enabled it to attack Russian fortifications from the sea. Moreover, it had already fought a war on the Liaodong Peninsula and was prepared to attack quickly. All of this came as a surprise to the Russian army, which had been confident that it would be able to secure southern Manchuria from its bases in Harbin and Port Arthur. The small Russian fleet found itself locked in the shallow waters surrounding Port Arthur. After the first Japanese attacks on Port Arthur in 1904, the Russian military command realized it needed more troops and naval power, which it did not have in the Russian Far East.

The Trans-Siberian Railway and its extension into Manchuria, the CER, were vital to the Russian war effort. Over nine months, the Russian military contingent in Manchuria grew from around 100,000 to 500,000, but this was not enough. The Siberian Railway and the CER were not efficient enough to meet Russia's military needs, and this led to delays in supplying troops and ammunition.[36] According to Kuropatkin, the war minister, the CER's low capacity led directly to the Russian military losses at the beginning of the war. He projected that at least fourteen military trains per day would have to arrive along the CER if the war was to be won, but in 1904, that line was handling only three military trains per day. A major reason for delays was the unfinished Xing'an Tunnel.[37] As a result of all this, Japan's land and naval forces exceeded those of Russia. At the beginning of the war, the Japanese had sent 442,000 soldiers to Manchuria. By the end of the war in 1905, their army there had grown to more than 1.185 million.[38]

The Russian forces on the Liaodong Peninsula and at Vladivostok waited for reinforcements from European Russia; meanwhile, they were unprepared for large-scale attacks. The Russian fort at Port Arthur had a good railway link with Vladivostok via Mukden and Harbin, which were patrolled by border troops.[39] However, Port Arthur and Vladivostok were far apart and separated by difficult terrain – the forests and mountains of the Qing–Korean frontier. Japan's occupation of Korea at the beginning of war gave it an advantage in launching land attacks on weak Russian positions along the Yalu River. Defeating the Russians, the Japanese forces crossed the Yalu and advanced to Liaoyang, where they won a major battle, seriously weakening Russian control over the peninsula.[40]

Russia's early losses in Manchuria exposed the gap between its grand colonial ambitions and its actual military strength. According to Korean historian Park Chong Hyo, Russia's cavalry, having lost momentum on the Qing–Korean border, preferred to "save" its forces from unnecessary losses while facing the Japanese army there. As a result of this lack of initiative, Russia retreated from this border after the Battle of Yalu, which gave the Japanese time to deploy their land forces.[41]

This war culminated in a protracted struggle for Port Arthur. From Russia's perspective, Port Arthur was the southern terminus of its Chinese railway as well as its warmest port on the Pacific. For Japan, Port Arthur was the gateway to southern Manchuria. In 1895, Japan had seized the southern tip of the Liaodong Peninsula but then lost it to European powers. Port Arthur, for them, was thus a symbolic jewel worth fighting for, besides being, in strategic terms, the crossroads of two theatres of war. Extended battles over this port lasted for eleven months and involved land and naval forces on both sides. Table 7.2 lists some of the major conflicts.

The Japanese attacks were persistent. The Japanese fleet efficiently defeated several attempts by the Russian fleet to break the blockade of Port Arthur; meanwhile, the Third Japanese Army approached the port from land. After several fierce attacks from land and sea, during which at least six Russian battleships were sunk, Port Arthur officially surrendered on January 1, 1905. The Japanese army had lost 112,000 men in its assaults on Port Arthur, compared to total Russian losses of 28,000 soldiers and sailors.[42] Official Russian accounts of this war mourned the loss of Port Arthur as a national tragedy: "It finally happened. Port Arthur is gone … Gone is the grand hill overlooking an abyss of misfortune and of bad luck brought to us by the Manchurian war … A child of Russia, so dear and so beloved during eleven months of this bloody battle, is dead."[43] The final defeat of Russian land forces occurred at Mukden. A two-month battle involving 750,000 troops ended in March 1905 with Japan's victory. Russia would no longer be able to gain further territories in Manchuria

TABLE 7.2 The Siege of Port Arthur

1904	Japanese initiatives	Russian initiatives
January 27	Sea battle near Port Arthur	
February 11, 14	Port blockaded by Japanese fleet	
February 21	Port bombardment from the sea	Russian fleet fires back
May 1	Permanent blockade announced	
July 4	Third Japanese Army launches an attack from rear of harbour	Russian army fights back
July 25, 27	Bombardment of Russian fleet from land	
August 6–11	Attempted attack by sea	Fleet and land troops fire back
September 1–17	Attack and bombardment by sea	Fleet fights back
November 13	3rd Japanese Army attacks again	Army fires back
December 20	Port Arthur taken by storm	Surrender

Source: D.N. Dubenskii, ed., *Letopis' voiny s Iaponiei, 1904–1905*, Vol. 40 (1904).

and Korea. The Russian defeat at sea was also striking. At the beginning of war, Japan's fleet was unified and ready to launch an attack, while Russia had only one-third of its entire fleet in the Pacific. Russia's strategic ports in Vladivostok and Port Arthur were 1,600 kilometres apart and separated by the Korean Peninsula. The waters around the peninsula were controlled by the Japanese navy, making it difficult for Russian ships to send support from one port to the other. In April 1905 the Russian government sent its Baltic fleet to the Sea of Japan. This entailed a long, costly voyage for three squadrons of Russian battleships. By the time the ships finally arrived in the unfamiliar waters of the Pacific Ocean, halfway around the world, the crews were exhausted. They also found themselves in an enemy trap. At the end of May 1905, the Japanese navy destroyed the Russian fleet while it was passing through the narrow Tsushima Strait between Korea and Japan. Defeated on land and sea, Russia was forced to sign a humiliating treaty with Japan. Under the terms of the Treaty of Portsmouth, which the United States helped negotiate, Russia lost its possessions and influence in southern Manchuria and Japan gained control over Port Arthur, Dalny, the South Manchuria Railway, and part of the southern Island of Sakhalin.

Russia's war with Japan had demanded more money, troops, and resources than its earlier occupation of Manchuria in 1900. The Amur's best Cossack units had been sent to southern Manchuria, and its existing resources had been sent to fortify military installations in Port Arthur and Vladivostok. Prices in the towns of the Amur during and after the war remained high, and labour shortages were common. The war delayed the development of the Russian Far East, forcing its economy to rely on imported goods from either European Russia or overseas.

Local Dimension of War: Shattered Frontier

When the Russo-Japanese War began, the Qing government declared itself neutral, instructing its forces in Manchuria not to involve themselves in hostilities between the two foreign powers. However, the local population, against its will, became involved in this war in several ways. Government non-involvement left them unprotected and with few choices for survival. Many Chinese peasants stayed in hideouts or escaped when they could. Most unfortunate were those in the epicentre of the most violent battles, such as at Port Arthur, Liaoyang, and Mukden. For them, one obvious choice was to temporarily offer their services to the occupiers.

The Russian army in Manchuria relied on Chinese labour to dig trenches and to transport casualties, arms, ammunition, and food (see Figures 7.3 and 7.4). Lacking a strong material base in the Amur frontier, the Russians relied on local resources to support their army. They purchased horses, meat, grain, vegetables, and clothing from merchants and from the local population in western and central Manchuria.[44] Also, the Russian railway administration continued to use Chinese labour to maintain and repair the CER and the Amur and Ussuri railways, whose strategic role increased during the war. The Chinese built houses and warehouses for the newly arriving Russian army; they were also indispensable in fortifying Port Arthur during the siege there.

Beyond the railway zone, the Chinese in southern Manchuria were more hostile to the Russians. After the Russo-Chinese War, Chinese peasants were reluctant to cooperate with foreigners. Impoverished, and finding themselves in a war zone, the local people did not hide their anti-Russian sentiments. Russian officer and writer Petr Nikolaevich Krasnov recalled the events in Southern Manchuria: "Unreliable local population adds to the horror of this war. We are surrounded by ill-wishing people who do not want to do anything for us. They stubbornly say 'no' to any request to sell food for our troops or animals. They have nothing for us.

FIGURE 7.3 Chinese horse carts with provisions for the Russian troops in southern Manchuria | From D.N. Dubenskii, ed., *Letopis' voiny s Iaponiei, 1904–1905* , Vol. 14 (1904)

Empty villages have no owners, nobody to make inquiries, nobody to buy from, nobody to pay ... Our people and horses are often hungry."[45] Requisition of goods and food from the local population became widespread among the Russian troops.

The Chinese population saw in Japan yet another intruder, albeit a slightly more familiar one. Having its material base near the Liaodong Peninsula, and a strong fleet, the Japanese did not rely as much as the Russians did on the local Chinese for food and labour. Partly due to growing anti-Russian sentiment, and partly due to Japanese propaganda, the Chinese population did not feel as threatened by the Japanese forces. The Russians learned from Chinese captives that the Japanese were employing Chinese to gather intelligence about the location, numbers, and movements of Russian forces in the rear. According to the Russian officer Arkadii Gusev, Chinese spies used various signals such as fires, flags, mirrors, and marks on trees to inform the Japanese about the location of Russian troops. The Russian military headquarters in Manchuria learned that Japanese officers had trained special units of Chinese bandits to instigate guerrilla attacks on Russian couriers and soldiers. These bandits had been recruited from the impoverished local population in the Songhua and Liao river valleys.[46]

But not all anti-Russian activities of Chinese bandits in Manchuria were supported by the Japanese. Local bandits had been attacking Russian officials and personnel in Manchuria since the beginning of the construction of the CER in 1898. During the war, in search of money

ПРОДАЖА КИТАЙЦАМИ РУБАШЕКЪ ВЪ ЛЯОЯНѢ.
РИСУНОКЪ ХУДОЖНИКА А. САФОНОВА СЪ ТЕАТРА ВОЙНЫ. СОБСТВЕННОСТЬ «ЛѢТОПИСИ».

FIGURE 7.4 Chinese traders and Russian soldiers in Liaoyang, Manchuria | From D.N. Dubenskii, ed., *Letopis' voiny s Iaponiei, 1904–1905*, Vol. 15 (1904)

and ammunition, they had intensified their attacks in Manchuria against foreigners and Chinese alike, ravaging major transportation routes near the Songhua and Liaohe rivers. On October 20, 1904, near Harbin, they captured and killed Vice-General Aleksei Bogdanov, the Russian military commissar of the Qiqiha'er region. There was no evidence of Japanese involvement in his death.[47]

This war was catastrophic for Chinese peasants in southern Manchuria, who fled from the military conflict zones, leaving everything behind. Frightened by the arrival of Russian and Japanese troops, and sometimes forced from their villages, the Chinese went into hiding in the mountains, leaving their fields unattended.[48] Local property worth 28 million silver taels was destroyed.[49] According to Chinese official accounts, there were more than 1,150 Chinese civilian casualties in twenty-one locations in southern Manchuria. Actual numbers were probably higher. Mukden and Harbin became magnets for thousands of hungry Chinese refugees. After the Battle of Shahe in October 1904, the retreating Russian army occupied several Chinese villages, displacing their populations. The inhabitants of these villages poured into Mukden. According to the Reverend Dugald Christie (1855–1936), a Presbyterian missionary in Mukden since the 1880s, in the first quarter of 1905 his mission supported over

10,000 refugees, and the Chinese government supported 38,000. During this war, Mukden alone became home to 90,000 refugees.[50]

The war seriously weakened Russian positions in Manchuria. By its end, the Russian army, having suffered a string of defeats, was demoralized. Russian soldiers took out their anger over military losses on the local population. As a result, hostility towards the Russian presence festered in Manchuria long after the war. The low morale of the Russian army in Manchuria coincided with the 1905 Revolution in European Russia. Soldiers and officers alike questioned the purpose of the war and wondered why they had suffered such a humiliating defeat. Demobilized soldiers who either remained in Manchuria or returned to the Russian side of the Amur frontier often harboured feelings of bitterness and hostility towards the Japanese, the Chinese, and Asians in general.

The most immediate outcome of the Russo-Japanese War was a change in spheres of influence in Manchuria between two foreign powers: Russia retained its semi-colonial enterprise in northern Manchuria, and Japan launched its gradual colonization of southern Manchuria. The Russo-Japanese War demonstrated that Russia's position in Manchuria was vulnerable and that the empire's efforts (and funds) to establish ice-free ports on the Pacific and to construct the longest railway in the world were being wasted. The loss of Port Arthur, Dalny, and the South Manchuria Railway was the immediate price Russia paid for dreaming big about expanding beyond Manchuria into the Korean Peninsula. After 1905, Russia was forced to revise its expansionist policy and focus on the less ambitious goal of retaining its economic privileges in the railway zone in northern Manchuria.

Military conflicts affected the Chinese population of the Amur frontier region in different ways. Among those who benefited were the local Chinese merchants who had supplied the Russian army during its stay in Manchuria and the local labourers who had been hired by the Russian army and the CER for war-related needs. But at the same time, the war had disrupted local trade and labour networks in the gold mines of the Amur and the fur markets of the Ussuri frontier, besides reinforcing anti-Russian and anti-Chinese sentiments on both sides of the Amur frontier. The Qing–Russian war of 1900 restricted the movement of Chinese subjects to and from the Amur frontier region, and after 1905, the Chinese presence on the Russian side would never be the same, as the local Russian administration introduced further measures to control the inflow of labour from China and tightened cross-border trade rules. Moreover, the

Russo-Japanese War of 1904–05 had reinforced the general suspicion and official mistrust of the Asian population in the Russian Far East; the notion of the "yellow peril" was widely discussed on the Russian side of the Amur border.

These two conflicts distracted Russian attention from the economic development of Amur and Maritime provinces, which remained backward. Russian military failures in Manchuria left less enthusiasm in St. Petersburg for grand plans in its Far East; meanwhile, the provincial administration of Amur and Maritime provinces faced uncertainty and the bleak prospect of trying to revive the local economy and attract new Russian settlers and businesses. After 1905, talk of a "Siberian Mississipi" along the Amur would excite few people. Meanwhile, the provincial governments of Manchuria and the Russian Far East moved to re-establish their authority over the growing population of this frontier by introducing administrative and economic reforms.

8
Fading Frontiers

After the Russo-Japanese War, the regional governments of Manchuria and the Russian Far East, backed by Peking and St. Petersburg, viewed each other with great mistrust.[1] Imperial Russia did not give up its commercial interests in northern Manchuria, and the Qing government, aware of the constant threat to its northeastern borders, encouraged Chinese migration to Manchuria. This chapter describes the efforts of central and provincial governments on both sides of the Amur River to strengthen their shared borders and borderland regions by economic and administrative means. Political centres were becoming increasingly weak and faced the daunting task of keeping their overextended empires afloat; in these circumstances, the provincial administrations came to play a pivotal role in bringing modernization and elements of civilian rule to the Amur frontier region. This chapter argues that at various times the provincial governments were able to re-exert strong regional authority and secure short periods of relative stability and economic revival. It also shows that these efforts were interrupted by dynastic collapse, changing political regimes, and enduring civil conflict, all of which disrupted this region's economic revival and created permanent tensions between civilian and military elements in administration and society.

In the first half of the twentieth century, no border settlement, village, or town escaped the unrest and destruction caused by revolution, civil war, warlord rule, ideological campaigns, purges, and state-sponsored (or forced) resettlements. Long periods of violence and foreign occupation were followed by efforts by the newly established central and regional governments to maintain order and modernize local economies. After the fall of the Qing in 1911 and of the Romanov dynasty in 1917, the Amur frontier was subjected to bitter national and international rivalries. From 1918 to 1921, the Russian Far East was ravaged by civil war and foreign intervention. In late 1920s and early 1930s, Manchuria became what Owen Lattimore termed a "Cradle of Conflict," suffering military clashes with the Soviet Union in 1929, the Japanese occupation from 1931 to 1945, and brief occupation by Soviet forces from 1945 to 1947.

Despite the efforts of the Qing/Chinese and Russian/Soviet governments to incorporate their border regions into their respective states, the international boundary between them remained porous. Developments on one side of the Amur River affected the other. The movement of people, ideas, and goods across this border continued despite restrictions on migration and international hostilities. By the 1920s, the governments of the Soviet Union and China, each facing growing tensions between the political centre and the periphery, were struggling to re-exert authority over their borderlands. The Soviet government was finally able to do so in the late 1930s, when it faced an imminent threat from Japan. The Nationalist government of China was less successful in controlling its Three Eastern Provinces in Manchuria, which was dominated by a powerful warlord and, after 1931, by the Japanese-sponsored puppet state of Manchukuo.

For most people on this frontier, the years 1911 to 1949 were full of uncertainty. The towns, local economy, and trade were all growing, but the dangers of robbery, kidnapping, civil war, and foreign occupation were constant. Social mobility worked both ways, making it possible for the former bandit Zhang Zuolin (1875–1928) to become the ruler of Manchuria and for the Qing dynasty's last Manchu emperor Henry Aixin-Gioro Puyi (1908–67) to become a figurehead of Manchukuo and, later, a prisoner in the Soviet Union. The efforts of the Soviet Union and Japan to shape the new regional order resulted in the gradual disappearance of the Amur frontier and the emergence, in the mid-1930s, of a tightly controlled border.

New Policy in Manchuria

In the first decade after the Russo-Japanese War, the Amur River region was relatively peaceful, and change was slow to come. Manchuria continued in its semi-colonial status, with the territories along and to the north of the CER controlled by Imperial Russian interests, and the territory along the South Manchuria Railway subjected to growing Japanese influence. The Qing government, alarmed by increasing Russian and Japanese power in Manchuria, attempted to introduce administrative and political reforms there. Since 1905, the New Policy (*xin zheng*) reforms, part of an empire-wide effort to modernize the ailing Qing institutions of power and governance, had started to shake the old structure of Manchuria's government and society. The Qing recognized that the dynasty's political and economic revival would depend on the establishment of a capable administration, and the reforms aimed to make all levels of government more efficient.

In Manchuria, the initial call to strengthen the civilian administration came from two Han Chinese military officials. Cheng Dequan (1860–1930), the military governor of Heilongjiang since 1906, was an open critic of the military government's personnel abuses in distant parts of Heilongjiang; he called for the introduction of a civilian administration.[2] Zhao Erxun (1844–1927), the military governor of Fengtian in 1906, was another advocate of radical reform in Manchuria. With the backing of the Qing government, Zhao Erxun reorganized Fengtian's administration by merging the positions of military governor (*jiangjun*) of Shengjing (the first Qing capital), Fengtian regional governor (*zongdu*), and five traditional bureaux under the authority of one provincial department (*Shengjing xingsheng bu*).[3] Both Cheng and Zhao tried to balance the military and civilian authority in these provinces in order to address growing civilian needs. Their efforts were only the first steps in reforming the administration of Manchuria's three provinces, a project that continued in 1907 with the appointment of new officials.

The most far-reaching reorganization of Manchuria's administration was carried out by a seasoned Qing official, Xu Shichang (1855–1939). A holder of the highest degree (*jin-shi*) under China's traditional examination system, Xu previously served as police minister, as civil affairs minister, and as a grand councillor. He had close ties with the viceroy of Zhili Province, Yuan Shikai (1859–1916) and had earlier served as the chief of staff of the Beiyang Army, founded by Yuan.[4] In April 1907, Xu was appointed to the newly created post of governor-general of the Three Eastern Provinces, replacing the military governors of Fengtian, Jilin, and Heilongjiang. The post of governor-general served to unify and thereby strengthen military and civilian authority in Manchuria in the hands of one person. Xu had supreme control over the military, civil, financial, and diplomatic affairs of the three provinces. Provincial governors (*xun fu*), a new level of civilian authority established in each province that same year, were subordinate to the governor-general. Xu established the following seven bureaux (*si*) to carry out the reorganization of Manchuria's administration: foreign affairs (*jiao she*), banner affairs (*qi wu*), civil affairs (*minzheng*), education (*ti xue*), finance (*du zhi*), industries (*quan ye*), and Mongol affairs (*meng wu*).[5]

Xu's reorganization reinvigorated the authority of the regional government, which had been seriously weakened under the old banner system and by the Russian occupation since 1900. The goal of these reforms was to make the government structure of Manchuria's three provinces similar to that of the provinces in China Proper. One significant measure involved regulating the transfer of lands previously owned by Manchu banner troops and the Qing court by selling them to private owners and thereby gaining revenue for the local government.[6] New Policy reforms aimed to strengthen the civil government down to the county level and to abolish separate administration for banners and civilians. These reforms narrowed the gap between the banner and civilian populations and facilitated the supervision of increasing numbers of Han migrants and farmers, who were coming to Manchuria to cultivate, rent, or purchase newly available arable lands.[7] Administrative reforms allowed the regional government to begin modernizing Manchuria by addressing the most pressing problems of governance and the economy.

The reform of financial institutions and policies was crucial to the New Policy reforms in Manchuria. New, modern-style banks were established in each province, replacing traditional money-exchange shops and remittance offices. Their most urgent task was to unify the multitude of currencies that were in circulation as a result of Russian and Japanese influence. The Fengtian Government Bank (1905), renamed the Three Eastern Provinces Bank in 1909, as well as Kirin Provincial Government Bank (1909) and Heilongjiang Provincial Government Bank (1909), became government enterprises that regulated the monetary market, supervised commercial transactions, conducted foreign currency exchange, and issued their own currencies. The Fengtian dollar (*Fengtian piao*), issued by the government of Fengtian, became a major currency in Manchuria during the Republican period.[8] Since 1906, new taxation bureaux had been established in each province of Manchuria to collect new taxes on animals, land, housing, alcohol, and tobacco in order to raise more revenue for the provincial government.[9] These financial measures were intended to strengthen the provincial government's role in the local economy and to curb the growing influence of Imperial Japanese and Russian banks and currencies in Manchuria.

Xu Shichang oversaw the establishment of a unified military administration in Manchuria to address the weakening of Manchuria's traditional banner forces. In 1908, a Military Training Staff for the Three Eastern Provinces was established in Fengtian with the aim of reducing banner forces, centralizing regional military administration, and creating a new professional army. A special Office of Military Schools supervised the creation of new centres for military training in the three provinces. Backed by Yuan Shikai, Xu secured temporary reallocation of several divisions of Beiyang troops to help defend Manchuria and train a professional army. The old armies were reorganized into patrol and defence troops (*xun fang dui*); new armies were trained as infantry and artillery.[10] Creating a new army was crucial for safeguarding Manchuria's fragile borders and for securing general order. In addition, a professional police force was established in the growing towns and along the main railway lines. These measures were a response to the imperialist ambitions of Russia and Japan in Manchuria, which did not disappear after the Russo-Japanese War, but took new forms. According to historian Blaine Chiasson, the Chinese institutions of administrative and military control established in Manchuria during this time provided a solid foundation for protecting Chinese sovereignty and expanding Chinese jurisdiction in the Special District of Three Eastern Provinces, which had replaced the CER concession in 1921.[11]

During the last several years of Qing rule, the economy, trade, and urban development were all growing in Manchuria. Russian and Japanese economic influence remained strong, but Chinese industries and companies were starting to expand their operations in railway building, urban planning and construction, and agricultural commerce. In 1906, Zhao Erxun announced the opening of Fengtian for foreign trade. Within two years, dozens of Manchurian towns had received the status of "open port" (*shangbu*). Like treaty ports in the rest of China, open ports were established as a result of foreign pressure and unequal treaties. Yet provincial governments in Manchuria had more bargaining power in these open ports compared to treaty ports in matters of administration, construction, policing, and hygiene.[12] Each town with open port status was administered by a "special bureau" (*shangbu ju*), which supervised urban planning and land development. This bureau also supervised newly built roads, quarries, and brick kilns, all of which were vital for urban construction. As the towns grew in size, local provincial and municipal administrations offered urban and rural land for rent, competing with Russian and Japanese railway concession zones in Manchuria, which also rented land. This policy proved successful as local rents were cheaper than those charged by either the CER or the South Manchuria Railway. In 1907, open port land (*shangbu di*) was offered for rent in Fengtian, Tieling, and Changchun; within one year, the deals had been completed.[13]

Trade and commerce intensified in the growing towns. Local wineries and oil-producing factories were established. Hundreds of shops appeared, selling food, tobacco, alcohol, agricultural products, and consumer goods. In 1911, Changchun alone had 1,000 small shops and businesses, and the largest ones joined municipal chambers of commerce (*shanghui*).[14] A lack of funding and unfair competition from Russian and Japanese firms prevented local industrialists and companies from establishing large, independent enterprises in Manchuria; even so, the New Policy reforms provided the impetus for the future economic development of Manchuria.

These reforms had several implications for the Qing–Russian frontier. On the one hand, the establishment of a strong regional authority enabled the government of Manchuria to take more initiative in strengthening border defences and in making decisions during border negotiations with Russia. The new provincial government introduced measures to encourage Han Chinese migration to the border areas, which were either underpopulated, like most of northern Heilongjiang Province, or populated by ethnic Mongols, as in western Heilongjiang Province. New Policy reforms turned a new page in the further Sinification of the Manchurian frontier. On the other hand, strong regional authority could not be achieved overnight. Divisions between military and civilian authorities in Manchuria were difficult to maintain, as political uncertainty in China Proper and power struggles in Manchuria in the years following the collapse of the Qing dynasty delayed the growth of civilian institutions and practices. Fiscal difficulties and the search for funding produced competition between the civilian and military elites, who saw economic opportunity as a means to strengthen their own power in this region. Hans Van de Ven has demonstrated that after new taxes were introduced in 1907, the government of Manchuria was confronted by strong popular anti-tax sentiment and, after 1911, by violent resistance to new taxes. The military took the initiative in suppressing popular protests and gained an upper hand in Manchurian politics.[15] The civil government was too frail to survive on its own in the presence of resurging armed banditry in the rural areas and recurring international threats. But the cooperation between the civil and military authorities helped address these challenges and was crucial for the emergence of Manchuria's new regional identity as part of China Proper.

Reforming Russia's Far East

The government of the Russian Far East also faced new challenges. Since its establishment in 1884, the Priamur Governor-Generalship had been administered by a succession of governor-generals, appointed by the tsar. They were accountable to the tsar and to the Ministry of the Interior (Ministerstvo Vnutrennikh Del). Chosen from the military elite, they oversaw all military, civilian, and diplomatic affairs in the region. At the beginning of the twentieth century, the Priamur Governor-Generalship was one of the largest in the Russian Empire and included Amur (Amurskii) and Maritime (Primorskii) provinces, the northern part of the Island of Sakhalin, Kamchatka, and Chukotka. The territories bordering China were more heavily populated and better developed than the territories to the north, where extreme cold prevented agricultural settlement. After Russia's defeat in the Russo-Japanese War, it became clear that the existing policy of government-sponsored settlement and military administration was insufficient for the economic development of this region. Existing industrial development, especially in mining, the fisheries, and forestry, contributed to the growth of towns; however, economic integration within this vast region was poor. For example, not even a dirt road existed between Blagoveshchensk and Khabarovsk, two of the most important regional towns. Poor infrastructure and the lack of funding slowed development of the region's natural resources. The military significance of Vladivostok was an impediment to turning it into a commercial port and to the development of Russian commerce. The Russian Far East remained economically isolated from the rest of the Russian empire. For poor Russian peasants, it remained an uninviting and unwelcoming place.

Imperial Russia's failures in Manchuria and the revolutionary unrest of 1905–06 forced the Russian government to adopt a new approach to developing its own Far East. Prime Minister Petr Arkad'evich Stolypin (1906–11) launched a policy of strengthening the Russian Far East by developing its economy and making it more attractive for settlement. The old idea of building a railway from Trans-Baikal to Khabarovsk, which would enable the Trans-Siberian Railway to run entirely on Russian territory, gained weight in St. Petersburg. In March 1908, with Stolypin's backing, the Russian Duma approved the construction of the Amur Railway, which started the same year. The railway would bring new settlers, revive the regional economy, and strengthen Russia's strategic position along its eastern borders. Like the Ussuri Railway, the Amur Railway would run parallel to the Sino-Russian border, making it easier to regulate cross-border trade, migration, and border defence. In 1909, Stolypin organized a special committee to settle the Russian Far East (Komitet po zaseleniiu i pereseleniiu Dal'nego Vostoka) and facilitated the government's financing of the Amur Expedition (1909–10) to study the territory around the future railway with the prospect of attracting agricultural settlers and developing trade, infrastructure, and the economy.[16]

A capable regional administration was crucial for carrying out the central government's plans. Stolypin's civilian agenda resulted in the appointment in 1911 of Nikolai L'vovich Gondatti (1860–1946) as the first non-military governor-general of the Priamur region. A graduate of Moscow State University, Gondatti was a professional ethnographer with intimate knowledge of the Russian Far East and its peoples. Before being appointed governor-general, he had served in the administration of several Siberian and Far Eastern districts. As head of the Amur Expedition (1909–11), he was familiar with the problems of the Far Eastern towns and settlements, their faltering economies, and their lack of infrastructure and civilian institutions. He also understood the limits of his new appointment, in that decision-making would depend on final approval and funding from St. Petersburg, where, despite Stolypin's efforts, government bureaucracies had limited understanding of and interest in the future of the Far East. Gondatti lost his supporter in St. Petersburg in September 1911, when Stolypin was assassinated by a revolutionary in Kiev. An experienced provincial administrator, Gondatti had learned to follow orders from the tsar and also how to deal with several direct representatives of central government ministries in Siberia and the Russian Far East.[17] Gondatti's disapproval of Russia's economic expansionism in Manchuria at the expense of the Russian Far East led him to support the construction of the Amur Railway, backed by St. Petersburg. This project became a major test of his administrative abilities and of his promise to revive this region's administration and economy.

The limits of Gondatti's efforts became apparent during the construction of the Amur Railway, which required a supply of qualified workers. Gondatti, like Stolypin, was in favour of using only Russian labour in the Russian Far East in order to create jobs for new migrants and prevent

Russian out-migration from the region. Yet it proved to be very difficult to attract Russian migrants to build the railway, which ran through a challenging landscape of thick forests, swift-flowing rivers, and permafrost and where winters were long and brutal. The main challenge was to improve the working conditions of Russian workers and to provide them with sufficient benefits. This was difficult to accomplish for several reasons. First, the territory between Lake Baikal and Khabarovsk was unevenly and sparsely populated, making it difficult to develop new settlements, industries, and services to support the railway. For example, in 1913, Blagoveshchensk's population was only 70,000, while Khabarovsk's was just 56,000.[18] Second, the wave of revolutionary protests since 1905 had inspired railway workers from Siberia to Manchuria to strike, delaying the construction of the Amur Railway. To address labour shortages and prevent the spread of revolutionary ideas among newly hired railway workers, Gondatti's government resorted to the use of Russian convicts (an old tradition in Siberia); at the same time, police and military convoys reinforced discipline and suppressed discontent.

During Gondatti's governorship, the Priamur Region did not see the fruits of his modernization efforts, apart from railway construction, despite the wealth brought by gold mining and businesses in Blagoveshchensk and Vladivostok. Recurrent unrest and rampant crime demanded the imposition of martial law, which lasted for most of Gondatti's tenure.[19] In 1913, a Khabarovsk agricultural exhibition to celebrate three hundred years of Romanov rule highlighted the Priamur region's potential to impress St. Petersburg, rather than its real achievements (see Figure 8.1). Businessmen and industrialists gained influence in municipal governments, but the institutions of rural self-government (*zemvsto*) appeared in the Russian Far East only in 1916, too late to address growing civilian needs in education, health, and legal matters. Moreover, Russia's involvement in the First World War (1914–18), distracted the central government from investing in the regional economy and deprived this region of workers, many of whom were conscripted.[20] As a result, the Russian Far East under Gondatti did not become self-sufficient. Its cities continued to rely on Chinese labour and on Manchuria's agricultural products well into the 1920s. The Sino-Russian border remained porous, and cross-border regulations were rarely enforced on either side.

The Amur Railway was finally completed in 1916. It became an important part of the Trans-Siberian Railway, connecting St. Petersburg with Vladivostok and promising a great future for regional economic development by linking European Russia with Siberia and its Far East. A

FIGURE 8.1 Stamp commemorating the Khabarovsk Exhibition of 1913 | Author's personal collection

3 kilometre railway bridge across the Amur River at Khabarovsk was the longest railway bridge in Russia, surpassing in length the railway bridge across the Volga. Gondatti declared that with the completion of the Amur Railway, "Russia could feel secure about its distant lands."[21] Yet the newly routed Trans-Siberian Railway also became what historian John Stephan called "the lightning rod" for revolution, which broke out in European Russia in February 1917.[22] This railway helped spread revolutionary sentiments and forces to the Russian Far East. The Trans-Siberian Railway was a site of brutal fighting during the Civil War, and of both White and

Red terror, which slowed the development of this region. Like the CER, the Amur Railway was fought over by both civilians and the military, and in the final years of the Qing and Russian empires, on both sides of the Amur River, the struggle to control it generated tensions between various political groups, which remained unresolved.

Revolution

The Amur frontier region was far from being a hotbed of revolution, but it was transformed by revolutionary fever in China and European Russia. The Xinhai Revolution (1911) had its beginnings in southern China and spread through the industrial centres of central China to the north. The February and October Revolutions (1917) took place in European Russia, with the first worker strikes and military clashes taking place in St. Petersburg and Moscow and spreading eastward. Railway workers, dissatisfied soldiers, and poor migrants were a perfect recruiting ground for the revolutionaries, who established cells in major urban centres of the Amur frontier. In both countries, revolutions overturned monarchies, ending several hundred years of Romanov and Qing dynastic rule. In Manchuria, as in the rest of China, the banner system and Manchu privileges came to an end. In the Russian Far East, Siberia, and the rest of the country, the system of governor-generals and provincial assemblies likewise crumbled.

The revolutions of 1911 and 1917 brought the Amur frontier region out of seeming isolation, forcing the provincial governments of Manchuria and the Russian Far East to involve themselves in national politics. Ongoing struggles between provincial and central authorities distracted them from establishing a strong international border for more than a decade. In China, the revolution resulted in a republican government and the fragmentation of political authority. Before the Northern Expedition of 1926, central political authority was divided between governments in Canton and Beijing, which were constantly challenged by self-proclaimed warlords, who dominated various parts of China. In Russia, the October Revolution signalled the founding of a socialist state, but it took the Bolsheviks four years of Civil War, accompanied by foreign intervention, to claim a final victory in the Russian Far East and the rest of the country.

In Manchuria, the 1911 revolution was less violent than in the south. Despite the New Policy reforms, a growing Chinese population, and weak

Manchu influence, Manchuria remained home to Qing loyalists, who occupied powerful positions in the old army, in the provincial assembly, and among the gentry. When the revolutionary forces, guided by the clandestine Alliance Society (Tongmenghui) and backed by New Army officers and radical reformers, attempted to overthrow the existing order, they were crushed by the acting military governor of Fengtian, Zhao Erxun (during his second posting in Manchuria in 1911–12). Zhao relied on conservative elites like Yuan Jinkai, a vice-president of the provincial assembly, and on the old army units under the command of Zhang Zuolin. In 1912, the last Qing emperor abdicated and the new Republican government appointed General Zhang Xiluan (1843–1922) governor of Fengtian Province and the top military authority in Manchuria.[23] The appointment of Zhang, who was a military commander of the old army and a protégé of Yuan Shikai, was a clear sign that the old political forces in Manchuria remained intact. In 1915, Zhang Xiluan was replaced by Zhang Zuolin, who gradually gained unlimited power. In 1918 he proclaimed himself governor-general of the northeastern provinces, marking the beginning of warlord rule in Manchuria. The military remained the dominant force in Manchuria's politics for a decade.

The end of Romanov rule in the Russian Far East was more violent than the end of the Qing dynasty in Manchuria. The October Revolution of 1917 triggered inevitable armed conflicts, because the Bolshevik program of political and social change included the eradication of privileged classes, the transfer of power to workers' soviets, and the transfer of land to poor peasants. The Bolshevik attempt to seize power in the Russian Far East met armed opposition from provincial leaders, White armies, Cossacks, and monarchists. Russia's anti-Bolshevik forces in Siberia and the Russian Far East united in opposition to Bolshevik rule and maintained power east of the Ural Mountains, from Omsk to Irkutsk. Fierce domestic opposition to the Bolsheviks was backed by foreign powers. In August 1918, British, Chinese, Japanese, and American troops landed in Vladivostok, starting an intervention that lasted several years.

In the fall of 1919, under Bolshevik assault, the White forces began to retreat in Siberia. In 1920 the Bolsheviks reclaimed power in Irkutsk, where they executed the leader of the White movement, Admiral Alexandr Vasil'ievich Kolchak (1847–1920). By the end of 1920, the Red Army had claimed victory in the Urals, Siberia, and Trans-Baikal, and the White armies had been pushed to the Sino-Russian border. The fragmented White forces would hold on in Maritime and Khabarovsk provinces, their last stronghold, for two more years. Meanwhile, the Far Eastern Republic

(1920–22) was established in Chita. This was a buffer state established by Soviet Russia as a temporary measure to solidify its armed forces before attacking the remaining White and Japanese armies in the Russian Far East. In August 1922, in Vladivostok, the Priamur provisional government (called Priamurskii zemskii krai), headed by White Major General Mikhail Konstantinovich Diterikhs (1874–1937), attempted to revive one of the Imperial Russian organs of rural self-government, the *zemskii sobor* (assembly of the land).[24] He appealed to the local nobles and bourgeoisie, and to the Cossacks and White officers, to overthrow Soviet power in the region in the name of the Romanov dynasty and of God.[25] It was too late. The defeated White armies and groups were demoralized, having been deprived of leadership and popular support. Two months later, pressured by the Red Army, the remaining Japanese troops left Vladivostok, and the remaining White Russians were forced to flee, destroying Diterikhs's dream of civilian self-government and of restoring the monarchy. The Russian Far Eastern Republic became part of the Soviet state.

The Russian Revolution and Civil War had an unsettling effect on the Amur frontier region. First, the combination of Red and White terror had seriously compromised provincial authority in the Russian Far East. The Japanese and British governments exploited the fragmentation of the White movement to further their own interests in the region.[26] Retreating White Russian armies and Cossack units crossed the Sino-Russian border into Manchuria and Mongol territory, robbing and terrorizing civilian populations there. Between Chinese bandits and the remains of the White Russian armies, the corridor from Trans-Baikal to Manchuria turned into a lawless land ruled by guns and violence. Provincial Chinese forces failed to restore order along the Sino-Russian border. The final collapse of the White movement in 1922 resulted in waves of Russian refugees, who fled to Manchuria.

Russian influence along the CER was also affected by the October Revolution. In 1920 the new Bolshevik government denounced all tsarist unequal treaties with China. As a result, the Russian management of the CER and the Russians residing in Manchuria lost their extraterritorial rights and became vulnerable to the new Chinese authorities. The greatest blow to the former tsarist subjects came in 1924, when the Chinese government in Beijing recognized the government of Soviet Russia and signed a new railway agreement for the joint commercial management of the railway. In Harbin, hostile groups of Russians were forced to live side by side. All the while, new Soviet employers, old tsarist engineers and entrepreneurs, and impoverished White Russian émigrés were finding it increasingly difficult to find decent jobs in Manchuria. Very few former tsarist subjects in Manchuria took seriously an invitation to acquire Soviet citizenship and return to what was now the Soviet Union. Most of them preferred to remain stateless and started planning to move to Tianjin, Shanghai, Hong Kong, or overseas.

The Closing of the Border

The Civil War and foreign intervention had devastated the economy of the Russian Far East, yet Manchuria in the 1920s seemed to thrive, as migration from China Proper increased and trade along the CER remained stable. Russian and Japanese companies reported profits and continued to invest in Chinese railways, enterprises, and services. Zhang Zuolin solidified his rule in Manchuria and for a short time allowed his civilian administration to manage the regional economy. In September 1924 he signed a separate agreement with the Soviet Union regarding the joint management of the CER – a clear demonstration of his independence from the central government and his interest in gaining more control over the railway's commercial operations.

In the mid-1920s, Manchuria's regional economy and trade grew, to the envy of provincial and warlord governments in China Proper. Historian Ronald Suleski has shown that under the leadership of Wang Yongjiang (1872–1927), civil governor of Fengtian Province, Shenyang and southern Manchuria boasted a vibrant economy with expanding Chinese businesses and agriculture, the latter producing soybeans for the global market.[27] Mining and manufacturing were on the rise. The construction of new roads, buildings, railways, and trams, and the expansion of telephone, telegraph, and postal services, were backed by strong financial institutions and mixed investment from domestic and foreign companies. Local schools, hospitals, and newspapers were established. After 1926, Zhang Zuolin used the gains from economic development to expand his military power beyond Manchuria, hoping to become a key player in the Republican government in China Proper.[28] As a result, many civilian projects were abandoned. Inflation led to more and more frequent strikes by railway and industrial workers. In 1927 and 1928 there were ninety-four and seventy-nine labour strikes in Manchuria, respectively, the highest yearly incidence of labour unrest in a decade.[29]

In the late 1920s, Manchuria was becoming a site of international conflict. In June 1928, while travelling on his private train outside Shenyang, Zhang Zuolin was assassinated by an explosion organized by the Japanese army. His son, Zhang Xueliang (1901–2001), succeeded him as the new military ruler of Manchuria. In May 1929, backed by Chiang Kai-shek (1887–1975), the head of the newly established Nationalist government in Nanjing, Zhang Xueliang attempted to limit Soviet influence in northern Manchuria by raiding Soviet diplomatic offices suspected of harbouring Communist elements and by taking control over different departments of the CER. In the fall of 1929, the Soviet Union responded by sending its troops across the border. Soviet forces occupied several towns in northern and western Manchuria and defeated Zhang Xueliang's army. The Khabarovsk Protocol, signed on December 22, 1929, was followed by lengthy Sino-Soviet negotiations in Moscow in 1930, which failed to resolve the differences between two sides. Soviet control over the CER was temporarily restored, despite the refusal of the Chinese negotiators to return to the conditions of the 1924 railway agreement.[30] Soviet Russia had demonstrated once more that it was not entirely giving up its predecessor regime's imperial gains in Manchuria.

This cross-border conflict damaged local trade and forced many Chinese migrant workers and small businesses to withdraw from the Russian Far East and from northern Manchuria.[31] It also afforded the Soviet Red Army an opportunity to conduct a campaign of terror against White Russian and Cossack settlements in northern and western Manchuria, creating a new wave of refugees to Harbin and intensifying the standoff between Red and White Russians there.[32] Finally, the blow suffered by Zhang Xueliang's regional authority in Manchuria as a result of the Soviet armed forces' activities exacerbated international rivalries between the Chinese Nationalist government, the Soviet Union, and Japan.

The growing hostility between Moscow and Tokyo contributed to the closing of the border along the Amur and Ussuri rivers. Japan's threat to the Soviet Union's eastern borders was increasing. In the years following the October Revolution, Japan supported the White Russian opposition to Soviet rule in the Russian Far East financially and by recruiting White Russians, planting spies, and provoking border tensions. By 1930, more and more Soviet troops and military intelligence agents were being posted on the Sino-Soviet border. Stalin strengthened his grip on Siberia and the Soviet Far East in 1928 with the introduction of his first five-year plan for economic development. In the Soviet Union, this period was characterized by renewed class struggle, forced collectivization, and purges of potential enemies and of ethnic groups with questionable loyalties to the Soviet regime. Strong regional authority and expanded punitive organs became a fact of life in the Soviet Union and its borderlands.

After 1929 it was increasingly difficult to cross the Sino-Soviet border, but desperate victims of Stalinist policies attempted to escape. Among them were peasants who had refused to join collective farms (*kolkhoz*). Another group were ethnic German peasants, who had arrived in the Amur region in 1926, attracted, like other peasants, by the Soviet policy of settling the empty lands on the north bank of the Amur River and having been promised financial support and fifteen acres of land per family. These agriculturalists founded several small villages, only to discover that their freedoms and religious practices (most of them were Mennonites) were denied to them by the Soviet authorities. Between 1927 and 1930, they gradually fled the Soviet Far East for Manchuria, having carefully planned their escapes months in advance. Crossing the Amur border was an ordeal: they suffered from frostbite and risked being caught by the border patrol. In December 1930, the largest group (217 people) left their village of Shumanovka and travelled to the border in horse-drawn sleds in extreme cold. One of them, Abram Friesen, described the experience of crossing the frozen Amur River:

> After a long and troubled journey with all its nerve-wracking stops, we reached the area of the Amur and had to pass the Russian village of Orlovka. The trip thus far had seemed like an eternity – and now Orlovka, with its border patrol of 20 men and machine gun. Morning was dawning and the cocks were crowing. At any moment we expected the machine-gun fire to begin and mow us down.[33]

The Chinese side of the border was not guarded and posed less of a threat to the refugees. This group arrived safely in Harbin, where further help was available from émigré organizations. Other refugees were less lucky; they were caught while attempting to escape the Soviet Union and faced imprisonment, forced labour, or death.

The Sino-Russian border remained flexible and poorly defended when it was free from military conflicts or domestic upheavals in neighbouring provinces. During the periods of relative tranquility between the revolutions of 1905, 1911, and 1917, as well during the 1920s, economies and trade revived, and civilian provincial authorities emerged to deal with the arrival of new migrants and the infrastructural demands posed by fast-growing towns. Yet civil war, warlord politics, and international rivalries brought more violence and military clashes to this border. After the Sino-Soviet conflict of 1929, this border would remain heavily militarized for several decades. Japan's occupation of Manchuria in 1931 and establishment of the puppet state of Manchukuo virtually sealed the Sino-Soviet border, which the Soviet forces guarded with tanks and airplanes. The arrival of modern weapons and means of transportation changed the nature of border clashes, which increased in frequency. Soviet and Japanese forces challenged each other with sudden attacks on land and in the air. No one with conflicting loyalties was tolerated on either side of the border, and ideological war was accompanied by harsh ethnic policies that resulted in the purge or resettlement of entire ethnic groups. For example, in the wake of Japan's all-out attack on China Proper in 1937, Stalin ordered the deportation to Kazakhstan of more than 175,000 ethnic Koreans and Chinese residing in the Russian Far East.[34] The Soviet government saw them as a possible destabilizing factor along the Sino-Soviet border in the event of war between the Soviet Union and Japan.

From 1932 to 1945, life in Manchukuo was controlled by various Japanese state and military agencies, which relied on the collaboration of the last Qing emperor Puyi, who was "restored" as emperor of the new dynasty in 1934, and on surviving Qing loyalists with anti-Republican leanings. Japan also relied on anti-Bolshevik groups among the Russian émigrés and on Cossack leaders, such as Ataman Grigorii Mikhailovich Semenov (1890–1946), who lived under Japanese patronage and were promised support in restoring White rule in Siberia and the Soviet Far East. Yet these groups soon realized that a return to the past was impossible and that Japan's actions in Manchukuo, the Soviet Far East, and elsewhere in East Asia were more about its own imperial and military expansion than about pan-Asian, anti-Bolshevik, or monarchic solidarity.[35] After 1931, Manchuria and the Soviet Far East had neither civilian rule nor independent economic structures. These regions were subject to the politics of Imperial Japan, the Soviet Union, and, after 1945, China. A new, militarized political order across the Amur frontier region had replaced earlier attempts at civilian reform.

Conclusion

Before the Amur region became an imperial frontier for the Qing Empire and Tsarist Russia, it had a life of its own. The climate and topography shaped the local society and economy. Pioneer migrants, traders, and exiles relied on the indigenous peoples, who knew the local conditions best. Each group borrowed from others and influenced other groups' ways of life. Even after an international boundary was nominally drawn along the Amur River in 1858, local populations manipulated and altered state policies to their advantage and maintained informal social and trading networks beyond state control.

From 1850 to 1930, a single lifetime, the Amur frontier region experienced unprecedented transformation: new people, ideas, and institutions arrived, and competing claims were made on its rich natural resources. Railways, new towns, and industries brought the modern age to parts of this region. This transformation created new opportunities for peasants escaping poverty and natural disasters in European Russia and northern China. Expanding commercial agriculture and trade invigorated the local economy. Over time, the newcomers and their descendants became agents of economic and cultural change, having brought with them their own agricultural practices and their own languages, religions, and social habits.

In the five decades after 1858, the Russian empire grew to its greatest size. The Qing Empire, expanded by the Kangxi and Qianlong emperors in the eighteenth century, faced new threats from Russia and the European powers. With the Russian occupation of the lands north of the

Amur River and east of the Ussuri, the Amur frontier became the meeting point of the two empires. Russia, and to a lesser extent China, organized military and scientific expeditions to this frontier. In the 1890s, Imperial Russia launched a series of administrative, economic, and military policies to populate this region and boost its economy. The Trans-Siberian Railway, the region's most ambitious project, aimed to connect European Russia with the Pacific Ocean and eventually turn the Amur frontier region into a corridor linking eastern Siberia with international markets. A further aim of Russia's colonization of the Amur was to strengthen its Far Eastern frontiers. Qing rulers, concerned about the increasing Russian presence on their northeastern frontier, followed suit. Overturning a long-standing ban, they began encouraging Han Chinese agricultural migration to Manchuria; they also introduced new economic policies, including the sale of land to Han Chinese settlers and merchants, the development of the mining industry, the promotion of urban development, and the introduction of banking systems. All of these policies were influenced by the growing Russian presence in Amur and Maritime provinces, and over times, they would strengthen the Qing borderlands.

Historians tend to see Russian colonization of the Amur region and Chinese colonization of Manchuria in the late nineteenth century as two separate processes, happening one after another. This study suggests, however, that Russian and Qing colonization occurred simultaneously and that the two processes overlapped, fusing with local developments. While the Russians moved to colonize Manchuria, the Qing government opened its ancestral lands northeast of the Great Wall. Chinese traders and migrants travelled through Manchuria to Russian towns, the river valleys of the Amur frontier, and already existing Chinese trading networks in the Ussuri forests. On Russian territory, they joined Russians in gold mining, seasonal labour, and services. Along with indigenous peoples, Koreans, and Mongols, they served as go-betweens in mixed Chinese and Russian communities. To the dismay of the Russian government, they also smuggled alcohol, opium, and gold. These activities, which ignored cross-border trade regulations, constantly irritated provincial officials even though they themselves often took bribes and closed their eyes to illegal trade.

Recent studies have emphasized the economic and cultural dimensions of cross-border encounters and stress that they were not always on an equal footing. Chinese historian Zhang Fengming argues that economic incentives drove the history of official cross-border contacts between the Russian Far East and Manchuria; this trade went through several stages, with long periods of stability and mutual benefit.[1] Qing and Russian contact zones existed on both sides of the Amur border. Several studies assert that such contact zones between Qing and Russian subjects existed in semi-colonial urban settings like Harbin.[2] Despite Russian administrative, architectural, and economic dominance in that town, Chinese played an important role in its development. Russians and Chinese formed alliances, to the benefit to both. The CER's enterprises and Russian companies relied on Chinese services and compradors. Chinese companies expanded small trade along the CER and in the major towns of the Russian Far East. Trade and industrial development, centred in Harbin, had a positive influence on the wider local economy, inspiring Chinese trade and industry and attracting international capital. Russian colonial efforts transformed Harbin into a cosmopolitan enclave that was home to fifty-three different nationalities by 1913.[3] Chinese traders and labourers also contributed to the economic development of the Amur frontier towns, providing food and services to Russian businesses and government organizations.

The Amur frontier region was a place where imperial (and later nation-state) peripheries overlapped. Why, then, did this region fail to achieve its promise during much of the twentieth century? Why did local trading networks and cross-cultural dialogue not prevail over mistrust and animosity? I suggest that several factors contributed to this frontier's failure to develop further economically.

First, despite eventual economic stagnation, there were several successful developments. For several decades, the CER and Harbin were dominant symbols of the Russian presence in Manchuria. Economic planners and engineers built and operated this railway in the harsh conditions of Manchuria. Strong foundations in administration and management before the October Revolution allowed the CER to make a smooth transition to a Soviet–Chinese joint venture in 1924, when mutual profit became a priority. Similarly, Harbin became the most successful city in the Amur frontier region, overshadowing regional centres such as Vladivostok, Khabarovsk, Jilin, and Changchun (before it flourished as the capital of Manchukuo). Harbin became a place where Chinese, Russian, and international economic and trading interests converged. Also, Imperial Russia's dominant economic position in Harbin provided an example for the Chinese provincial government in railway and urban development.

Second, the frontier's failure to develop further was embedded in its geography, local experience, and weak imperial policies. Difficult terrain and harsh climate made parts of this region unsuitable for human activity. The steep mountains covered by taiga, and the marshy delta at the confluence of the Ussuri and Amur rivers, were more attractive to mosquitoes than to humans. Vast territories in northern Manchuria along the Greater Xing'an and Sikhote Alin mountain ranges remained unsettled. Unofficial associations between local people and newcomers in pursuit of mutual economic gain, in either the fur trade or gold exploration, posed challenges for the frontier administrators and provincial authorities. Traders, labourers, and exiles established their own networks and rules, often ignoring the authorities. For them, the border did not exist. They had their own armed protection and were capable of defending themselves from the authorities. Local administrators on both sides of the border, lured by the prospect of extra income, became partners in unregulated trade and other economic activities. As a result, large but unrecorded amounts of gold, furs, alcohol, and valuable animal parts circulated in the Amur frontier region, creating an shadow economy and weakening state-sponsored administrative reforms aimed at strengthening the Qing–Russian frontier. It is small wonder that Russian authorities in Khabarovsk and Vladivostok consistently complained about the unregulated Chinese presence and the outflows of gold and cash, while Chinese migrants complained about the corruption of the Russian police.

Third, Qing and Russian expansion in the region had limits. State economic policies in the Amur frontier region and its settlements were not well thought out and were not well funded. By 1900, both Tsarist Russia and the Qing Empire had significant experience in territorial expansion and colonization. Yet these overextended empires, occupying vast territories, had weak control over their frontiers. Both faced hostile environments as well as indigenous peoples with divided loyalties. As a result, the Amur frontier became a breeding ground of lawlessness and violence. Moreover, Russia's appetite for imperial expansion and its desire to link eastern Siberia to international markets on the Pacific did not stop at the Amur basin. The CER stretched all the way to Lüshun. Russian economic penetration reached the Qing–Korean frontier and challenged Japan's imperial claims to Korea. It was Japan that demonstrated to the Qing and Russian empires (in 1895 and again in 1904) how weak their positions were at the southernmost extension of the Amur frontier region.

Other elements contributing to this frontier's endemic weakness came from outside. The Qing collapse in 1911, the First World War, the October Revolution and Civil War in Russia, warlord conflicts, and foreign interventions contributed to instability on the Amur frontier. Waves of refugees, exiles, demoralized soldiers, and impoverished peasants washed over the region. Warlords, bandits, and the new Soviet authorities could claim this region only in theory. Control of this region was left largely to frequently changing local regimes, and its borders were poorly guarded for several decades.

One persistent feature of this frontier region was inconsistent and insufficient support from central governments. The initiatives of provincial officials in developing this frontier often raised suspicions in the centres of power. There were short periods of revival in the 1920s that resulted in sound provincial policies in Manchuria and the Soviet Far Eastern Republic. The CER and Harbin even blossomed commercially. Yet peaceful economic development did not last long. In the first half of the twentieth century, civil war and international rivalries militarized this frontier, rolling back the efforts of local civilian administrations to stabilize the region and make it prosperous. The Japanese occupation of Manchuria after 1931, which is beyond the scope of this study, marked China's loss of its sovereignty there and brought more Japanese settlers, companies, banks, and industries. In 1935, Japan purchased the CER, formally ending Soviet influence in Manchuria and allowing Japan to extend control over former tsarist subjects. Stalin's unease over the Soviet borders in Siberia and the Russian Far East, and Japan's war in China in 1937, marked the end of the frontier era and the emergence of stronger states that closely watched their border regions. New military technology (tanks, military aircraft, and heavy artillery) facilitated this task.

This study has demonstrated that the Amur frontier region was shaped by the interplay of natural features and human activities. The region's topography and climate are central to understanding the complex interactions among indigenous populations, the frontier society, and state-sponsored colonizers. Railway and economic expansion, urban development, and war transformed this region's environment as well as the lives of local people and their trading practices. In the twentieth century, the collapse of the Russian and Qing empires resulted in new political regimes that had different visions for their borderlands. All the while, the political centres found it very difficult to transform this frontier and assimilate its people into the mainstream society of China Proper or European Russia. The geographic remoteness of this region, which was relatively free from the conventions of traditional Chinese or Russian cultural centres, created a frontier spirit, one characterized by high mobility, defiance of authority, and sporadic violence.[4] This study suggests that the emerging regional culture of the Amur frontier to some degree defied state policies. Until the 1930s, neither Soviet Russia nor Republican China was strong enough to control every aspect of life in this frontier region, to impose an ideology on its people, or even to police the border.

While I consider the Amur frontier region to be a unique geographic and historical place, I also suggest that Imperial Russia's colonization of Manchuria is comparable to the British, German, French, and Japanese colonization of China. The Russian presence in Manchuria, despite being semi-colonial (along the railway zone and in leased territories) and short-lived, used methods similar to those resorted to by other colonial powers, such as military conflict, railway imperialism, unequal treaties, concessions, and the imposition of spheres of influence and extraterritorial rights for its citizens.[5] Russian internal colonization of its new Amur frontier region spilled over into Manchuria. European powers and Japan competed and negotiated with one another over their spheres of influence in China. Russia had one important geographic advantage over other European empires: it shared borders with China and was able to expand directly into Manchuria without having to ship people and supplies thousands of miles by sea, as other powers had to do. As a result, Russia's sphere of influence in Manchuria was larger than in any other territory in China claimed by any other European state.

The railways were crucial to colonization; they were also catalysts of modernization. Imperial Russia pioneered railway expansion on the Amur frontier by linking the Trans-Siberian and Chinese Eastern railways, and the Russian example was followed by Japanese railway expansion in southern Manchuria. The railways spurred industrial development in mining, steelworks, and shipping and contributed to the commercialization of the agricultural economy by facilitating the export and import of wheat, beans, livestock, and other food products. The railways also changed travel and transportation in this region. In times of peace, they brought new settlers; in times of war, they carried troops and munitions. The railways also contributed to the growth of towns such as Changchun and Harbin. They linked older towns with new ones, turning the local population into a workforce for the railway and for new economic enterprises. Booming towns attracted seasonal workers, migrants, and traders from Siberia and China Proper; poor farmers, hunters, and fishermen found new jobs in manufacturing, construction, and trade. Even military conflicts brought commerce to the towns, for troops travelling by rail to and from the conflict zones used towns as bases, which supplied them with provisions and services besides being sites for military hospitals. After the Sino-Japanese War, many demobilized soldiers stayed in the region, having found more opportunities there than were available back home.

At the same time, the railways brought new challenges to the region. First, they favoured large companies and enterprises backed by the state, thus squeezing out smaller companies and creating near-monopolies in some sectors. Second, by attracting larger companies, the railways disrupted traditional patterns of local trade, which had long been conducted in town markets and at rural fairs, and which relied on traditional modes of transportation, such as horse and donkey carts. Third, the railways and their enterprises created a new class of industrial workers, who introduced strikes as a new form of protest and disrupted rail traffic. Railway strikes in this region were directed against the state's economic monopoly and, for Chinese workers, against the foreign powers of Russia and Japan.

Finally, the railways intensified international competition between China, Russia, and Japan. Control over railways meant control over the provinces through which they ran. In this regard, the ownership and operatings costs of the railways, as well as their location and direction, remained at the centre of diplomatic controversies between the governments of the three countries. The building of the CER had been the result of a secret treaty between Russia and China in May 1896, which promised to protect China from a possible Japanese threat. The treaty made it clear that Russia would be able to use this railway at any time to transport its troops.[6] In the decade following the Russo-Japanese War, two railway enterprises divided Manchuria into Russian and Japanese spheres of influence. Between them, the CER and the South Manchuria Railway controlled most of Manchuria's economy, allowing only limited participation by Chinese administrations and companies. These restrictions did not prevent the Chinese from supporting local railway enterprises.[7] Yet during the first half of the twentieth century, the CER did not became a truly Chinese enterprise. In 1924 it became a joint venture between the Soviet Union and Republican China and, as such, was closely watched by Japan. In 1935, Japan purchased the railway from the Soviet Union and controlled it for the rest of its occupation of Manchuria until 1945, at which point it fell back under the Soviet control until well into the early 1950s. For Chinese nationalists, the railways in Manchuria were a permanent reminder of foreign dominance in this region. For the national governments, the railways transformed the strategic balance in this region, which only added to their concerns about border security.

Far from the political centre, this frontier region came to symbolize the ambiguity of imperial attitudes, which ranged from high expectations to neglect. The international boundary drawn along the Amur River in 1858 enticed the Russian and Qing states to populate nearly empty lands and to maintain frontier administrations capable of keeping an eye on each other. For Imperial Russia and subsequently the Soviet Union, this region remained an extension of Siberia: cold and uninviting. It never experienced a true population boom. The Qing and Republican governments saw it as a place under constant threat from its northern neighbour. The fact that Imperial Russia had occupied former Qing territory haunted Chinese nationalists during much of the twentieth century. Sino-Soviet hostilities from the 1960s to the 1980s and border clashes along the Amur and Ussuri rivers in 1969 are still fresh in the minds of people on either side of the border. Despite the improvement in bilateral relations in the 1990s, strategic partnerships, and a flourishing cross-border trade, Beijing and Moscow view this border with mistrust, just as imperial governments did more than 150 years ago. The last border dispute over the islands at the confluence of the Amur and Ussuri rivers was resolved only in 2004. Chinese and Russian historians disagree over their shared history in this region, reflecting divergent versions of officially sponsored history acceptable by their respective states. In 2006, a new 5,000-ruble banknote was issued in Russia with the image of Murav'ev-Amurskii overlooking the Amur River – an official nod to Russia's imperial past in this region.

Today, more than one hundred years after the period described in this book, seasonal economic migrants from China's Northeast to the Russian Far East are subject to politically driven xenophobia, which is common from Moscow to Vladivostok. China's northeastern provinces are enjoying a booming economy and have a total population larger than that of the Russian Far East and Siberia combined. Russian politicians are concerned that the demographic disparity between overpopulated China's Northeast and the sparsely populated Russian Far East will inevitably result in mass migration of Chinese peasants into Russian territory. These concerns do not take into account that most of the Chinese migrants to this region come for seasonal jobs and that existing Russian and Chinese regulations make it very difficult for Chinese migrants to settle permanently in Russia. Since the 1990s, provincial administrations on both sides of the Amur River have talked about building a bridge between Heihe and Blagoveshchenk to facilitate cross-border trade between Heilongjiang and Amur provinces, but they have been reluctant to move forward.[8] Despite this apparent mutual mistrust, the Sino-Russian border along the Amur and Ussuri rivers remains open for cross-border trade. Access to cheap Chinese clothes, agricultural products, manufactured goods, and labour are vital for the struggling economy of the Russian Far East. Timber, minerals, and arms from Russia cross this border into China.

The biggest challenges to the future of this region may come neither from history nor from politics, but once again from the natural environment, granted that this time the change is a result of human activity. The effects of deforestation and climate change are already being felt in the region. The volume of the Amur River has declined over the last century, and global warming may exacerbate this problem. The Amur and its tributaries are crucial to the lives and local economies of people on both sides of the border. The river may change its course, generating new territorial disputes over emerging and disappearing islands and creating the potential for renewed conflict. But for now, the Sino-Russian border bustles with business, and the Amur River conveniently divides two distinct political and cultural worlds.

Appendix A

Chronology

1616 – Nurhaci establishes the Later Jin dynasty in Manchuria
1636 – Hong Taiji establishes the Qing dynasty in Manchuria
1643 – Vasilii Poyarkov's expedition to Amur
1644 – The Manchu rulers conquer Beijing, starting Qing rule in China
1689 – Nerchinsk Treaty demarcates the border between China and Russia
1699 – Qiqiha'er becomes the headquarters of the Heilongjiang military region
1727 – Kiakhta Treaty establishes Sino-Russian caravan trade
1740 – Qing government bans Chinese immigration to Manchuria
1822 – Eastern Siberia's governor-generalship established
1856 – Maritime Province in the Russian Far East established
1858 – Amur Province established
1858 – Aigun Treaty. Russia acquires north bank of the Amur River. Khabarovka is founded as a military outpost.
1860 – Treaty of Peking. Russia acquires the Ussuri region. Vladivostok is founded as a military outpost.
1884 – Governor-generalship is established for the Priamur (Amur, Maritime, Sakhalin, and Trans-Baikal provinces)
1890 – Prince Nicholas (son of Tsar Alexander III) travels to Asia
1891 – The construction of the Trans-Siberian Railway starts
1894–95 – Sino-Japanese War

1894 – Nicholas II crowned as tsar
1896 – China and Russia form secret alliance against Japan
1897 – Russia leases Lüshun (Port Arthur) as a naval base
1898 – Construction of the Chinese Eastern Railway starts. Harbin is established.
1900 – Boxer Rebellion starts. Joint Allied forces land in China to suppress Boxers. Russia invades Manchuria to protect its railway.
1901 – Boxer Protocol. Russian troops remain in Manchuria.
1903 – Chinese Eastern Railway is completed
1904 – Japan attacks Russian naval base at Port Arthur. Russo-Japanese War starts.
1905 – Treaty of Portsmouth ends the Sino-Japanese War
1906 – South Manchuria Railway Company founded. Japan establishes Kwantung governor-generalship in Lüshun.
1907 – Manchuria's military government is replaced with a civilian government. Three Eastern Provinces established (Fengtian, Jilin, and Heilongjiang).
1910 – Priamur governor-generalship divided into civilian and military administrations
1911 – Xinhai Revolution marks the end of the Qing dynasty
1913 – Agricultural exhibition in Khabarovsk
1916 – Amur Railway is completed. Zhang Zuolin starts independent rule in Manchuria.
1917 – October Revolution in Russia. Priamur governor-generalship abolished.
1918–20 – Civil War in Russia. Anti-Bolshevik forces take the Russian Far East.
1920–22 – Far Eastern Republic established by the Bolsheviks
1922 – Far Eastern Province established (renamed Far Eastern Region in 1926)
1924 – Sino-Soviet Treaty establishes joint management of the Chinese Eastern Railway
1928 – Zhang Zuolin murdered by Japanese military
1929 – Sino-Soviet conflict over Chinese Eastern Railway
1931 – Japan occupies Manchuria

Appendix B

Chinese Terms

Aigun	瑷珲
Beiyang Shuishi	北洋水师
bianjiang	边疆
bianjiang qu	边疆区
bianjie	边界
bianjie xian	边界线
Boli	伯力
Cao Tingjie	曹廷杰
Changbai Shan	长白山
Changchun	长春
Chang Shun	长顺
Chengde	承德
Cheng Dequan	程德全
Cheng Enze	程恩泽
Dalian	大连
daofei	盗匪
Dongbei	东北
Dongsansheng	东三省
Duluhe Jinkuang	都鲁河金矿
duzhi si	度支司
fei	匪
feibang	匪帮
Fengtian piao	奉天票
Fengtian	奉天
fudutong	副都统
gongdiao	贡貂
gufei	股匪
guantun	官屯
Haila'er	海拉尔
Haishenwei	海参崴
Ha'erbin	哈尔滨
Heihe	黑河
Heilongjiang	黑龙江
Heixiazi Dao	黑瞎子岛
Hezhe	赫哲
hong huzi	红胡子
Hong Jun	洪 钧
huagong	华工
hufei	胡匪
huiguan	会馆
Hulun Bei'er	呼伦贝尔
Ji Fengtai	纪凤台
jiang	疆
jiaoshe si	交涉司

Jilin	吉林
jinshi	進士
kenwu zongju	垦务总局
kuli	苦力
Kuanhe Jinkuang	宽和金矿
Li Hongzhang	李鸿章
Li Jinyong	李金镛
Liaodong Bandao	辽东半岛
Liaoning	辽宁
Lüshunkou	旅顺口
Manzhouli	满洲里
mengwu si	蒙务司
minzheng si	民政司
Mohe	漠河
Mohe Jinkuang	漠河金矿
Niehaihua	孽海花
nanmin	难民
ni	逆
Nie Shicheng	聂士成
Nenjiang	嫩江
Ningguta	宁古塔
pan	叛
Qiqiha'er	齐齐哈尔
qiwu si	旗务司
quanye si	劝业司
Sanjiang pingyuan	三江平原
Sanxing	三星
Sanxing Jinkuang	三星金矿
Shandong Sheng	山东省
shangbu	商埠
shangbu di	商埠地
Shanhai Guan	山海关
Shengjing	盛京
Shou Shan	寿山
shuhai	树海
Songhua Jiang	松花江
Song Xiaolian	宋小濂
tixue si	提学司
Tianjin	天津
Tianshan	天山
Tongmenghui	同盟会
Yantai	烟台
Yingkou	营口
Yuan Jinkai	袁金铠
Yuan Shikai	袁世凯
Yupi Dazi	鱼皮鞑子
Wang Yongjiang	王永江
Wei Yuan	魏源
xinzheng	新政
Xing'an Ling	兴安岭
Xingkai Hu	兴凯湖
Xu Shichang	徐世昌
xunfangdui	巡防队
xunfu	巡抚
zei	贼
Zeng Pu	曾樸
Zeng Qi	增祺
Zhang Zuolin	张作霖
Zhang Xiluan	张锡銮
Zhang Xueliang	张学良
Zhili	直隶

Notes

Introduction

1 On Manchuria as a distinct geographic place invented by Qing rulers and the evolution of this term in different languages, see Mark Elliot, "The Limits of Tartary: Manchuria in Imperial and National Geographies," *Journal of Asian Studies* 59, 3 (2000): 603–46.

2 Zhili ("directly ruled" in Chinese) was a northern province during the Qing dynasty that included Beijing and Tianjin. In 1928 it was renamed Hebei.

3 For a discussion of Chinese terms referring to the Qing and Chinese frontier, see Mark Elliott, "Frontier Stories: Periphery as Center in Qing History," *Frontiers of History in China* 9, 3 (2014): 336–60.

4 Frederick Jackson Turner, *The Significance of the Frontier in American History* (New York: Henry Holt and Company, 1921).

5 Harold A. Innis, *Essays in Canadian Economic History* (Toronto: University of Toronto Press, 1956); Innis, *The Fur Trade in Canada* (Toronto: University of Toronto Press, 1967). Charles M. Studness builds on Innis's economic approach while analyzing economic incentive as a driving force behind migrations of individual settlers and state companies from the east coast westward to the Canadian prairies. In the nineteenth century, the direction of human migration depended not only on the location of fur or gold, but also on available fertile land, railways, and publicity. Studness, "Economic Opportunity and Westward Migration of Canadians during the Late Nineteenth Century," *Canadian Journal* of *Economics and Political Science* 30, 4 (November 1964): 570–84.

6 Arthur J. Ray, *Indians in the Fur Trade: Their Role as Trappers, Hunters, and Middlemen in the Lands Southwest of Hudson Bay, 1660–1870* (Toronto: University of Toronto Press, 1974).

7 William Cronon, "Revisiting the Vanishing Frontier: The Legacy of Frederick Jackson Turner," *Western Historical Quarterly* 18, 2 (April 1987): 157–76.

8 David J. Weber, *The Mexican Frontier, 1821–1846: The American Southwest under Mexico* (Albuquerque: University of New Mexico Press, 1982), 277–85.

9 Andrew Malozemoff, *Russian Far Eastern Policy, 1881–1904: With Special Emphasis on the Causes of the Russo-Japanese War* (Berkley: University of California Press, 1958).

10 Sarah C.M. Paine, *Imperial Rivals: China, Russia, and Their Disputed Frontier* (Armonk: M.E. Sharpe, 1996). For earlier work on Russian "predatory" policies in Manchuria, see Peter S.H. Tang, *Russian and Soviet Policy in Manchuria and Outer Mongolia, 1911–1913* (Durham: Duke University Press, 1959).

11 Mark Bassin, *Imperial Visions: Nationalist Imagination and Geographical Expansion in the Russian Far East, 1840–1865* (Cambridge: Cambridge University Press, 1999).

12 David Schimmelpenninck van der Oye, *Toward the Rising Sun: Russian Ideologies of Empire and the Path to War with Japan* (DeKalb: Northern Illinois University Press 2001).

13 For example, in his study of Harbin's history, David Wolff demonstrates that Russian railway expansion in Manchuria was accompanied by rivalries among the diplomatic, economic, and military interest groups within the Russian government. Wolff, *To the Harbin Station: The Liberal Alternative in Russian Manchuria, 1898–1914* (Stanford: Stanford University Press, 1999), 49–62.

14 Robert H.G.Lee's study of the late Qing policy towards its Manchurian frontier challanges the assumptions made by diplomatic historians of Russia about Qing passivity. See Robert H.G. Lee, *The Manchurian Frontier in Ch'ing History* (Cambridge, MA: Harvard University Press, 1970), 138–81.

15 Zhongguo shehui kexueyuan jindai shi yanjiusuo [Institute of Modern History, Chinese Academy of Social Sciences], ed., *Sha E Qin Hua Shi* [History of the Tsarist Russia's aggression against China], 4 vols. (Beijing: Renmin chubanshe, 1978–90).

16 Tong Dong, *Sha E yu Dongbei* [Tsarist Russia and the Northeast] (Changchun: Jilin wenhua chubanshe, 1985).

17 Xue Xiantian, *Zhongdong tielu hulujun yu Dongbei bianjiang zhengju* [Chinese Eastern Railway patrol police and the political situation of the northeastern frontier] (Beijing: Shehui kexueyuan chubanshe, 1993); Guo Yunshen, "Zhongdong tielu yu Eluosi wenhua de chuanbo" [Chinese Eastern Railway and Russian cultural influence] *Xuexi yu Tansuo* 5 (1994): 139–42; Shi Yan and Sun Guangmei, "Zhongdong tielu guanliju de jigou shezhi jiqi xingzhi" [Formation of the administrative divisions of the Chinese Eastern Railway] *Beifang Weiwu* 1 (1997): 88–90.

18 For example, Soviet historian Evgenii Leodinovich Besprozvannykh argues that until the mid-nineteenth century, the territory north of the Amur River had been an empty land with no links to Imperial China and that Russia did not annex this territory but only regained what had once belonged to it. Besprozvannykh, *Priamur'e v sisteme Russko-Kitaiskikh otnoshenii, XVII- seredina XIX v.* [Priamur region in Sino-Russian relations, from the seventeenth to the mid-nineteenth century] (Khabarovsk: Khabarovsk knizhnoe izdatel'stvo, 1983).

19 The term "contact zone" is attributed to the work of Mary Pratt in her classic book *Imperial Eyes: Travel Writing and Transculturation* (London: Routledge, 1992). Aleksei D. Voskresenskii interprets theoretical models of *balance* or *equilibrium* in international relations defined by George Liska and Morton A. Kaplan. He sees Sino-Russian relations as driven by overlapping interests: universal, state/national, and those of government agencies and of society at large. See Voskresenskii, *Rossiia i Kitai: Teoriia i istoriia mezhgosudarstvennykh otnoshenii* [Russia and China: Theory and history of interstate relations] (Moscow: Moskovskii obshchestvennyi nauchnyi fond, 1999), 104–45.

20 A.N. Yakovlev, *Rossiia i SShA: diplomaticheskie otnosheniia, 1900–1917* [Russia and the United States: Diplomatic relations, 1900–1917] (Moscow: Mezhdunarodnyi fond demokratiia, 1999). On Japanese imperialism in Manchuria before 1932, see Yoshihisa Tak Matsusaka, *The Making of Japanese Manchuria, 1904–1932* (Cambridge, MA: Harvard University Press, 2001).

21 For example, see V.S. Myasnikov, ed., *Granitsy Kitaia: Istoriia formirovaniia* [China's borders: Historical development] (Moscow: Pamiatniki istoricheskoi mysli, 2001); Aleksei D. Voskresenskii, *Diplomaticheskaia istoriia Russko-Kitaiskogo Sankt Peterburgskogo dogovora 1881 g.* [Diplomatic history of Sino-Russian Treaty of St. Petersburg, 1881] (Moscow: Pamiatniki istoricheskoi mysli, 1995); and Iu.M. Galenovich, *"Belye piatna" i "bolevye tochki" v istorii Sovetsko-Kitaiskikh otnoshenii* ["White spots" and "friction points" in the history of the Sino-Soviet relations] (Moscow: Institut Dal'nego Vostoka, 1992).

22 For example, see Guan Guihai and Luan Jinghe, eds., *Zhong-E guanxi de lishi yu xianshi (di er ji)* [The history and reality of the Sino-Russian relations, vol. 2] (Beijing: Shehui kexue wenxian chubanshe, 2009).

23 On Chinese primary and secondary sources on the history of Sino-Russian relations and on their classification, see Xue Xiantian and Zhou Xinmin, eds., *Zhong-E guanxi Zhongwen wenxian mulu, 17–20 shiji* [Catalogue of Chinese documents on Sino-Russian relations, from the seventeenth to the twentieth century] (Chengdu: Sichuan renmin chubanshe, 2002).

24 Owen Lattimore, *Inner Asian Frontiers of China* (New York: American Geographic Society, 1940).

25 Owen Lattimore, *Manchuria, Cradle of Conflict* (New York: Macmillan, 1932).

26 Lee, *The Manchurian Frontier.*

27 For example, see James Reardon-Anderson, *Reluctant Pioneers: China's Expansion Northward, 1644–1937* (Stanford: Stanford University Press, 2005)

28 For discussion of Wei Yuan's work, the *Record of Sacred Military Campaigns (Shengwuji),* published in 1842, see Peter C. Perdue, "Embracing Victory, Effacing Defeat: Rewriting the Qing Frontier Campaigns," in *The Chinese State at the Borders,* ed. Diana Lary (Vancouver: UBC Press, 2007), 113–14. On Cheng Enze, see Twitchett and Fairbank, *The Cambridge History of China,* vol. 10, 155–57.

29 Xu Shichang, *Dongsansheng shenglue* [Brief administrative account of the Three Eastern Provinces, vol. 12] (Taipei: Weihai chubanshe, 1965).

30 For an overview of trends in frontier studies in the PRC, see Lu Yiran, "Zhongguo bianjiang shidi yanjiu huigu yu zhanwang" [Research on the historical geography of China's borderland: Past and future], *Zhongguo bianjiang shidi yanjiu* 4 (1991): 1–9; Lu Yiran, Ma Dazheng, and Xing Yulin, eds., *Zhongguo bianjiang shidi lunji* [Collection of articles on the history and geography of China's borderland] (Ha'erbin: Heilongjiang jiaoyu chubanshe, 1991); Ma Ruheng and Ma Dazheng, *Qingdai de bianjiang zhengce* [Qing dynasty policies towards the borderlands] (Beijing: Zhongguo shehui kexue chubanshe, 1994); and Lu Yiran, ed., *Zhongguo jindai bianjie shi* [Modern history of Chinese borders] (Sichuan: Sichuan renmin chubanshe, 2007).

31 For recent trends in research on China's northeastern frontiers, see Ma Dazheng, *Zhongguo Dongbei bianjiang yanjiu* [Studies on China's northeastern borderland] (Beijing: Zhongguo shehui kexueyuan chubanshe, 2003). On recent studies of historical geography of the Chinese frontiers, see Li Sheng and Li Guoqiang, eds., *Zhongguo*

bianjiang yanjiu zongshu (1989–1998) [Summary of border studies in China, 1989–1998], (Ha'erbin: Heilongjiang jiaoyu chubanshe, 2002).

32 For example, V.M. Kabuzan, *Dal'nevostochnyi krai v XVII-nachale XX veka* [Far Eastern region in the nineteenth and early twentieth century] (Moscow: Nauka, 1985); John J. Stephan, *The Russian Far East: A History* (Stanford: Stanford University Press 1994); Lu Mnghui, ed., *Zhong E bianjiang maoyi de qiyuan yu yange* [The rise and development of the Sino-Russian border trade] (Beijing: Zhongguo jingji chubanshe, 1991); and Dan Ben-Canaan, Frank Grüner, and Ines Prodöhl, eds., *Entangled Histories: The Transcultural Past of Northeast China* (Heidelberg: Springer, 2014).

33 For recent general history of Manchuria, see Li Zhiting, ed., *Dongbei tongshi* [General history of the Northeast] (Zhengzhou: Zhongzhou guji chubanshe, 2003); Chen Fangzhi, *Dongbei shi tantao* [Discussing the history of the Northeast] (Beijing: Zhongguo shehui kexue chubanshe, 1995). For the history of Heilongjiang Province, see Xin Peilin, Zhang Fenming, and Gao Xiaoyan, eds., *Heilongjiang kaifa shi* [Historical development of Heilongjiang province] (Ha'erbin: Heilongjiang renmin chubanshe, 1999); Liu Wenxin, ed., *Heilongjiang jindai lishi dashiji, 1860–1949* [Chronology of events in Heilongjiang modern history, 1840–1949] (Ha'erbin: Heilongjiang renmin chubanshe, 1987). On Manchuria's cities, see Qu Xiaofan, *Jindai Dongbei chengshi lishi bianqian* [Historical change in China's northeastern cities during modern times] (Changchun: Dongbei shifan daxue, 2001); Li Shuxiao, ed., *Ha'erbin lishi biannian* [Harbin's historical chronicle] (Ha'erbin: Ha'erbin chubanshe, 2000).

34 Kong Jingwei, *Zhongguo Dongbei diqu jingji shi* [Economic history of China's Northeast] (Changchun: Jilin jiaoyu chubanshe, 1994); Kong Jingwei, *Qingdai Dongbei diqu jingji shi* [Economic history of the Northeast region during the Qing dynasty] (Ha'erbin: Heilongjiang renmin chubanshe, 1990).

35 Reardon-Anderson, *Reluctant Pioneers,* 3–7.

36 For analysis of Japanese sources on Manchuria, see Ronald Suleski, *The Modernization of Manchuria: An Annotated Bibliography* (Hong Kong: Chinese University Press, 1995). For documents collected by the administration of the Kwantung Leased Territory up to 1918, see Kantō totokufu, ed., *Man-Mō keizai tōkei zuhyō* [Economic statistics and graphs for Manchuria–Mongolia], vols. 1 and 2 (Tokyo: Kantō totokufu, 1918).

37 For example, see South Manchuria Railway Company ed., *Man-Mō no taisei: Jinkō, kōchi oyobi nōsanbutsu yori mitaru* [General conditions of Manchuria: From the standpoint of population, arable land, and agricultural products] (Dalian: SMRC, 1919); and John Young, *The Research Activities of the South Manchuria Railway Company, 1907–1945: A History and Bibliography* (New York: East Asian Institute, Columbia University, 1966).

38 For example, the Japanese journalist Kikuchi Teiji moved to Shenyang in the final years of the Qing dynasty and stayed in Manchuria for forty years, observing local politics and society. See Kikuchi Teiji, *Kikuchi Gōsō-an zuihitsu: Shūfū sanzenri* [Essays of Kikutchi "Gōsō-an": The autumn wind blows three thousand *li*] (Tokyo: Kikutchi Teiji sensei kankōkai, 1966).

39 For example, Sarah C.M. Paine, *The Sino-Japanese War of 1894–1895: Perceptions, Power, and Primacy* (Cambridge: Cambridge University Press, 2005); Louise Young, *Japan's Total Empire: Manchuria and the Culture of Wartime Imperialism* (Berkeley: University of California Press, 1999); and Matsusaka, *Making of Japanese Manchuria.*

40 See Edward J.M. Rhoads, *Manchus and Han: Ethnic Relations and Political Power in Late Qing and Early Republican China, 1861–1928* (Seattle: University of Washington Press,

2000); Pamela Kyle Crossley, *A Translucent Mirror: History and Identity in Qing Imperial Ideology* (Berkeley: University of California Press, 1999); and, most recently, Dan Shao, *Remote Homeland, Recovered Borderland: Manchus, Manchoukuo, and Manchuria, 1907–1985* (Honolulu: University of Hawai'i Press, 2011).

Chapter 1: A River Runs through It

1 Perry McDonough Collins, *Siberian Journey: Down the Amur to the Pacific, 1856–1857* (Madison: University of Wisconsin Press, 1962), 261.
2 S.I. Vavilov, ed., *Bol'shaia Sovetskaia entsiklopediia,* vol. 2 [The Great Soviet Encyclopedia, vol. 2] (Moscow: Bol'shaia Sovetskaia Entsiklopediia, 1950), 307; N.K. Shul'man, ed., *Amurskaia oblast'* [Amur Province]. (Blagoveshchensk: Khabarovskoe knizhnoe izdatel'stvo, 1989), 40.
3 *Zhongguo gujin diming da cidian* [Dictionary of China's ancient and modern place names]. (Shanghai: Shouwu shuguan, 1933), 995.
4 Petr P. Semenov, *Geograficheskо-statisticheskii slovar' Rossiiskoi Imperii,* vol. 1 [Geographic-statistical dictionary of the Russian Empire] (St. Petersburg: Tipografiia Bezobrasova, 1863), 88; Aleksandr Kirillov, *Geografichesko-statisticheskii slovar' Amurskoi i Primorskoi oblastei s vklyucheniem nekotorykh punktov sopredel'nykh s nimi stran* [Geographic-statistical dictionary of the Amur and Maritime Provinces including several locations of the adjacent countries] (Blagoveshchensk: D.O. Mokin i Ko, 1894), 48–49; Shul'man, *Amurskaia oblast* (1989), 42.
5 Owen Lattimore, "The Gold Tribe, 'Fishskin Tatars' of the Lower Sungari," *Memoirs of the American Anthropological Association* 40 (1933): 75.
6 A.A. Bolotov, *Amur i ego bassein* [Amur River and its basin] (Harbin: Obshchestvo izucheniia Man'chzhurskogo kraia, 1925), 18.
7 Ibid., 21–23.
8 Pëtr Kropotkin, *Memoirs of a Revolutionist* (Montreal: Black Rose Books, 1989), 178.
9 P.N. Men'shikov, *Otchet kommercheskogo agenta Kitaiskoi Vostochnoi zheleznoi dorogi P. N. Men'shikova po obsledovaniiu Heilongjiang provintsii i chasti Zharimskogo seima Vnutrennei Mongolii* [Report of P.N. Menshikov, commercial agent of the Chinese Eastern Railway on the Heilongjiang Province and part of Inner Mongolia] (Harbin: Tipografiia Kitaiskoi Vostochnoi zheleznoi dorogi, 1913), 27–29; Zhu Daren, *Zhongguo dituce* [China atlas] (Beijing: Zhongguo ditu chubanshe, 2001), 10; Bolotov, *Amur i ego bassein,* 25.
10 Ibid., 1–2.
11 On the mountains of the Amur province, see Kirillov, *Geografichesko-statisticheskii,* 14.
12 Zhao Songqiao, *Geography of China: Environment, Resources, Population, and Development* (New York: John Wiley and Sons, Inc., 1994), 185–86.
13 Lattimore, *Manchuria,* 15.
14 Owen Lattimore, *The Mongols of Manchuria* (New York: Howard Fertig, 1969), 156.
15 V.A. Anuchin, *Geograficheskie ocherki Manchzhurii* [Essays on the geography of Manchuria] (Moscow: Gosudarstvennoe izdatel'stvo geograficheskoi literatury, 1948), 142.
16 Ibid., 140.
17 Zhao, *Geography of China,* 82–83.
18 Vladimir K. Arsen'ev, *V debriakh Ussuriiskogo kraia* [In the depths of the Ussuri region] (Moscow: Gosudarstvennoe izdatel'stvo geograficheskoi litaratury, 1951), 84, 87, 104;

Arsen'ev, *Kitaitsy v Ussuriiskom krae* [The Chinese in the Ussuri region] (Moscow: Izdatel'stvo Kraft, 2004), 17–21.

19 Nikolai A. Baikov, *V debriakh Manchzhurii: Ocherki i rasskazy iz byta obitatelei taigi* [In the depths of Manchuria: Essays and stories from daily life of taiga] (Harbin: Ofset-press, 1934), 9, 36–38, 67.

20 Arsen'ev, *V debriakh Ussuriiskogo kraia,* 99.

21 Zhao, *Geography of China,* 28; Ernest G. Ravenstein, *The Russians on the Amur* (London: Trubner and Co., 1861), 315–16.

22 Lattimore, "The Gold Tribe," 19, 33–34.

23 There are several theories about the origins of the word *Orochen.* According to one theory, the Tungus word *oron* means reindeer. According to another, *Orochen* referred to the person who lived along the Oro River, a tributary of the Amur. See G.M. Vasilevich, *Evenki: Istoriko-etnograficheskie ocherki (XVIII–nachalo XX vv.)* [The Evenks: Historical and ethnographic essays] (Leningrad: Nauka, 1969), 11–12; Ravenstein, *Russians on the Amur,* 318.

24 Vasilevich, *Evenki,* 75.

25 Alexander Hosie, *Manchuria: Its People, Resources and Recent History* (Boston: J.B. Millet, 1910), 107; Lattimore, "The Gold Tribe," 31–32. According to Lattimore, horses and cattle were difficult to maintain in the natural conditions of Manchuria.

26 See Vladimir K. Arsen'ev, "Kratkii fiziko-geograficheskii ocherk basseina reki Amura" [Essay on the geography of the Amur River basin] (public meeting protocol of the ORO) Harbin, June 6, 1916.

27 Hosie, *Manchuria,* 86–88.

28 Mixed Chinese–Russian ownership of coal mines started in Manchuria in 1901 with the unequal Qing–Russian joint agreement on coal mining in Jilin and Heilongjiang provinces, in which the actual right to explore coal resources belonged to the Russian-controlled Chinese Eastern Railway Company. See Kong, *Zhongguo Dongbei,* 127.

29 Lee, *Manchurian Frontier,* 91.

30 Average annual precipitation in the Amur region in summer and in winter has a ratio of 50 to 1 and more. See L.M. Bolkhovitinov, *Reka Amur ot Blagoveshchenska do Khabarovska* [Amur River from Blagoveshchensk to Khabarovsk] (St. Petersburg: Voennaia tipografiia, 1910), 64; Zhao, *Geography of China,* 175.

31 E.E. Anert, "Ezhegodnye polovod'ia v severnoi Manchzhurii i navodnenie 1932 goda" [Yearly floods in Northern Manchuria and the flood of 1932], *Ezhegodnik,* Annual of the Club of Natural Science and Geography of the YMCA, 1 (1933): 66.

32 Ravenstein, *Russians on the Amur,* 80–81.

33 Liu Zheming and Shi Ye, *Dongbei da di* [Manchuria's great land] (Beijing: Dizhi chubanshe, 1989), 19.

34 Anuchin, *Geograficheskiie ocherki Manchzhurii,* 151.

35 D.A. Davidov, *Kolonizatsiia Manchzhurii i severo-vostochnoi Mongolii* [Colonization of Manchuria and northeastern Mongolia] (Vladivostok: Vostochnyi institut, 1911), 125.

36 Lattimore, *Manchuria,* 19.

37 E.O. Pauer, *Manchzhuriia [Manchuria]* (St. Petersburg: Slovo, 1904), 63.

38 For the cultural adaptation of the Chinese to winter in Manchuria, see the unpublished paper by Diana Lary, "The Manchurian Winter," University of British Columbia, October 1999.

39 Shi Fang and Gao Ling, *Chuantong yu biange* [Tradition and change] (Harbin: Heilongjiang renmin chubanshe, 1995), 37–39.

40 Wu Lien-teh (G.L. Tuck) and Hulun Taotai, "First Report of the North Manchurian Plague Prevention Service," *Journal of Hygiene,* 13, 3 (October 1913), 243–44.

41 According to Baikov, the fur of infected animals passed the plague to humans. Infected lice were a vector, and people shared the same bed or a hut, usually during cold winters. Chinese peasants got infected by adding rodent's fat or meat to their food. See Baikov, *V debriakh Manchzhurii,* 20–24; and Dugald C.M.G. Christie, *Thirty Years in Moukden, 1883–1913: Being the Experiences and Recollections of Dugald Christie* (London: Constable, 1914), 234–235. Christie distinguishes between bubonic and pneumonic plague, explaining that bubonic plague passed from rats and fleas, whereas pneumonic plague could be transmitted from person to person.

Chapter 2: They Came from Everywhere

1 For historical and cultural context of Chinese migrations to Manchuria, see Thomas R. Gottschang and Diana Lary, *Swallows and Settlers: The Great Migration from North China to Manchuria* (Ann Arbor: University of Michigan, Center for Chinese Studies, 2000), 45–48, 69–73. For discussion of Chinese terms for external and internal migration, see Gungwu Wang, *The Chinese Overseas: From Earthbound China to the Quest for Autonomy* (Cambridge, MA: Harvard University Press, 2000), 42–50.

2 Willard Sunderland, *The Baron's Cloak: A History of the Russian Empire in War and Revolution* (Ithaca: Cornell University Press, 2014), 90–94.

3 Lattimore, *Inner Asian Frontiers of China,* 129–31.

4 Juna Janhunen, *Manchuria: An Ethnic History* (Helsinki: Finno-Ugrian Society, 1996), 187.

5 Semenov, *Geograficheskо-statisticheskii,* vol. 1, 89.

6 For a detailed description of Manchurian indigenous tribes, see Janhunen, *Manchuria,* 41–76. On Tungus tribes of the Russian Far East, see Vasilevich, *Evenki,* 3–41.

7 D. Pozdneev, *Opisanie Manchzhurii* [Description of Manchuria] (St. Petersburg: Kantseliariia Ministerstva Finansov, 1897), 234.

8 Kira Van Deusen, *The Flying Tiger: Women Shamans and Storytellers of the Amur* (Montreal and Kingston: McGill–Queen's University Press, 2001), 23–25, 78, 170–72.

9 Czaplicka referred to shamanism as partly a primitive religion and partly a practice of observing nature and spirits. According to her, shamanism was widespread in Northern and Central Asia among Tungusic and Mongol people. Maria A. Czaplicka, *Aboriginal Siberia: A Study in Social Anthropology* (Oxford: Clarendon Press, 1914), 166–68.

10 Sergei M. Shirokogoroff, "What Is Shamanism?" *China Journal of Science and Arts* 3 (May 1924): 275–79; 4 (July 1924): 368–71; Anna V. Smoliak, "Osnovnye cherty shamanizma nanaitsev i ul'chei" [Main features of shamanism among the Nanai and the Ul'chi], in *Antropologiia i istoricheskaia etnografiia Sibiri* [Anthropology and historical ethnography of Siberia], ed. V.A. Dremov, R.F. Its, and N.A. Tomilov (Omsk: Omsk University, 1990), 141–48.

11 Ling Chunsheng, *Songhuajiang xiayoude Hezhe zu* [Hezhe nationality in the lower reaches of the Songhua River] (Shanghai: Shanghai wenyi chubanshe, 1990), 49–51.

12 A.P. Bogaevskii, *Sansin'skoe fudutunstvo* [Sanxing fudutun county] (Khabarovsk: Tipografiia Priamurskogo voennogo okruga, 1903), 32–34.
13 Arsen'ev, *V debriakh Ussuriiskogo kraia,* 49–57.
14 Kuzmichev, *Pisatel' Arsen'ev* [Writer Arsen'ev] (Leningrad: Sovetskii pisatel', 1977), 144–65.
15 Lattimore, "The Gold Tribe," 8, 75.
16 Ibid., 55–56.
17 Lee, *Manchurian Frontier,* 16–19.
18 Rhoads, *Manchus and Han,* 8.
19 David M. Farquhar, "Emperor as Bodhisattva in the Governance of the Ch'ing Empire," *Harvard Journal of Asiatic Studies* 38 (June 1978): 5–34.
20 R. Kent Guy, "Who Were the Manchus? A Review Essay," *Journal of Asian Studies* 61, 1 (February 2002): 160–63; Zhao Yuntian, "Qingmo bianjiang diqu xinzheng juyao" [Highlight study on the new policy towards borderlands in the late Qing dynasty], *Zhongguo bianjiang shidi yanjiu* 4 (1996): 64–66.
21 Petr Rossov, *Sushchestvuiut li Manchzhury?* [Do the Manchus exist?] (Harbin: Tipografiia gazety Novy Krai, 1903), 12–15.
22 Shao, *Remote Homeland*
23 N.P. Mat'khanova, *Graf N.N. Murav'ev-Amurskii v vospominaniiakh sovremennikov* [Count N.N. Murav'ev-Amurskii in the memoirs of his contemporaries] (Novosibirsk: Sibirskii khronograph, 1998), 190–99.
24 T.F. Kolykhalova, *Sotsial-demokraticheskoe dvizhenie na Amure v period revoliutsionnoi bor'by s samoderzhaviem* [Social-democratic movement in the Amur during the revolutionary struggle against the autocracy] (Tomsk: Izdanie Tomskogo Universiteta, 1979), 13.
25 Kabuzan, *Dal'nevostochnyi krai,* 96. Stephan, *Russian Far East,* 65.
26 Stephan, *Russian Far East,* 310.
27 Kolykhalova, *Sotsial-demokraticheskoe dvizhenie na Amure,* 19.
28 Kirillov, *Geograficheskо-statisticheskii,* 48.
29 T.I. Polner, *Priamur'e: Fakty, tsyfry, nabliudeniia* [Priamur'e: Facts, numbers, observations] (Moscow: Gorodskaia tipografiia 1909), 720–22.
30 Ibid., 816, 846.
31 Stephan, *Russian Far East,* 67–68.
32 George Woodcock, and Ivan Avakumovic, *The Doukhobors* (Toronto: Oxford University Press, 1968), 149–51.
33 After 1879, the convicts also arrived from Odessa by sea. In 1889, the number of prisoners on Sakhalin Island reached nearly 12,000. Kirillov, *Geograficheskо-statisticheskii,* 362.
34 Baikov, *V debriakh Manchzhurii,* 60–61.
35 George Kennan, "Siberia – The Exiles' Abode," *Journal of the American Geographic Society of New York* 14 (1882): 44–52.
36 On the role of Korean peasants in developing paddy fields in Manchuria, see Yi Baozhong, "Lun Qingmo Dongbei diqude shuitian kaifa" [Development of paddy fields in the Northeastern region in the late Qing dynasty], *Jilin Daxue Shehui Kexue Xuebao* 1 (January 2002): 96–97.
37 Changyu Piao, "The History of Koreans in China and the Yanbian Korean Autonomous Prefecture," in *Koreans in China,* ed. Dae-Sook Suh and Edward J. Shultz. Papers of the Center for Korean Studies, no. 16 (Honolulu: University of Hawai'i, 1990), 49.

38 Yan Junguang, *Chaoxian Zu* [The Korean nationality] (Beijing: Renmin chubanshe, 1996), 10. For a detailed history of Korean migration to Manchuria in modern times, see Sun Chunri, *Zhongguo chaoxianzu yimin shi* [The history of migration by China's ethnic Koreans] (Beijing: Zhonghua shuju, 2009).

39 O.I. Sergeev, S.I. Lazareva, and G.Ya. Trigub, *Mestnoe samoupravlenie na Dal'nem Vostoke Rossii vo vtoroi polovine XIX – nachale XX v.* [Local self-government in the Russian Far East from the late nineteenth to the early twentieth century] (Vladivostok: Dal'nauka, 2002), 229; Stephan, *Russian Far East,* 75.

40 A.V. Zagorul'ko, "Koreitsy na Rossiiskom Dal'nem Vostoke, 1863–1938 gg.," [Koreans in the Russian Far East, 1863–1938], *Narody Sibiri* [People of Siberia], ed. Iu. B. Simchenko (Moscow: Institut etnografii i antropologii im N.N. Miklukho-Maklaia, 1997), 69; Ross King, "Blagoslovennoe: Korean Village on the Amur, 1871–1937," *Review of Korean Studies* 4, 2 (2001): 139–40, 147–50.

41 Lattimore, *Manchuria,* 45–47.

42 Lee, *Manchurian Frontier,* 79–80.

43 Gottschang and Lary, *Swallows and Settlers,* 46.

44 An official Russian military survey of 1906 estimated the population of Heilongjiang Province to be 1.53 million. However, this number was based on outdated local statistics of the banner population and did not include the seasonal Chinese labourers involved in railway construction and in the mines. See I.A. Dobrolovskii, *Heiluntszianskaia provintsiia Manchzhurii* [Heilongjiang Province of Manchuria] (Harbin: Tipo-litografiia shtaba Zaamurskogo okruga pogranichnoi strazhi, 1906), 98–100; Qu, *Jindai Dongbei,* 224.

45 Ibid., 225.

46 Lee, *Manchurian Frontier,* 93–94.

47 Shi Fang, *Heilongjiang quyu shehui shi yanjiu* [Research on social history of the Heilongjiang region] (Harbin: Heilongjiang renmin chubanshe, 2002), 467.

48 Ibid., 468.

49 E.I. Martynov, *Rabota nashih zheleznodorozhnyh del'tsov v Manchzhurii* [Activities of our railway dealers in Manchuria] (Moscow: Tipografiia Riabushinskogo, 1914), 72–73.

50 Arsen'ev, *Kitaitsy v Ussuriiskom krae,* 197. Translated by the author.

51 Shi, *Heilongjiang,* 494–95.

52 Anton P. Chekhov, *Ostrov Sakhalin: iz putevykh zapisok* [Sakhalin Island: From traveler's notes], Collected Works, vol. 10 (Moscow: Khudozhestvennaia literatura, 1963), 45. Translated by the author.

Chapter 3: Fur, Gold, and Local Trade

1 The emergence of trade between the Qing and Russians in the Amur Basin coincided with the gradual decline of the Kiakhta trade system (1728–1850), which was an extension of the caravan trade between Russian and Mongol merchants. Kiakhta trade contributed to the growth of the fur business in Siberia and Kamchatka, and to China's manufacturing industries producing silk, porcelain, tobacco, and tea. See M.I. Sladkovskii, *The Long Road: Sino-Russian Economic Contacts from Ancient Times to 1917* (Moscow: Progress Publishers, 1981), 136–50; Mi Zhenbo, Qingdai *Zhong-E Qiaketu*

bianjiang maoyi [Sino-Russian Kiakhta border trade during the Qing dynasty] (Tianjin: Nankai daxue chubanshe, 2003), 158–69.

2 Lee, *Manchurian Frontier,* 34, 55.

3 For the full text of Aigun Treaty, see V.S. Myasnikov, ed., *Russko-Kitaiskie dogovorno-pravovye akty (1689–1916)* [Sino-Russian treaties and legal acts, 1689–1916] (Moscow: Pamiatniki istoricheskoi mysli, 2004), 62–65. Under the Treaty of Tianjin (1858), Russia gained rights to conduct trade with China by land and by sea, in the "free" ports of Shanghai, Ningbo, Fuzhou, Amoy (Xiamen), Canton, Taiwan-fu, and other places open for foreign trade.

4 Ibid., 72.

5 Myasnikov, *Russko-Kitaiskie dogovorno-pravovye akty,* 91.

6 Ren Jiahe, "Qingchu Dongbei bianjing gezu diaogong kaolü" [Rethinking fur tribute among the nationalities in China's northeast frontier during the early Qing dynasty], *Heilongjiang Minzu Congkan* 1 (1994): 80–85.

7 Shuyler Cammann, "Origins of the Court and Official Robes of the Ch'ing Dynasty," *Artibus Asiae* 12, 3 (1949): 200; James L. Hevia, *English Lessons: The Pedagogy of Imperialism in Nineteenth-Century China* (Durham: Duke University Press, 2003), 79, 85.

8 Zhou Xifeng, "Jian shu Qingdai Nenjiang liuyu de Ewenke zu" [Brief account of the Evenk people in the Nen River valley], *Heilongjiang Minzu Congkan* 4 (2002): 79–80.

9 N.K. Lavrov, *Pushnoi promysel na Russkom Dal'nem Vostoke* [Fur trade in the Russian Far East] (Tokyo: n.p., 1923), 24.

10 Ibid., 228. S.N. Liupov, *Hulan'skoe fudutunstvo Heiluntszianskoi provintsii* [Hulan administrative region of the Heilongjiang province] (Khabarovsk: n.p., 1903), 199.

11 Ibid., 1.

12 Vladimir K. Arsen'ev, *Dorogoi hishchnik: Okhota na sobolia v Ussuriiskom krae* [Valuable beast of prey: Sable hunt in the Ussuri region] (Vladivostok: Aktsyonernoe knizhnoe obshchestvo, 1925), 4–7.

13 Arsen'ev, *Kitaitsy v Ussuriiskom krae,* 128–29.

14 Ibid., 22–23.

15 The amount of Kamchatka sable hunted in 1916 accounted for 20 percent of all officially hunted sable in Russia. See Lavrov, *Pushnoi promysel,* 11.

16 Hosie, *Manchuria,* 110.

17 Vladimir K. Arsen'ev, *Po Ussuriiskomu kraiu* [Across the Ussuri region] (Moscow: Gosudarstvennoe izdatel'stvo geograficheskoi literatury, 1960), 18.

18 Ibid., 232.

19 Mikhail I. Sladkovskii, *Istoriia torgovo-ekonomicheskikh otnoshenii narodov Rossii s Kitaem* [The history of trade and economic relations between Russians and Chinese people] (Moscow: Nauka, 1974), 284, 285.

20 Ibid., 341, 345; Pozdneev, *Opisanie Manchzhurii,* 554.

21 L.L. Tove and D.V. Ivanov, *Otchet po statistiko-ekonomicheskomu i tekhnicheskomu issledovaniiu zolotopromyshlennosti Amursko-Primorskogo raiona* [The report on statistical, economic, and technical research about the gold mining industry in the Amur and Maritime regions], vol. 2, pt. 1: *Amurskaia oblast'* (St. Petersburg: Iakor', 1905), 56–57.

22 N.V. Sliunin, *Sovremennoe polozhenie nashego Dal'nego Vostoka* [Current affairs of our Far East] (St. Petersburg: Tipografiia Ministerstva Finansov, 1908), 107–8.

23 Kirillov, *Geograficheskо-statisticheskii,* 153.
24 "Guangxu nianjian kaiban Heilongjiang Mohe jinkuang shiliao" [Historical materials on the Mohe gold mine in Heilongjiang during the Guangxu reign], pt. 1, in *Lishi Dang'an.* Zhongguo diyi lishi dang'an zhuban (2004): 1, 38–44.
25 Kong, *Zhongguo Dongbei,* 79.
26 Zhang Fengming, "19 shiji hou ban Heilongjiang diqu jinkuangye de xingqi he fazhan" [The rise and development of gold mining in Heilongjiang region during the late nineteenth century], *Heilongjiang shehui kexue* 6 (2008): 140–42.
27 V.D. Riazanov, *Otchet po statistiko-ekonomicheskomu i tekhnicheskomu issledovaniiu zolotopromyshlennosti Amursko-Primorskogo kraia* [Report on the statistical, economic, and technical investigations of gold mining in the Amur-Maritime regions], vol. 2, pt. 2: *Amurskaia oblast'* [Amur Province] (St. Petersburg: Iakor', 1903), 828–29.
28 *Protokoly vtorogo Amurskogo s'ezda zolotopromyshlennikov, 25–30 ianvaria, 1899* [The Protocol of the second Amur congress of gold miners, January 25–30, 1899] (Blagoveshchensk: Tipografiia opeki Artamonova i ko., 1899), 18–25.
29 Bronislav L. Grombchevskii, "Kitaiskie zolotye Priiski na pravom beregu Amura" [Chinese goldfields on the right bank of the Amur River], *Priamurskie Vegomosti* (1897): 245–246.
30 Tove and Ivanov, *Otchet po statistiko-ekonomicheskomu,* 300–7.
31 Pavel F. Unterberger, *Priamurskii krai,* 1906–1910 [Priamur region, 1906–1910] (St. Petersburg, 1912), 180–82.

Chapter 4: Imperial Russian Expansionism

1 Mark Mancall, *Russia and China: Their Diplomatic Relations to 1728* (Cambridge, MA: Harvard University Press, 1971), 28–31.
2 On Peter the Great's foreign policy, see E.V. Anisimov, "The Imperial Heritage of Peter the Great in the Foreign Policy of his Early Successors," in *Imperial Russian Foreign Policy,* ed. Hugh Ragsdale (Cambridge: Cambridge University Press, 1993), 21–35. On Yongzheng's military campaigns, see Jonathan Spence, *In Search of Modern China* (New York: W.W. Norton, 1990), 74–89.
3 The negotiations were facilitated by two Jesuit interpreters, Jean-Francois Gerbillion and Thomas Pereira. The Latin version served as the official text of the treaty. Emmanuel C.Y. Hsü, *The Rise of Modern China* (Oxford: Oxford University Press, 1983), 111–12.
4 Liu Yuantu, ed., *Zaoqi Zhong-E dongduan bianjie yanjiu* [Research on the early period of the eastern section of the Sino-Russian border] (Beijing: Zhongguo shehui kexue chubanshe, 1993), 1, 38, 267–68.
5 G.V. Melikhov, *Manchzhury na severo-vostoke, XVII v.* [The Manchus of the Northeast in the seventeenth century] (Moscow: Nauka, 1974), 107–9.
6 Peter C. Perdue, *China Marches West: The Qing Conquest of Central Eurasia* (Cambridge, MA: Harvard University Press, 2005), 87–89.
7 Stephan, *Russian Far East,* 21.
8 On the Russian state's changing perceptions about Siberia, see Mark Bassin, "Inventing Siberia: Visions of the Russian Far East in the Early Nineteenth Century," *American Geographic Review* 96, 3 (June 1991), 763–94. On the Siberian exile system, see Kennan, "Siberia – the Exiles' Abode."

9 Russia's two major state-sponsored naval expeditions to the North Pacific were called the Kamchatka Expeditions, and lasted from 1725 to 1744. The first Russian settlement in North America was in 1775. Stephan, *Russian Far East,* 33–35.

10 James R. Gibson, "Russian Expansion in Siberia and America," *Geographic Review* 70, 2 (April 1980), 130–31.

11 A.I. Alekseev, *Amurskaia expeditsiia, 1849–1855* [The Amur expedition, 1849–1855] (Moscow: Mysl', 1974), 14.

12 Ivan Barsukov, *Graf Nikolai Nikolaevich Murav'ev-Amurskii po ego pis'mam, ofitsial'nym dokumentam, rasskazam sovremennikov i pechatnym istochnikam* [Count Nikolai Nikolayevich Murav'ev-Amurskii: His letters, official documents, contemporary accounts and published sources], vol. 1 (Moscow: Sinodal'naia tip., 1891), 211–12, cited in Mark Bassin, "The Russian Geographical Society, the 'Amur Epoch,' and the Great Siberian Expedition 1855–1863," *Annals of the Association of American Geographers* 73, 2 (June 1983), 246.

13 Richard L. Edmonds, "The Willow Palisade," *Annals of the Association of American Geographers* 69, 4 (December 1979): 611–21.

14 A.I. Alekseev, *Russkie geograficheskie issledovaniia na Dal'nem Vostoke i v severnoi Amerike, XIX – nachalo XX veka* [Russian geographic explorations in the Far East and in North America, from the nineteenth to the early twentieth century] (Moscow: Nauka, 1976), 8.

15 Petr Petrovich Semenov-Tianshansky was a president of the Russian Geographical Society from 1873 to 1914.

16 Petr P. Semenov-Tianshansky, *Puteshestvie v Tianshan* [Journey to Tianshan] (Moscow: Gosudarstvennoe isdatel'stvo geograficheskoi literatury, 1946); Schimmelpenninck van der Oye, *Toward the Rising Sun,* 28–30; Bassin, *Imperial Visions,* 97–99.

17 Mat'khanova, *Graf N.N. Murav'ev-Amurskii,* 7–18. On Murav'ev's contacts with American merchants, see Norman Saul, "An American's Siberian Dream," *Russian Review* 37, 4 (October 1978), 406, 416–19.

18 Arthur W. Hummel, *Eminent Chinese of the Ch'ing Period (1644–1912)* (Washington, DC: Government Publication Office, 1943), vol. 1, 392–93.

19 The earliest Russian map of Siberia was produced by Semion Remezov in 1697; one of the earliest Qing maps of the Manchu ancestral lands was produced in 1760. See Leo Bagrow, *History of Cartography* (Cambridge, MA: Harvard University Press, 1964), 202–3, App. C, 107. For historical comparisons between the Qing, Russian, and European cartography, see Laura Hostetler, *Qing Colonial Enterprise: Ethnography and Cartography in Early Modern China.* (Chicago: University of Chicago Press, 2001), 51–80.

20 Liu, *Zaoqi Zhong-E dongduan bianjie yanjiu,* 38.

21 See Alekseev, *Russkie geograficheskie issledovaniia,* 29; Stephan, *Russian Far East,* 43.

22 G.F. Starikov and A.A. Stepanov, "Important Monument to Far Eastern Cartography," *Voprosy geografii Dal'nego Vostoka* 6 (1963), 292.

23 Cong Peiyuan and Zhao Mingqi, eds., *Cao Tingjie ji* [Collected works of Cao Tingjie] (Beijing: Zhonghua shuju, 1985) vol. 2, 508–10.

24 Xue and Zhou, *Zhong-E guanxi,* 276.

25 Myasnikov, *Granitsy Kitaia,* 173–77; Fucheng Hsieh, *The European Diary of Hsieh Fucheng: Envoy Extraordinary of Imperial China,* trans. Helen Hsieh Chien (New York: St. Martin's Press, 1993), 85–87.

26 Zeng Pu, *Nie Hai Hua* [Flowers in the sea of sin] (Shanghai: Shanghai guji chubanshe, 1979), 99–100.

27 *Alfavitnyi ukazatel' geograficheskikh imen pomeshchennykh na karte Manchzhurii L. Borodovskogo* [Index of geographic names on the map of Manchuria by L. Borodovsky] (St. Petersburg: The Ministry of Finance, 1901).
28 Myasnikov, *Russko-Kitaiskie dogovorno-pravovye akty,* 71.
29 Myasnikov, *Granitsy Kitaia,* 113.
30 Neville Maxwell, "A Note on the Amur/Ussuri Sector of the Sino-Soviet Boundaries," *Modern China* 1, 1 (January 1975), 116–26.
31 Dmitrii I. Stakheev, *Za Baikalom i na Amure* [Beyond the Baikal Lake and along the Amur River] (St. Petersburg: Tipografiia K. Vul'fa, 1869), 281.
32 Myasnikov, *Russko-Kitaiskie dogovorno-pravovye akty,* 371.
33 Hosie, *Manchuria,* 274.
34 The official Russian account of Nicholas's trip to Asia is by E.E. Ukhtomskii, *Puteshestvie gosudaria imperatora Nikolaia II na Vostok (v 1890–1891)* [The tour of the Tsar Nicholas II to the East, 1890–1891] (Leipzig: F.A. Brokgauz, 1897). Also see Schimmelpenninck van der Oye, *Toward the Rising Sun,* 15–23.
35 For the texts of the treaties, see P.E. Skachkov and V.S. Myasnikov, eds., *Russko-Kitaiskie otnosheniia, 1689–1916: Ofitsyal'nye dokumenty* [Sino-Russian relations, 1689–1916: Official documents] (Moscow: Vostochnaia literatura, 1958), 73–80.
36 C. Walter Young, *The International Relations of Manchuria* (Chicago: University of Chicago Press, 1929), 49–53; Tang, *Russian and Soviet Policy,* 36–37.
37 See Tolstoy's letter to Nicholas II in S.P. Melgunov, ed., *Nicholas II: Materialy dlia kharakteristiki lichnosti i tsarstvovaniia* [Nicholas II: Materials describing his personality and reign] (Moscow: Izdanie zhurnala Golos Minuvshego, 1917), 117–23.
38 Under the Russo-Japanese Treaty of Shimoda (1855), Japan and Russia jointly occupied Sakhalin Island. After 1881, Sakhalin Island was turned into a Russian penal colony. After 1905, the Japanese ruled Southern Sakhalin for another forty years. John J. Stephan, "Sakhalin Island: Soviet Outpost in Northeast Asia," *Asian Survey* 10, 12 (1970): 1090–100.
39 Tessa Morris-Suzuki, "Lines in the Snow: Imagining the Russo-Japanese Frontier," *Pacific Affairs,* 72, 1 (Spring 1999): 67–70.
40 Russia acquired the Liaodong Peninsula in 1898 under a twenty-five-year lease. Myasnikov, *Russko-kitaiskie dogovorno pravovye akty,* 221–24.
41 Between 1906 and 1909, twenty-one new treaty ports were established in Manchuria. Herbert P. Bix, "Japanese Imperialism and the Manchurian Economy, 1900–31," *China Quarterly* 51 (July 1972), 433.
42 C. Walter Young, "Economic Factors in Manchurian Diplomacy," *Annals of the American Academy of Political and Social Science* 152 (November 1930), 303; Prasenjit Duara, *Sovereignty and Authenticity: Manchukuo and the East Asian Modern* (Lanham, MD: Rowman and Littlefield, 2003), 48.

Chapter 5: Chinese Migrants in Frontier Towns

1 See Russian text of the Aigun Treaty (1858) in Myasnikov, *Russko-Kitaiskie dogovorno-pravovye akty,* 62, 63.
2 Ibid., 125–30. According to the St. Petersburg Treaty, arms, salt, and opium were forbidden for cross-border trade. The export of rice and Chinese copper coins from China was also banned.

3 For a detailed historical account of Chinese migration to Manchuria, see Reardon-Anderson, *Reluctant Pioneers;* and Patrick Fuliang Shan, *Taming China's Wilderness: Immigration, Settlement, and Shaping of the Heilongjiang Frontier, 1900–1931* (Burlington: Ashgate, 2014).

4 Pozdneev, *Opisanie Manchzhurii,* 550.

5 The Priamur governor-generalship included Trans-Baikal, Amur, Maritime, and Sakhalin provinces. Stephan, *Russian Far East,* 55; Kirillov, *Geograficheskо-statisticheskii,* 330.

6 Kabuzan, *Dal'nevostochnyi krai,* 228.

7 P.R. Volnogorskii, *Velikii put'* [The great route] (Moscow: Izdanie Tikhomirova, 1904), 187.

8 Bolkhovitinov, *Reka Amur,* 64.

9 Wolff, *To the Harbin Station,* 31.

10 Sergeev, Lazareva, and Trigub, *Mestnoe samoupravlenie,* 229.

11 A.G. Larin, *Kitaitsy v Rossii vchera i segodnia* [The Chinese in Russia: Past and present] (Moscow: Muravei, 2003), 18–21. The Russian Far East then included a vast territory: part of east Siberia, Trans-Baikal, Amur, and Maritime Provinces, Kamchatka, and Sakhalin. In 1909, Kamchatka and Sakhalin formed separate provinces within the region.

12 N.I. Dubinina, *Priamurskii general-gubernator N.L. Gondatti* [Priamur Governor-General N.L. Gondatti] (Khabarovsk: Priamurskie Vedomosti, 1997), 113. In 1914, there were 50,000 Chinese in the Ussuri taiga, or roughly the population of Khabarovsk at that time.

13 Pozdneev, *Opisanie Manchzhurii,* 564.

14 L. Bogoslovskii, "Krepost'-gorod Vladivostok i kitaitsy" [Fortress Vladivostok and the Chinese], in *Vestnik Azii* (1913), 21.

15 The Chinese term for sojourners, *qiao,* refers to Chinese migrations overseas. It is usually used in the context of the long history of Chinese migration to Southeast Asia and, since the nineteenth century, to the Western countries. Wang, *Chinese Overseas,* 39–77.

16 Dubinina, *Priamurskii general-gubernator, N. I. Grodekov* [Priamur Governor-General N.I. Grodekov] (Khabarovsk: Priamurskie Vedomosti, 2001), 82.

17 Arsen'ev, *Kitaitsy v Ussuriiskom krae,* 115–117.

18 For junk trade figures, see Pozdneev, *Opisanie Manchzhurii,* 558–62.

19 L. Eve Armentrout Ma distinguishes several types of *huiguan,* especially merchant and resettlement. In Manchuria, which saw rapid Chinese migration from Shandong and Zhili provinces, settlement *huiguan* prevailed. Manchurian *huiguan* included railway workers, Chinese loggers, ginseng seekers, and fur trappers. Russian frontier towns along the Amur probably had mixed types of *huiguan,* combining merchant and resettlement types. They included men coming from more than one province in China Proper. Ma, "Fellow-Regional Associations in the Qing Dynasty: Organizations in Flux for Mobile People," *Modern Asian Studies* 18, 2 (1984), 321–325.

20 Arsen'ev, *Kitaitsy v Ussuriiskom krae,* 233–35.

21 Volnogorskii, *Velikii put',* 203.

22 Pozdneev, *Opisanie Manchzhurii,* 37–40.

23 Larin, *Kitaitsy v Rossii,* 62.

24 Ibid., 63; Wolff, *To the Harbin Station,* 16.

25 Mikhail V. Grulev, *V shtabakh i na poliakh Dal'nego Vostoka* [In military headquarters and in the fields of the Far East] (Moscow: Gosudarstvennaia publichnaia istoricheskaia biblioteka Rossii, 2007), 122.

26 See Qing–Russian protocol on border negotiation, 1886, in Myasnikov, ed., *Russko-Kitaiskie dogovorno-pravovye akty,* 173.

27 A.I. Petrov, "Russkii 'kitaets' Nikolai Ivanovich Tifontai (Ji Fengtai)" [A Russian "Chinese": Nikolai Ivanovich Tifontai], *Rossiia i ATR* 2 (2005): 141–51; Maria Burilova, "Vliublennyi v Rossiiu" [In love with Russia], *Svoe Delo* 4 (2010). http://dv-delo.ru/2010/08/01/vlyublennyj-v-rossiyu.

28 Arsen'ev, *Kitaitsy v Ussuriiskom krae,* 109–10.

29 Maria Burilova, "Kitaitsy v Priamurskom krae" [The Chinese in the Priamur region], *Turne* [Tour] 1–2 (2004), 31; A.P. Ivanova, "Torgovlia kak sterzhen' infrastruktury goroda" [Trade as a core of urban infrastructure], in *Arkhitektura vostochnoi Sibiri i Dal'nego Vostoka,* vol. 1, ed. N.P. Kradin (Khabarovsk: Dal'nauka, 2002), 68.

30 Sergeev, Lazareva, and Trigub, *Mestnoe samoupravlenie,* 234–38; Dubinina, *Priamurskii [...] Gondatti,* 133–34.

31 Burilova, "Kitaitsy v Priamurskom krae," 31.

32 Dubinina, *Priamurskii [...] Gondatti,* 8, 114–117.

33 A.V. Pliusnin's father, Vasilii Pliusnin, and uncle, Andrei Pliusnin, were prominent merchants who ran the Pliusnin trading house, based in Khabarovsk.

34 Sergeev, Lazareva, and Trigub, *Mestnoe Samoupravlenie,* 79; Stephan, *Russian Far East,* 330, 83.

Chapter 6: A Railway Runs through It

1 Sergei Witte, *Vospominaniia* [Memoirs] (Berlin: Slovo, 1922), 37–47.

2 Myasnikov, *Russko-Kitaiskie dogovorno-pravove akty,* 207–10, 212–16.

3 This and the next chapter refer to Lüshun and Dalian as Port Arthur and Dalny, respectively, to reflect Imperial Russia's jurisdiction over these ports, which lasted until the end of the Russo-Japanese War in 1905. After Russia's defeat in this war, these ports became part of Japanese-controlled Kwantung Leasehold and were called Ryojun and Dairen in Japanese.

4 Myasnikov, *Russko-Kitaiskie dogovorno-pravove akty,* 221–24, 233–36.

5 Witte, *Vospominaniia,* 119–133.

6 After the Russo-Japanese War, the Chinese Eastern Railway Company was in charge of the Ussuri Railway's construction.

7 Vladimir K. Arsen'ev, *Novyi entsyklopedicheskii slovar'* [New encyclopedic dictionary], vol. 2 (St. Petersburg: F.A. Brokgauz and I.A. Efron, 1911–1916), 437; Shul'man, *Amurskaia oblast',* 47.

8 After 1924, the Chinese Eastern Railway was jointly operated by the Chinese Republic and the Soviet Union. Myasnikov, *Russko-Kitaiskie dogovorno-pravovye akty,* 212; Chin-Chun Wang, "The Chinese Eastern Railway," *Annals of the American Academy of Political and Social Science* 122 (November 1925), 57–60.

9 According to this agreement, the Chinese Eastern Railway Company did not pay for the government-owned leased lands, but had to pay a yearly rent or one-time payment to the private owners of land. Myasnikov, *Russko-Kitaiskie dogovorno-pravovye akty,* 213.

10 Nearly a decade after the railway was built, disputes between the Chinese Eastern Railway Company and the local administration left the land concessions around the railway's major stations incomplete. According to the Qing Ministry of Foreign Affairs, or *Waiwubu,* in Heilongjiang Province only 65 of 94 railway stations in the province

had their land turned into concessions; in Jilin Province, only 47 of 62 railway stations had concession lands. Myasnikov, *Russko-Kitaiskie dogovorno-pravovye akty,* 370.

11 The original purchase of land for the construction of Harbin in 1898 was 200 *desiatinas.* Wolff, *To the Harbin Station,* 28–29, 202.

12 After the Russo-Japanese War, the Qing government questioned land concession agreements signed between the Chinese Eastern Railway Company and the administration of Heilongjiang and Jilin provinces. In 1910, the Russian Ministry of Finance notified the Qing Ministry of Foreign Affairs that it would agree to reduce the area of the company's land concessions in Manchuria by 30 percent. Myasnikov, *Russko-Kitaiskie dogovorno-pravovye akty,* 306–10, 319–23, 327–30.

13 Ibid., 323–326; Tang, *Russian and Soviet Policy,* 107–8.

14 Myasnikov, *Russko-Kitaiskie dogovorno-pravovye akty,* 330–34, 345–49.

15 Xue, *Zhongdong tielu,* 177; Evgenii Kh. Nilus, ed., *Istoricheskii obzor Kitaiskoi Vostochnoi Zheleznoi Dorogi, 1896–1923 gg.* [Historical overview of the Chinese Eastern Railway, 1896–1923], vol. 1 (Harbin: Tipografiia KVZhD, 1923), 527.

16 Tang, *Russian and Soviet Policy,* 53.

17 Quoted in N.P. Kradin, *Kharbin – Russkaia Atlantida* [Harbin – Russian Atlantis] (Khabarovsk: Khvorov A. Yu, 2001), 18.

18 Surveying the land took at least three years and was done just prior to the construction of each segment. The railway was officially opened on July 1, 1903. *North Manchuria and the Chinese Eastern Railway* (Harbin: CER Printing Office, 1924), 36; Nilus, *Istoricheskii,* 31.

19 Ibid., 59–64.

20 Ibid., 60.

21 *Sbornik dokumentov otnosiashchikhsia k Kitaiskoi Vostochnoi zheleznoi doroge* [Collection of documents related to the Chinese Eastern Railway] (Harbin: Tipografiia Kitaiskoi Vostochnoi zheleznoi dorogi, 1922), xvii.

22 Nilus, *Istoricheskii,* 23–28.

23 Kradin, *Kharbin,* 15, 44.

24 N.A. Vasilenko, "Kto stroil KVZhD: O chislennosti i natsional'nom sostave naseleniia KVZhD v 1897–1917" [Who built the CER: The size and national distribution of the population along the CER during 1897–1917], *Rossiia i ATR* 2 (1995), 66.

25 Nilus, *Istoricheskii,* 79–80.

26 The exact number of Chinese seasonal workers is difficult to calculate due to their mobility. In 1899 the Russian engineer Sergei Vladimirovich Ignatius personally recruited Chinese workers from Shanghai and Zhifu. In 1900, A.K. Karpov, the Chinese Eastern Railway's commercial agent, brought 100,000 Chinese workers for the main section. Nilus, *Istoricheskii,* 185.

27 *Priamurskie Vedomosti* [Priamur News], February 15, 1904. Quoted in Vasilenko, "Kto stroil KVZhD," 67.

28 Wolff, *To the Harbin Station,* 32; Nilus, *Istoricheskii,* 75–78.

29 Ibid., 39, 58.

30 Ibid, 50–51.

31 Kradin, *Kharbin,* 16.

32 Wolff, *To the Harbin Station,* 34; Nilus, *Istoricheskii,* 108.

33 For comparison, by early 1901, the Trans-Siberian Railway, including the CER section, had 9,670 kilometres and had cost 855.3 million rubles. Steven G. Marks, *Road*

to Power: The Trans-Siberian Railroad and the Colonization of Asian Russia 1850–1917 (Ithaca: Cornell University Press, 1991), 214–15; Nilus, *Istoricheskii,* 121–24.

34 G.P. Beloglazov, "Russkaia flotiliia na Sungari, konets XIX–nachalo XX vv." [Russian flotilla on the Songhua River, from the end of the nineteenth to the beginning of the twentieth century], *Rossiia i ATR* 2 (1995), 48–52.

35 Pozdneev, *Opisanie Manchzhurii,* 617.

36 "Lun E-ren zai Dongsansheng jingying zhi xinshi" [Discussion of new towns managed by the Russians in China's Three Eastern Provinces], *Dongfang zazhi* 1, 7 (1904), 140–42.

37 A.V. Tuzhilin, *Sovremennyi Kitai* [Modern China] (St. Petersburg: Tipografiia imperatorskogo uchilishcha glukhonemykh, 1910), 367.

38 Li Xinggeng, ed., *Fengyu fuping: Eguo qiaomin zai Zhongguo, 1917–1945* [Duckweed in the rain and wind: Russian immigrants in China, 1917–1945] (Beijing: Zhongyang bianyi chubanshe, 1997), 18; Kradin, *Kharbin,* 16.

39 Li, *Fengyu fuping,* 10–11.

40 Hosie, *Manchuria,* 268.

41 Olga Bakich, "A Russian City in China: Harbin before 1917," *Canadian Slavonic Papers,* 28: 2 (June 1986), 140.

42 According to Chang Huaisheng, Harbin's architectural styles included art nouveau, baroque, Byzantine, classical revival, Russian, Judaic, eclectic, and modern. Chang Huaisheng, *Ha'erbin jianzhu yishu* [Harbin's architectural art] (Ha'erbin: Ha'erbin kexue jishu chubanshe, 1990), 28–32.

43 Li, *Fengyu fuping,* 406; E.P. Taskina, *Russkii Kharbin* [Russian Harbin] (Moscow: Moscow University, 1998), 27–32.

44 Shi Fang, Liu Shuyang, and Gao Ling, eds., *Ha'erbin E-qiao shi* [History of the Russian emigrants in Harbin] (Ha'erbin: Heilongjiang renmin chubanshe, 2003), 96, 97.

45 Taskina, *Russkii Kharbin,* 11.

46 Bakich, "A Russian City in China," 134–36, 144.

47 Olga Bakich, "Émigré Identity: The Case of Harbin," *South Atlantic Quarterly* 99, 1 (Winter 2000), 50–53.

48 Qu, *Jindai Dongbei,* 49, 58–61.

49 Percy H. Kent, *Railway Enterprise in China* (London: Edward Arnold, 1907), 78.

50 Wang, "The Chinese Eastern Railway," 63.

51 Martynov, *Rabota nashikh,* 15–33.

52 Grulev, *V shtabakh,* 17.

53 Beloglazov, "Russkaia flotiliia na Sungari," 55.

Chapter 7: Conflict and War

1 Joseph Esherick, *The Origins of the Boxer Uprising* (Berkeley: University of California Press, 1987), 317–21.

2 For the full account and new perspectives on this war, see O.R. Airapetov, ed., *Russko-Iaponskaia voina, 1904–1905: Vzgliad cherez stoletie* [Russo-Japanese War, 1904–1905: An outlook a century later] (Moscow: Tri Kvadrata, 2004); Felix Patrikeev and Harry Shukman, *Railways and the Russo-Japanese War: Transporting War* (London: Routledge, 2007); and John H. Steinberg, Bruce W. Menning, David Schimmelpenninck van der Oye, David Wolff, and Shinji Yokote, eds., *The Russo-Japanese War in Global Perspective,* vol. 1 (Leiden: Brill, 2005).

3 Petr Rossov, *Russkii Kitai: Ocherki zaniatiia Kvantuna i byta tuzemnogo naselenia* [Russian China: essays on the occupation of Kwantung and life of the indigenous population] (Port Arthur: Novyi Krai, 1901), 1–2.

4 Railway guards were a substitute for the regular army, part of the Independent Corps of Frontier Guards under the Ministry of Finance. They performed the duties of railway police until November 1903, when a separate police force was established. Rosemary K.I. Quested, *"Matey" Imperialists? The Tsarist Russians in Manchuria 1895–1917* (Hong Kong: Center of Asian Studies, University of Hong Kong, 1982), 99–100.

5 Airapetov, *Russko-Iaponskaia voina,* 368–75.

6 On June 1, the Boxers surrounded Peking's foreign legations. The situation in Manchuria remained calm until the end of June, when the Boxers attacked the CER's southern line and occupied Mukden. They burned the city, beheading local Christian converts. They captured a Russian stationmaster and tortured and killed him. Christie, *Thirty Years in Moukden,* 130–39.

7 N.E. Ablova, "Rossiia i russkie v Manchzhurii v kontse XIX nachale XX vv." [Russia and the Russians in Manchuria from the later nineteenth to the early twentieth century], in Airapetov, *Russko-Iaponskaia voina,* 188.

8 Kirillov, *Geograficheсko-statisticheskii,* 75–76.

9 *Voennyi Sbornik* [Military collection] 6 (1908), 206–7.

10 I.Ia. Korostovets, *Rossiia na Dal'nem Vostoke* [Russia in the Far East] (Peking: Tipografia Rossiiskoi dukhovnoi missii, 1922), 109.

11 Zhang Zonghai, *Yuandong diqu shiji zhijiao de Zhong-E guanxi* [A century of change of Sino-Russian relations in the Far Eastern region] (Harbin: Heilongjiang renmin chubanshe, 2000), 132–35.

12 Ibid., 43.

13 George Alexander Lensen, *The Russo-Chinese War* (Tallahassee: Diplomatic Press, 1967), 111–13.

14 V., "Blagoveshchenskaia 'Utopiia'" [Blagoveshchensk "Utopia"] *Vestnik Evropy* 10 (1910), 236–37.

15 Zhongguo shehui kexueyuan jindai shi yanjiusuo [Institute of Modern History, Chinese Academy of Social Sciences], ed., *Sha E qin Hua shi* [History of the Tsarist Russia's aggression against China] (Beijing: Renmin chubanshe, 1990), vol. 4, Pt. 1, 252.

16 Lensen, *Russo-Chinese War,* 108.

17 Alexander V. Vereshchagin, *Po Manchzhurii (1900–1901). Vostominaniia i rasskasy* [Across Manchuria (1900–1901). Memoirs and short stories] (St. Petersburg: Sklad v knizhnykh magazinakh V.A. Berezovskogo, 1903), 19–21.

18 Ibid., 23–26.

19 V.N. Abelentsev, *Amurskoe kazachestvo, XIX–XX vv.* [Amur Cossacks, from the nineteenth to the twentieth century]. Blagoveshchensk: Amur Region Museum of Local History, 2004, 44–46.

20 Ibid., 49–53.

21 Airapetov, *Russko-Iaponskaia voina,* 362.

22 Xue, *Zhongdong tielu,* 48.

23 Lee, *Manchurian Frontier,* 140.

24 Lensen, *Russo-Chinese War,* 197.

25 Nilus, *Istoricheskii,* 192. The different reactions of the authorities in Jilin and Mukden to the Russian military occupation are remarkable. While the administration of Jilin

nearly welcomed the Russian troops, the military governor of Mukden fled with local officials, fearing Russian retribution for their support of the Boxers. Korostovets, *Rossiia na Dal'nem Vostoke,* 123–24.

26 Myasnikov, *Russko-Kitaiskie dogovorno-pravovye akty,* 62.

27 Between 1901 and 1905, Chinese patriotic societies, established in Shanghai and Tokyo, propagated anti-Russian and anti-Imperialist sentiment. Despite the Qing court's official ban on anti-Russian activities, Chinese students in Japan and Chinese merchants were central in organizing patriotic societies in treaty ports. Yang Tianshi, *Cong dizhi zou xiang gonghe* [From monarchy to republic] (Beijing: Shehui kexueyuan wenxian chubanshe, 2002), 87–101.

28 This agreement was negotiated between a Russian diplomat, I.Ia. Korostovets, and the military governor of Mukden, Zhou Mian. Both Zhou Mian and Zeng Qi were criticized by the Qing court for signing this agreement. Korostovets, *Rossiia na Dal'nem Vostoke,* 130–135.

29 Myasnikov, *Russko-Kitaiskie dogovorno-pravovye akty,* 290–293; Hsü, *Rise of Modern China,* 404.

30 In the 1890s, Korea became a contested ground between China, Russia, and Japan. After China's defeat in war with Japan in 1895, Japan and Russia replaced China as a dominant force in Korean court politics. After Queen Min was assassinated by the Japanese on October 8, 1895, Prince Kojong asked for Russia's protection and spent most of 1896 in the Russian Legation in Seoul. The rivalry between Russia and Japan over influence in Korea continued until 1904. Jinwung Kim, *A History of Korea* (Bloomington: Indiana University Press, 2012), 308.

31 Schimmelpenninck van der Oye, *Toward the Rising Sun,* 98, 183.

32 Kim, *History of Korea,* 311–13.

33 Chong Hyo Park, *Russko-Iaponskaia voina 1904–1905 gg. i Korea* [Russo-Japanese War of 1904–1905 and Korea] (Moscow: Vostochnaia literatura, 1997), 38–41, 66.

34 J.N. Westwood, *Russia against Japan, 1904–1905* (New York: SUNY Press, 1986), 15–16; Park, *Russko-Iaponskaia voina,* 120–36.

35 V.V. Glushkov and K.E. Cherevko, eds., *Russko-Iaponskaia voina 1904–1905 gg v dokumentakh vneshnepoliticheskogo vedomstva Rossii* [Russo-Japanese War, 1904–1905, in the documents of the Ministry of Foreign Affairs of Russia] (Moscow: IDEL, 2006), 86–89.

36 According to the Russian General M.S. Stolitsa, Russian troops had insufficient numbers and lost initiative. He blamed it on delays in sending the troops and arms by railway. Stolitsa, "Trudnye gody" [Difficult years], *Voennyi sbornik* 7 (July 1908), 70–72. Railway mismanagement also contributed to slow supply. Around 6,000 wagons of goods disappeared during the war. V.A. Zolotarev and Iu.F. Sokolov, *Tragediia na Dal'nem Vostoke* [The tragedy in the Far East] (Moscow: Animi Fortitudo, 2004), vol. 1, 557.

37 Aleksei N. Kuropatkin, *Russko-Iaponskaia voina, 1904–1905. Itogi voyny* [Russo-Japanese War, 1904–1905: The war's outcome] (St. Petersburg: Poligon, 2002), 216–32.

38 V.A. Zolotarev and I.A. Kozlov, *Russko-Iaponskaia voina, 1904–1905 gg. Bor'ba na more* [Russo-Japanese War, 1904–1905. Sea battles] (Moscow: Nauka, 1990), 64–65.

39 D.N. Dubenskii, ed., *Letopis' voiny s Iaponiei, 1904–1905* [Chronicle of war with Japan, 1904–1905], vol. 1 (St. Petersburg: Tov-vo Golike i Vil'burg, 1904), 12–13.

40 Peter Randall, *There Are No Victors Here: A Local Perspective on the Treaty of Portsmouth* (Portsmouth: Portsmouth Marine Society, 1985), 3.

41 Park, *Russko-Iaponskaia voina,* 206–8.

42 Ibid., 116, 220.
43 Dubenskii, *Letopis' voiny s Iaponiei,* vol. 40, 754.
44 Wolff, *To the Harbin Station,* 121–25.
45 Dubenskii, *Letopis' voiny s Iaponiei,* vol. 14, 258–59.
46 Arkadii Gusev, "Iz vospominanii uchastnika Russko-Iaponskoi voiny" [Recollections of a participant in the Russo-Japanese War], *Voennyi Sbornik* 9 (1910), 72–74; Dubenskii, *Letopis' voiny s Iaponiei,* vol. 15 (1904), 292; see also vol. 23 (1904), 424–27.
47 Dubenskii, *Letopis' voyny s Iaponiei,* vol. 33, 609.
48 Ibid., vol. 16, 292; Gusev, "Iz vospominanii uchastnika," 71.
49 Liaoning sheng dang'anguan bian, *Ri-E zhanzheng dang'an shiliao* [Archival historical materials about the Russo-Japanese War] (Shenyang: Liaoning guji chubanshe, 1995), 469.
50 Christie, *Thirty Years in Moukden,* 186–87.

Chapter 8: Fading Frontiers

1 This chapter, unless specified, uses "Manchuria" and "the Russian Far East" for consistency, while recognizing that changing political and administrative regimes called their regions different names, such as the Three Eastern Provinces (Dongsansheng), Northeast China (Dongbei), and Manchukuo (Manzouguo), and Priamur Governor-Generalship (Priamur'e), Far Eastern Republic (Dal'nevostochnaia Respublika), and Far Eastern region (Dal'nevostochnyi krai).
2 Lee, *Manchurian Frontier,* 141.
3 Li, *Dongbei tongshi,* 610.
4 Lee, *Manchurian Frontier,* 146.
5 Ibid., 153–55; Li, *Dongbei tongshi,* 611.
6 Yoshiki Enatsu, *Banner Legacy: The Rise of the Fengtian Local Elite at the End of the Qing Dynasty* (Ann Arbor: University of Michigan Press, 2004), 110.
7 Li, *Dongbei tongshi,* 611.
8 Yoshiro Sakatani, *Manchuria: A Survey of Its Economic Development,* revised by Grover Clark (New York: Garland, 1980), 38–39.
9 Qu, *Jindai Dongbei,* 113.
10 Lee, *Manchurian Frontier,* 170–71.
11 Blaine R. Chiasson, *Administering the Colonizer: Manchuria's Russians under Chinese Rule, 1918–29* (Vancouver: UBC Press, 2010), 39–49, 56–57.
12 Qu, *Jindai Dongbei,* 115–16.
13 For example, in 1907, a local company in Changchun auctioned land in three price categories, depending on location and quality, and costing 500, 400, and 300 *diao* (1 *diao* = 1,000 copper coins) per 1 *shang* (1 shang = 15 *mu* of land). The price in each category was 100 *diao* cheaper than prices offered in the South Manchuria Railway zone. Ibid., 119–21.
14 Xu Shuming, "Qing mo Jilin sheng Heilongjiang sheng de xinxing chengshi he gongshangye" [New towns and enterprises in Jilin and Heilongjiang provinces during the late Qing], *Qingshi yanjiu* 8 (1997), 325.
15 Hans J. Van de Ven, "Public Finance and the Rise of Warlordism," *Modern Asian Studies* 30, 4 (1996), 851, 867.
16 Dubinina, *Priamurskii [...] Gondatti,* 38–39.

17 Ibid., 52–59.
18 I.D. Penzin, "Gorodskie poseleniia Priamur'ia" [Town settlements of the Amur], *Voprosy Geografii Dal'nego Vostoka* 6 (1963), 56.
19 A.A. Stepanov, "Nekotorye voprosy istorii g. Khabarovska" [Several questions about the history of Khabarovsk], *Voprosy geografii Dal'nego Vostoka* 4 (1960): 344.
20 Kabuzan, *Dal'nevostochnyi krai,* 139.
21 Cited in Dubinina, *Priamurskii [...] Gondatti,* 96.
22 Stephan, *Russian Far East,* 109.
23 Lee, *Manchurian Frontier,* 174–78.
24 Diterikhs was the former commander of the Czech legionaries who, as part of the Allied forces, played a crucial effort in fighting the Red Army in the Russian Far East and controlling the Trans-Siberian Railway during the Civil War. He was also a commander of the armed forces in the government of Admiral Kolchak (1874–1920).
25 Vasilii Tsvetkov, ed., *General Diterikhs* (Moscow: Posev, 2004), 395–97, 426–27.
26 Jamie Bisher, *White Terror: Cossack Warlords of the Trans-Siberian* (London: Routledge, 2005), 72.
27 Ronald Suleski, *Civil Government in Warlord China: Tradition, Modernization, and Manchuria* (New York: Peter Lang, 2002), 210–11.
28 Ibid., 215–16.
29 Chong-Sik Lee, *Revolutionary Struggle in Manchuria: Chinese Communism and Soviet Interest, 1922–1945* (Berkeley: University of California Press, 1983), 45.
30 Wai Guizhong, "Guanyu Zhongdong tielu shijian de tanpan" [Negotiations about the Chinese Eastern Railway Incident], in *Zhongdong lu yü Zhongdong lu shijian* [Chinese Eastern Railway and Chinese Eastern Railway Incident], ed. Guo Junsheng, 228–30.
31 N.A. Sokolov, "Pereselencheskoe dvizhenie v severnuiu Manchzhuriiu," [Settlement movement in Northern Manchuria], *Vestnik Manchzhurii* 3 (1932), 58.
32 G.V. Melikhov, *Rossiiskaia emigratsiia v mezhdunarodnykh otnosheniiakh na Dal'nem Vostoke, 1925–1932* [Russian emigration in international relations of the Far East, 1925–1932] (Moscow: Russkii Put', 2007), 166–70.
33 Abraham Friesen and Abram J. Loewen, *Escape across the Amur River: A Mennonite Village Flees (1930) from Soviet Siberia to Chinese Manchuria,* trans. Victor G. Doerksen (Winnipeg: CMBC Publications, Manitoba Mennonite Historical Society, 2001), 26.
34 Michael Gelb, "An Early Soviet Ethnic Deportation: The Far Eastern Koreans," *Russian Review* 54 (July 1995), 390; N.L. Pobol' and P.N. Polyan, eds., *Stalinskie deportatsii,* 1928–1953 [Stalin's deportations, 1928–1953] (Moscow: Mezhdunarodnyi fond Demokratiia, 2005), 80–85.
35 Victor.V. Zatsepine, "An Uneasy Balancing Act: The Russian Émigré Community and Utopian Ideals of Manzhouguo," *Journal of Northeast Asian History* 10, 1 (2013): 132–45.

Conclusion

1 Zhang Fengming, *Zhongguo Dongbei yu Eguo (Sulian) jingji guanxi shi* [The history of economic relations between China's Northeast and Russia (Soviet Union)] (Beijing: Zhongguo shehui kexue chubanshe, 2003), 27–45. See Sladkovskii, *Istoriia torgovo-ekonomicheskikh,* 282.
2 Thomas Lahusen, ed., *Harbin and Manchuria: Place, Space, and Identity* (Durham: Duke University Press, 2000). On changing power relations in Harbin during the early

Republican Period, see Chiasson, *Administering the Colonizer;* and James H. Carter, *Creating a Chinese Harbin: Nationalism in an International City, 1916–1932* (Ithaca: Cornell University Press, 2002).

3 Bakich, "Émigré Identity," 53.

4 Historians of modern Manchuria disagree about the frontier spirit among Chinese migrants and the extent of their support for the Qing government's plans to incorporate Manchuria firmly into the Chinese state. For example, these contrasting views can be found in Reardon-Anderson, *Reluctant Pioneers;* and Shan, *Taming China's Wilderness.*

5 Robert Bickers, *The Scramble for China: Foreign Devils in the Qing Empire, 1832–1914* (London: Allen Lane, 2011); Laura Victoir and Victor Zatsepine, eds., *Harbin to Hanoi: The Colonial Built Environment in Asia, 1840 to 1940* (Hong Kong: Hong Kong University Press, 2013).

6 See "Moskovskii dogovor, zakliuchennyi mezhdu Rossiei i Kitaem o soiuze v otrazhenii Iaponskoi ekspansii v vostochnoi Azii i stroitel'sve KVZhD" [Moscow agreement between Russia and China about fighting off the Japanese expansion in East Asia and the construction of the Chinese Eastern Railway," in Myasnikov, *Russko-Kitaiskie dorovorno-pravovye akty,* 207–9.

7 Chang Jui-te, "Technology Transfer in Modern China: The Case of Railway Enterprises in Central China and Manchuria," in *Manchurian Railways and the Opening of China: An International History,* ed. Bruce A. Elleman and Stephen Kotkin (Armonk: M.E. Sharpe, 2010), 112–15.

8 In September 2015, the authorities of the Russian Far East announced plans to build an auto and railway bridge across the Amur to connect these cities. See "Rukovoditel' Priamur'ia nazval sroki stroitel'stva mosta v Kitai" [The leader of the Priamur region announced the plan to build the bridge to China], *Lenta.ru,* September 5, 2015, http://lenta.ru/news/2015/09/05/bridge.

Bibliography

Magazines and Newspapers

Dongfang Zazhi [Eastern miscellany], Shanghai (1904–48)
Izvestiia [News], Vostochnyi Institut, Vladivostok (1889–1921)
Priamurskie Vedomosti [Priamur news], Khabarovsk (1894–1917)
Vestnik Azii [Herald of Asia], Harbin (1909–26)
Vestnik Evropy [Herald of Europe], St. Petersburg (1866–1918)
Voennyi Sbornik [Military collection], St. Petersburg (1858–1917)
Zhongguo Bianjiang Shidi Yanjiu [China's borderland history and geography studies], Chinese Academy of Social Sciences, Beijing (1991–present)

Other Sources

Abelentsev, V.N. *Amurskoe kazachestvo, XIX–XX vv.* [Amur Cossacks, from the nineteenth to the twentieth century]. Blagoveshchensk: Amur Region Museum of Local History, 2004.

Airapetov, O.R., ed. *Russko-Iaponskaia voina, 1904–1905: Vzgliad cherez stoletie* [Russo-Japanese War, 1904–1905: An outlook a century later]. Moscow: Tri Kvadrata, 2004.

Alekseev, A.I. *Amurskaia ekspeditsyia, 1849–1855* [The Amur expedition, 1849–1855]. Moscow: Mysl', 1974.

—. *Russkie geograficheskie issledovaniia na Dal'nem Vostoke i v severnoi Amerike, XIX – nachalo XX vv.* [Russian geographic explorations in the Far East and in North America, from the nineteenth to the early twentieth century]. Moscow: Nauka, 1976.

Alfavitnyi ukazatel' geograficheskikh imen pomeshchennykh na karte Manchzhurii L. Borodovskogo [Index of geographic names on the map of Manchuria by L. Borodovsky]. St. Petersburg: Ministry of Finance, 1901.

Anert, E.E. "Ezhegodnye polovod'ia v severnoi Manchzhurii i navodnenie 1932 goda" [Yearly floods in Northern Manchuria and the flood of 1932]. *Ezhegodnik*, Annual of the Club of Natural Science and Geography of the YMCA, 1 (1933): 52–87.

Anisimov, E.V. "The Imperial Heritage of Peter the Great in the Foreign Policy of His Early Successors." In *Imperial Russian Foreign Policy*, edited by Hugh Ragsdale, 21–35. Cambridge: Cambridge University Press, 1993.

Anuchin, V.A. *Geograficheskiie ocherki Manchzhurii* [Essays on the geography of Manchuria]. Moscow: Gosudarstvennoe izdatel'stvo geograficheskoi literatury, 1948.

Arsen'ev, Vladimir K. *Dorogoi khishchnik: Okhota na sobolia v Ussuriiskom krae* [Valuable beast of prey: Sable hunt in the Ussuri region]. Vladivostok: Aktsyonernoe knizhnoe obshchestvo, 1925.

—. *Kitaitsy v Ussuriiskom krae* [The Chinese in the Ussuri region]. Moscow: Izdatel'stvo Kraft, 2004. Originally published in Khabarovsk, 1914.

—. "Kratkii fiziko-geograficheskii ocherk basseina reki Amura" [Essay on the geography of the Amur River basin]. Record of public meeting of the ORO, Harbin, June 6, 1916, *Vestnik Azii* 38–39 (1916): 324–30.

—. *Po Ussuriiskomu kraiu* [Across the Ussuri region]. Moscow: Gosudarstvennoe izdatel'stvo geograficheskoi literatury, 1960.

—. *V debriakh Ussuriiskogo kraia* [In the depths of the Ussuri region]. Moscow: Gosudarstvennoe iszdatel'stvo geograficheskoi literatury, 1951.

Bagrow, Leo. *History of Cartography*. Cambridge, MA: Harvard University Press, 1964.

Baikov, Nikolai A. *V debryakh Manchzhurii: Ocherki i rasskazy iz byta obitatelei taigi* [In the depths of Manchuria: Essays and stories from daily life of taiga]. Harbin: Ofset-press, 1934.

Bakich, Olga. "Émigré Identity: The Case of Harbin." *South Atlantic Quarterly* 99, 1 (2000): 51–78.

—. "A Russian City in China: Harbin before 1917." *Canadian Slavonic Papers* 28, 2 (June 1986): 129–48.

Barsukov, Ivan. *Graf Nikolai Nikolaevich Murav'ev-Amurskii po ego pis'mam, ofitsial'nym dokumentam, rasskazam sovremennikov i pechatnym istochnikam* [Count Nikolai Nikolayevich Murav'ev-Amurskii: His letters, official documents, contemporary accounts and published sources]. Vol. 1 (Moscow: Sinodal'naia tip., 1891).

Bassin, Mark. *Imperial Visions*. Cambridge: Cambridge University Press, 1999.

—. "Inventing Siberia: Visions of the Russian Far East in the Early Nineteenth Century." *American Geographic Review* 96, 3 (June 1991): 763–94.

—. "The Russian Geographical Society, the 'Amur Epoch,' and the Great Siberian Expedition 1855–1863." *Annals of the Association of American Geographers* 73, 2 (June 1983): 240–56.

Beloglazov, G.P. "Russkaia flotiliia na Sungari, konets XIX–nachalo XX vv" [Russian flotilla on the Songhua River, from the end of the nineteenth to the beginning of the twentieth century]. *Rossiia i ATR*, 2 (1995): 47–55.

Ben-Canaan, Dan, Frank Grüner, and Ines Prodöhl, eds. *Entangled Histories: The Transcultural Past of Northeast China*. Heidelberg: Springer, 2014.

Besprozvannykh, Evgenii L. *Priamur'e v sisteme Russko-Kitaiskikh otnoshenii, XVII–seredina XIX v.* [Priamur region in Sino-Russian relations, from the seventeenth to the mid-nineteenth century]. Khabarovsk: Khabarovsk knizhnoe izdatel'stvo, 1983.

Bickers, Robert. *The Scramble for China: Foreign Devils in the Qing Empire, 1832–1914*. London: Allen Lane, 2011.

Bisher, Jamie. *White Terror: Cossack Warlords of the Trans-Siberian*. London: Routledge, 2005.
Bix, Herbert P. "Japanese Imperialism and the Manchurian Economy, 1900–31." *China Quarterly* 51 (July 1972): 425–43.
Bogaevskii, A.P. *Sansin'skoe fudutunstvo* [Sanxing fudutong county]. Khabarovsk: Tipografiia Primorskogo voennogo okruga, 1903.
Bogoslovskii, L. "Krepost'-gorod Vladivostok i kitaitsy" [Fortress Vladivostok and the Chinese]. *Vestnik Azii* 13 (1913): 20–33.
Bolkhovitinov, L.M. *Reka Amur ot Blagoveshchenska do Khabarovska* [Amur River from Blagoveshchensk to Khabarovsk]. St. Petersburg: Voennaia tipografiia, 1910.
Bolotov, A.A. *Amur i ego bassein* [Amur River and its basin]. Harbin: Obshchestvo izucheniia Manchzhurskogo kraia, 1925.
Burilova, Maria. "Kitaitsy v Priamurskom krae" [The Chinese in the Priamur region]. *Turne* [Tour] 1–2 (2004): 30–32.
—. "Vliublennyi v Rossiiu" [In love with Russia]. *Svoe Delo* 4 (2010). http://dv-delo.ru/2010/08/01/vlyublennyj-v-rossiyu.
Cammann, Shuyler. "Origins of the Court and Official Robes of the Ch'ing Dynasty," *Artibus Asiae* 12, 3 (1949): 189–201.
Carter, James H. *Creating a Chinese Harbin: Nationalism in an International City, 1916–1932*. Ithaca: Cornell University Press, 2002.
Chang Huaisheng, ed. *Ha'erbin jianzhu yishu* [Harbin's architectural art]. Ha'erbin: Ha'erbin kexue jishu chubanshe, 1990.
Chang Jui-te. "Technology Transfer in Modern China: The Case of Railway Enterprises in Central China and Manchuria." In *Manchurian Railways and the Opening of China: An International History*, edited by Bruce A. Elleman and Stephen Kotkin, 105–22. Armonk: M.E. Sharpe, 2010.
Chekhov, Anton P. *Ostrov Sakhalin: Iz putevykh zapisok* [Sakhalin Island: From traveller's notes]. Collected works, vol. 10. Moscow: Khudozhestvennaia literatura, 1963.
Chen Fangzhi. *Dongbei shi tantao* [Discussing the history of the Northeast]. Beijing: Zhongguo shehui kexue chubanshe, 1995.
Chiasson, Blaine R. *Administering the Colonizer: Manchuria's Russians under Chinese Rule, 1918–29*. Vancouver: UBC Press, 2010.
Christie, Dugald C.M.G. *Thirty Years in Moukden, 1883–1913: Being the Experiences and Recollections of Dugald Christie*. London: Constable, 1914.
Collins, Perry McDonough. *Siberian Journey: Down the Amur to the Pacific, 1856–1857*. Madison: University of Wisconsin Press, 1962. Originally published in 1860.
Cong Peiyuan and Zhao Mingqi, eds. *Cao Tingjie ji* [Collected works of Cao Tingjie]. 2 vols. Beijing: Zhonghua shuju, 1985.
Cronon, William. "Revisiting the Vanishing Frontier: The Legacy of Frederick Jackson Turner." *Western Historical Quarterly* 18, 2 (April 1987): 157–76.
Crossley, Pamela Kyle. *A Translucent Mirror: History and Identity in Qing Imperial Ideology*. Berkeley: University of California Press, 1999.
Czaplicka, Maria A. *Aboriginal Siberia: A Study in Social Anthropology*. Oxford: Clarendon Press, 1914.
Dan Shao. *Remote Homeland, Recovered Borderland: Manchus, Manchoukuo, and Manchuria, 1907–1985*. Honolulu: University of Hawai'i Press, 2011.
Davidov, D.A. *Kolonizatsiia Manchzhurii i severo-vostochnoi Mongolii* [Colonization of Manchuria and northeastern Mongolia]. Vladivostok: Vostochnyi institut, 1911.

Dobrolovskii, I.A. *Heilonjiang provintsiia Manchzhurii* [Heilongjiang Province of Manchuria]. Harbin: Tipo-litografiia shtaba Zaamurskogo okruga pogranichnoi strazhi, 1906.

Duara, Prasenjit. *Sovereignty and Authenticity: Manchukuo and the East Asian Modern.* Lanham: Rowman and Littlefield, 2003.

Dubenskii, D.N., ed. *Letopis' voiny s Iaponiei, 1904–1905.* [Chronicle of war with Japan, 1904–1905], vols. 1–84. St. Petersburg: Tov-vo Golike i Vil'burg, 1904–1905.

Dubinina, N.I. *Priamurskii general-gubernator N.L. Gondatti* [Priamur governor-general N.L. Gondatti]. Khabarovsk: Priamurskie Vendomosti, 1997.

—. *Priamurskii general-gubernator N.I. Grodekov* [Priamur governor-general N.I. Grodekov]. Khabarovsk: Priamurskie Vedomosti, 2001.

Edmonds, Richard L. "The Willow Palisade." *Annals of the Association of American Geographers* 69, 4 (December 1979): 599–621.

Elliott, Mark. "Frontier Stories: Periphery as Center in Qing History." *Frontiers of History in China* 9, 3 (September 2014): 336–60.

—. "The Limits of Tartary: Manchuria in Imperial and National Geographies." *Journal of Asian Studies* 59, 3 (August 2000): 603–46.

Enatsu, Yoshiki. *Banner Legacy: The Rise of the Fengtian Local Elite at the End of the Qing Dynasty.* Ann Arbor: University of Michigan Press, 2004.

Esherick, Joseph. *The Origins of the Boxer Uprising.* Berkeley: University of California Press, 1987.

Farquhar, David M. "Emperor as Bodhisattva in the Governance of the Ch'ing Empire." *Harvard Journal of Asiatic Studies* 38 (June 1978): 5–34.

Friesen, Abraham, and Abram J. Loewen. *Escape across the Amur River: A Mennonite Village Flees (1930) from Soviet Siberia to Chinese Manchuria.* Translated by Victor G. Doerksen. Winnipeg: CMBC Publications, Manitoba Mennonite Historical Society, 2001.

Galenovich, Iu.M. *"Belye piatna" i "bolevye tochki" v istorii Sovetsko-Kitaiskikh otnoshenii* ["White spots" and "friction points" in the history of Sino-Soviet relations]. Moscow: Institut Dal'nego Vostoka, 1992.

Gelb, Michael. "An Early Soviet Ethnic Deportation: The Far Eastern Koreans." *Russian Review* 54 (July 1995): 389–412.

Gibson, James R. "Russian Expansion in Siberia and America." *Geographic Review* 70, 2 (April 1980): 127–36.

Glushkov, V.V., and K.E. Cherevko, eds. *Russko-Iaponskaia voina 1904–1905 gg v dokumentakh vneshnepoliticheskogo vedomstva Rossii* [Russo-Japanese War, 1904–1905, in the documents of the Ministry of Foreign Affairs of Russia]. Moscow: IDEL, 2006.

Gottschang, Thomas R. and Diana Lary. *Swallows and Settlers: The Great Migration from North China to Manchuria.* Ann Arbor: Center for Chinese Studies, University of Michigan, 2000.

Grombchevskii, Bronislav L. "Kitaiskie zolotye priiski na pravom beregu Amura" [Chinese goldfields on the right bank of the Amur River]. *Priamurskie Vedomosti* (1897): 245–47.

Grulev, Mikhail V. *V shtabakh i na poliakh Dal'nego Vostoka* [In military headquarters and in the fields of the Far East]. Moscow: Gosudarstvennaia publichnaia biblioteka Rossii, 2007. Reprint of 1908 publication.

Gruzdeva (Volgina), F. *Amur: Priroda i liudi Amurskogo kraia* [Amur: Nature and people of the Amur Region]. St. Petersburg: Izdanie P.P. Soikina, 1900.

Guan Guihai and Luan Jinghe, eds. *Zhong-E guanxi de lishi yu xianshi (di er ji)* [The history and reality of the Sino-Russian relations, vol. 2]. Beijing: Shehui kexue wenxian chubanshe, 2009.

"Guangxu nianjian kaiban Heilongjiang Mohe jinkuang shiliao" [Historical materials on Mohe gold mine in Heilongjiang during the Guangxu reign]. In *Lishi Dang'an.* Zhongguo diyi lishi dang' an zhuban 1 (2004): 33–44; and 2 (2004): 27–37.

Guo Junsheng, ed. *Zhongdong lu yü Zhongdong lu shijian* [Chinese Eastern Railway and Chinese Eastern Railway Incident]. Shenyang: Liaoning renmin chubanshe, 2010.

Guo Yunshen, "Zhongdong tielu yu Eluosi wenhua de chuanbo" [The Chinese Eastern Railway and the influence of Russian culture]. *Xuexi yu Tansuo* 5 (1994): 139–42.

Gusev, Arkadii. "Iz vospominanii uchastnika Russko-Iaponskoi voiny" [Recollections of a participant in the Russo-Japanese War]. *Voennyi Sbornik* 9 (1910): 67–88.

Guy, R. Kent. "Who Were the Manchus? A Review Essay." *Journal of Asian Studies* 61, 1 (February 2002): 151–64.

Hevia, James L. *English Lessons: The Pedagogy of Imperialism in Nineteenth-Century China.* Durham: Duke University Press, 2003.

Hong Jun, *Zhong-E jiaojie quantu* [Complete maps of the Sino-Russian border], n.p., 1890.

Hosie, Alexander. *Manchuria: Its People, Resource, and Recent History.* Boston: J.B. Millet, 1910.

Hostetler, Laura. *Qing Colonial Enterprise: Ethnography and Cartography in Early Modern China.* Chicago: University of Chicago Press, 2001.

Hsieh, Fucheng. *The European Diary of Hsieh Fucheng: Envoy Extraordinary of Imperial China.* Translated by Helen Hsieh Chien. New York: St. Martin's Press, 1993.

Hsü, Emmanuel C.Y. *The Rise of Modern China.* Oxford: Oxford University Press, 1983.

Hummel, Arthur W. *Eminent Chinese of the Ch'ing Period (1644–1912).* Vols. 1 and 2. Washington, DC: Government Publication Office, 1943-44.

Innis, Harold A. *Essays in Canadian Economic History.* Toronto: University of Toronto Press, 1956.

—. *The Fur Trade in Canada.* Toronto: University of Toronto Press, 1967.

Ivanova, A.P. "Torgovlia kak sterzhen' infrastruktury goroda" [Trade as a core of urban infrastructure]. In *Arkhitektura vostochnoi Sibiri i Dal'nego Vostoka,* vol. 1, edited by N.P. Kradin, 55–71. Khabarovsk: Dal'nauka, 2002.

Janhunen, Juna. *Manchuria: An Ethnic History.* Helsinki: Finno-Ugrian Society, 1996.

Kabuzan, V.M. *Dal'nevostochny kraii v XVII-nachale XX veka* [Far Eastern region in the nineteenth and early twentieth century]. Moscow: Nauka, 1985.

Kantō totokufu, ed. *Man-Mō keizai tōkei zuhyō* [Economic statistics and graphs for Manchuria–Mongolia] vols.1 and 2. Tokyo: Kantō totokufu, 1918.

Kennan, George. "Siberia – the Exiles' Abode." *Journal of the American Geographic Society of New York* 14 (1882): 13–68.

Kent, Percy H. *Railway Enterprise in China.* London: Edward Arnold, 1907.

Kikuchi, Teiji. *Kikuchi Gōso-an zuihitsu: Shūfū sanzenri* [Essays of Kikutchi "Gōsō-an": The autumn wind blows three thousand *li*]. Tokyo: Kikutchi Teiji sensei kankōkai, 1966.

Kim, Jinwung. *A History of Korea*. Bloomington: Indiana University Press, 2012.
King, Ross. "Blagoslovennoe: Korean Village on the Amur, 1871–1937." *Review of Korean Studies* 4, 2 (2001): 133–76.
Kirillov, Aleksandr. *Geograficheskо-statisticheskii slovar' Amurskoi i Primorskoi oblastei s vklyucheniem nekotorykh punktov sopredel'nykh s nimi stran* [Geographic-statistical dictionary of the Amur and Maritime Provinces including several locations of the adjacent countries]. Blagoveshchensk: Tipografiia t-va D.O. Mokin i K., 1894.
Kolykhalova, T.F. *Sotsial-demokraticheskoe dvizhenie na Amure v period revoliutsyonnoi bor'by s samoderzhaviem* [Social-democratic movement in the Amur during the revolutionary struggle against the autocracy]. Tomsk: Izdanie Tomksogo universiteta, 1979.
Kong Jingwei. *Qingdai Dongbei diqu jingji shi* [Economic history of the Northeast region during the Qing dynasty]. Ha'erbin: Heilongjiang renmin chubanshe, 1990.
—. *Zhongguo Dongbei diqu jingji shi* [Economic history of China's Northeast]. Changchun: Jilin jiaoyu chubanshe, 1994.
Korostovets, I.Ia. *Rossiia na Dal'nem Vostoke* [Russia in the Far East]. Peking: Tipografiia Rossiiskoi dukhovnoi missii, 1922.
Kradin, N.P. *Kharbin – Russkaia Atlantida* [Harbin – Russian Atlantis]. Khabarovsk: Khvorov A. Yu, 2001.
Kropotkin, Pëtr. *Memoirs of a Revolutionist.* Montreal: Black Rose Books, 1989. Originally published in 1899.
Kuropatkin, Aleksei N. *Russko-Iaponskaia voina, 1904–1905: Itogi voiny* [Russo-Japanese War, 1904–1905: The war's outcome]. St. Petersburg: Poligon, 2002. Originally published in 1906.
Kuzmichev, Igor. *Pisatel' Arsen'ev* [Writer Arsen'ev]. Leningrad: Sovetskii pisatel', 1977.
Lahusen, Thomas, ed. *Harbin and Manchuria: Place, Space, and Identity*. Durham: Duke University Press, 2000.
Larin, A.G. *Kitaitsy v Rossii: Vchera i segodnia* [The Chinese in Russia: Past and present]. Moscow: Muravei, 2003.
Lary, Diana, ed. *The Chinese State at the Borders*. Vancouver: UBC Press, 2007.
—. "The Manchurian Winter." Unpublished paper, University of British Columbia, October 1999.
Lattimore, Owen. "The Gold Tribe, 'Fishskin Tatars' of the Lower Sungari." *Memoirs of the American Anthropological Association* 40 (1933): 1–77.
—. *Inner Asian Frontiers of China.* London: Oxford University Press, 1940.
—. *Manchuria: Cradle of Conflict.* New York: Macmillan, 1932.
—. *The Mongols of Manchuria.* London: George Allen and Unwin, 1935.
Lavrov, N.K. *Pushnoi promysel na Russkom Dal'nem Vostoke* [Fur trade in the Russian Far East]. Tokyo: n.p., 1923.
Lee, Chong-Sik. *Revolutionary Struggle in Manchuria: Chinese Communism and Soviet Interest, 1922–1945*. Berkeley: University of California Press, 1983.
Lee, Robert H.G. *The Manchurian Frontier in Ch'ing History.* Harvard East Asian Series 43. Cambridge, MA: Harvard University Press, 1970.
Lensen, George Alexander. *The Russo-Chinese War.* Tallahassee: Diplomatic Press, 1967.
Li Sheng and Li Guoqiang, eds. *Zhongguo bianjiang yanjiu zongshu, 1989–1998* [Summary of border studies in China, 1989–1998]. Ha'erbin: Heilongjiang jiaoyu chubanshe, 2002.

Li Shuxiao, ed. *Ha'erbin lishi biannian* [Harbin's historical chronicle]. Ha'erbin: Ha'erbin chubanshe, 2000.

Li Xinggeng, ed. *Fengyu fuping: Eguo qiaomin zai Zhongguo, 1917–1945* [Duckweed in the rain and wind: Russian immigrants in China, 1917–1945] Beijing: Zhongyang bianyi chubanshe, 1997.

Li Zhiting, ed. *Dongbei tongshi* [General History of the Northeast]. Zhengzhou: Zhongzhou guji chubanshe, 2003.

Liaoning sheng dang'anguan bian. *Ri-E zhanzheng dang'an shiliao* [Archival historical materials about the Russo-Japanese War]. Shenyang: Liaoning guji chubanshe, 1995.

Ling Chunsheng. *Songhuajiang xiayoude Hezhe zu* [Hezhe nationality in the lower reaches of the Songhua River]. Shanghai: Shanghai wenyi chubanshe, 1990. Originally published in Nanjing in 1934.

Liu Wenxin ed. *Heilongjiang jindai lishi dashiji, 1840–1949* [Chronology of events in Heilongjiang modern history, 1840–1949]. Ha'erbin: Heilongjiang renmin chubanshe, 1987.

Liu Yuantu, ed. *Zaoqi Zhong-E Dongduan bianjie yanjiu* [Research on the early period of the eastern section of the Sino-Russian border]. Beijing: Chinese Academy of Social Sciences, 1993.

Liu Zheming and Shi Ye. *Dongbei da di* [Manchuria's great land]. Beijing: Beijing Dizhi chubanshe, 1989.

Lu Minghui, ed. *Zhong E bianjiang maoyi de qiyuan yu yange* [The rise and development of the Sino-Russian border trade]. Beijing: Zhongguo jingji chubanshe, 1991.

Lu Yiran. "Zhongguo bianjiang shidi yanjiu huigu yu zhanwang" [Research on the borderland historical geography of China: Past and future]. *Zhongguo bianjiang shidi yanjiu* 4 (1991): 1–9.

—, ed. *Zhongguo jindai bianjie shi* [Modern history of Chinese borders]. Sichuan: Sichuan renmin chubanshe, 2007.

Lu Yiran, Ma Dazheng, and Xing Yulin, eds. *Zhongguo bianjiang shidi lunji* [Collection of articles on the history and geography of China's borderland]. Ha'erbin: Heilongjiang jiaoyu chubanshe, 1991.

"Lun E-ren zai Dongsansheng jingying zhi xinshi" [Discussion of new towns managed by the Russians in China's Three Eastern Provinces]. *Dongfang zazhi* 1, 7 (1904): 140–42.

Liupov, S.N. *Hulan'skoe fudutunstvo Heiluntszianskoi provintsii* [Hulan administrative region of the Heilongjiang province]. Khabarovsk: n.p., 1903.

Ma Dazheng. *Zhongguo Dongbei bianjiang yanjiu* [Studies on China's northeastern borderland]. Beijing: Zhongguo shehui kexueyuan chubanshe, 2003.

Ma, L. Eve Armentrout. "Fellow-Regional Associations in the Qing Dynasty: Organizations in Flux for Mobile People." *Modern Asian Studies* 18, 2 (1984): 307–30.

Ma Ruheng and Ma Dazheng. *Qingdai de bianjiang zhengce* [Qing dynasty policies towards the borderlands]. Beijing: Zhongguo shehui kexue chubanshe, 1994.

Malozemoff, Andrew. *Russian Far Eastern Policy 1881–1904*. Berkeley: University of California Press, 1958.

Mancall, Mark. *Russia and China: Their Diplomatic Relations to 1728*. Cambridge, MA: Harvard University Press, 1971.

Marks, Steven G. *Road to Power: The Trans-Siberian Railroad and the Colonization of Asian Russia, 1850–1917*. Ithaca: Cornell University Press, 1991.

—. *Rabota nashikh zheleznodorozhnykh del'tsov v Manchzhurii* [Activities of our railway dealers in Manchuria]. Moscow: Tipografiia P.P. Riabushinskogo, 1914.

Mat'khanova, N.P. *Graf N. N. Murav'ev-Amurskii v vospominaniiakh sovremennikov* [Count N.N. Murav'ev-Amurskii in the memoirs of his contemporaries]. Novosibirsk: Sibirskii khronograf, 1998.

Matsusaka, Yoshihisa Tak. *The Making of Japanese Manchuria, 1904–1932*. Cambridge, MA: Harvard University Press, 2001.

Maxwell, Neville. "A Note on the Amur/Ussuri sector of the Sino-Russian Boundaries." *Modern China* 1, 1 (January 1975): 116–26.

Melgunov, S.P., ed. *Nicholas II: Materialy dlia kharakteristiki lichnosti i tsarstvovaniia* [Nicholas II: Materials describing his personality and reign]. Moscow: Izdanie zhurnala Golos Minuvshego, 1917.

Melikhov, G.V. *Man'chzhury na severo-vostoke, XVII v.* [The Manchus of the Northeast in the seventeenth century]. Moscow: Nauka, 1974.

—. *Rossiiskaia emigratsiia v mezhdunarodnykh otnosheniyakh na Dal'nem Vostoke, 1925–1932* [Russian emigration in international relations of the Far East, 1925–1932]. Moscow: Russkii Put', 2007.

Men'shikov, P.N. *Otchet kommercheskogo agenta Kitaiskoi Vostochnoi zheleznoi dogori P. N. Men'shikova po obsledovaniiu Heiluntszianskoi provintsii i chasti Zharimskogo seima Vnutrennei Mongolii* [Report of P.N. Menshikov, commercial agent of the Chinese Eastern Railway on the Heilongjiang Province and part of Inner Mongolia]. Harbin: Tipografiia Kitaiskoi Vostochnoi zheleznoi dogori, 1913.

Mi Zhenbo. *Qingdai Zhong-E Qiaketu bianjiang maoyi* [Sino-Russian Kiakhta border trade during the Qing dynasty]. Tianjin: Nankai daxue chubanshe, 2003.

Morris-Suzuki, Tessa. "Lines in the Snow: Imagining the Russo-Japanese Frontier." *Pacific Affairs*, 72, 1 (Spring 1999): 57–77.

Myasnikov, V.S., ed. *Granitsy Kitaia: Istoriia formirovaniia* [China's borders: Historical development]. Moscow: Pamiatniki istoricheskoi mysli, 2001.

—. *Russko-Kitaiskie dogovorno-pravovye akty (1689–1916)* [Sino-Russian treaties and legal acts (1689–1916)]. Moscow: Pamiatniki istoricheskoi mysli, 2004.

Nilus, Evgenii Kh., ed. *Istoricheskii obzor Kitaiskoi Vostochnoi Zheleznoi Dorogi, 1896–1923 gg.* [Historical overview of the Chinese Eastern Railway, 1896–1923], vol. 1. Harbin: Tipografiia KVZhD, 1923.

North Manchuria and the Chinese Eastern Railway. Harbin: CER Printing Office, 1924.

Paine, Sarah C.M. *Imperial Rivals: China, Russia, and Their Disputed Frontier.* Armonk: M.E. Sharpe, 1996.

—. *The Sino-Japanese War of 1894–1895: Perceptions, Power, and Primacy*. Cambridge: Cambridge University Press, 2005.

Park, Chong Hyo. *Russko-Iaponskaia voina 1904–1905 gg. i Korea* [Russo-Japanese War of 1904–1905 and Korea]. Moscow: Vostochnaia literatura, 1997.

Patrikeev, Felix, and Harry Shukman. *Railways and the Russo-Japanese War: Transporting War*. London: Routledge, 2007.

Pauer, E.O. *Manchzhuriia* [Manchuria]. St. Petersburg: Slovo, 1904.

Penzin, I.D. "Gorodskie poseleniia Priamur'ia" [Town settlements of the Amur]. *Voprosy Geografii Dal'nego Vostoka* 6 (1963): 55–70.

Perdue, Peter C. *China Marches West: The Qing Conquest of Central Eurasia.* Cambridge, MA: Harvard University Press, 2005.

—. "Embracing Victory, Effacing Defeat: Rewriting the Qing Frontier Campaigns." In *The Chinese State at the Borders,* edited by Diana Lary, 105–25. Vancouver: UBC Press, 2007.

Petrov A.I. "Russkii 'kitaets' Nikolai Ivanovich Tifontai (Ji Fengtai)" [A Russian "Chinese": Nikolai Ivanovich Tifontai]. *Rossiia i ATR* 2 (2005): 141–51.

Piao, Changyu. "The History of Koreans in China and the Yanbian Korean Autonomous Prefecture." In *Koreans in China,* edited by Dae-Sook Suh and Edward J. Shultz, 44–77. Papers of the Center for Korean Studies, no. 16. Honolulu: University of Hawai'i Press, 1990.

Pobol', N.L., and P.M. Polyan, eds. *Stalinskie deportatsii, 1928–1953* [Stalin's deportations, 1928–1953]. Moscow: Mezhdunarodnyi fond Demokratiia, 2005.

Polner, T.I., *Priamur'e: Fakty, tsyfry, nabliudeniia* [Priamur'e: Facts, numbers, observations]. Moscow: Gorodskaia tipografiia, 1909.

Pozdneev, D. *Opisanie Manchzhurii* [Description of Manchuria]. St. Petersburg: Kantseliariia Ministerstva Finansov, 1897.

Pratt, Mary. *Imperial Eyes: Travel Writing and Transculturation.* London: Routledge, 1992.

Protokoly vtorogo Amurskogo s'ezda zolotopromyshlennikov, 25–30 ianvaria, 1899 [Protocol of the second Amur congress of gold miners, January 25–30, 1899]. Blagoveshchensk: Tipografiia opeki Artamonova i ko., 1899.

Qu Xiaofan. *Jindai Dongbei chengshi de lishi bianqian* [Historical change in China's northeastern cities during modern times]. Changchun: Dongbei shifan daxue, 2001.

Quested, Rosemary K.I. *"Matey" Imperialists? The Tsarist Russians in Manchuria, 1895–1917.* Hong Kong: Center of Asian Studies, University of Hong Kong, 1982.

Randall, Peter. *There Are No Victors Here: A Local Perspective on the Treaty of Portsmouth.* Portsmouth: Published for the Portsmouth Marine Society by P.E. Randall, 1985.

Ravenstein, Ernest G. *The Russians on the Amur.* London: Trubner, 1861.

Ray, Arthur J. *Indians in the Fur Trade: Their Role as Trappers, Hunters, and Middlemen in the Lands Southwest of Hudson Bay, 1660–1870.* Toronto: University of Toronto Press, 1974.

Reardon-Anderson, James. *Reluctant Pioneers: China's Expansion Northward, 1664–1937.* Stanford: Stanford University Press, 2005.

Ren Jiahe, "Qingchu Dongbei bianjing ge zu diaogong kaolü" [Rethinking fur tribute among the nationalities in China's northeast frontier during the early Qing dynasty]. *Heilongjiang minzu congkan* 1 (1994): 80–85.

Rhoads, Edward J.M. *Manchus and Han: Ethnic Relations and Political Power in Late Qing and Early Republican China, 1861–1928.* Seattle: University of Washington Press, 2000.

Riazanov, V.D. *Otchet po statistiko-ekonomicheskomu i tekhnicheskomu issledovaniiu zolotopromyshlennosti Amursko-Primorskogo kraiia* [Report on the statistical, economic, and technical investigations of gold mining in the Amur-Maritime regions], vol 2., pt. 2. *Amurskaia oblast'* [Amur Province]. St. Petersburg: Iakor', 1903.

Rossov, Petr. *Russkii Kitai: Ocherki zaniatiia Kvantuna i byta tuzemnogo naseleniia* [Russian China: Essays on the occupation of Kwantung and its local population]. Port Arthur: Novyi Krai, 1901.

—. *Sushchestvuiut li Manchzhury?* [Do the Manchus exist?] Harbin: Tipografiia gazety Novyi Krai, 1903.

"Rukovoditel' Priamur'ia nazval sroki stroitel'stva mosta v Kitai" [The leader of the Priamur region announced the plan to build the bridge to China]. *Lenta.ru,* September 5, 2015. http://lenta.ru/news/2015/09/05/bridge.

Sakatani, Yoshiro. *Manchuria: A Survey of Its Economic Development.* Revised by Grover Clark. New York: Garland, 1980. Originally published by Carnegie Endowment for Peace in 1932.

Saul, Norman. "An American's Siberian Dream." *Russian Review* 37, 4 (October 1978): 405–20.

Sbornik dokumentov otnosiashchikhsia k Kitaiskoi Vostochnoi zheleznoi doroge [Collection of documents related to the Chinese Eastern Railway]. Harbin: Tipografiia Kitaiskoi Vostochnoi zheleznoi dorogi, 1922.

Schimmelpenninck van der Oye, David. *Toward the Rising Sun: Russian Ideologies of Empire and the Part to War with Japan.* DeKalb: Northern Illinois University Press, 2001.

Semenov, Petr P. *Geograficheskо-statisticheskii slovar' Rossiiskoi Imperii,* vol. 1 [Geographic-statistical dictionary of the Russian Empire]. St. Petersburg: Tip. Bezobrazova, 1863.

Semenov-Tianshansky, Petr P. *Puteshestvie v Tianshan* [Journey to Tianshan] Moscow: Gosudarstvennoe isdatel'stvo geograficheskoi literatury, 1946.

Sergeev, O.I., S.I. Lazareva, and G.Ya. Trigub. *Mestnoe samoupravlenie na Dal'nem Vostoke Rossii vo vtoroi polovine XIX – nachale XX v.* [Local self-government in the Russian Far East from the late nineteenth to the early twentieth century]. Vladivostok: Dal'nauka, 2002.

Shan, Patrick Fuliang. *Taming China's Wilderness: Immigration, Settlement, and Shaping of the Heilongjiang Frontier, 1900–1931.* Burlington: Ashgate, 2014.

Shi Fang. *Heilongjiang quyu shehui shi yanjiu* [Research on social history of the Heilongjiang region]. Ha'erbin: Heilongjiang renmin chubanshe, 2002.

Shi Fang and Gao Ling. *Chuantong yu biange* [Tradition and change]. Ha'erbin: Heilongjiang renmin chubanshe, 1995.

Shi Fang, Liu Shuyang, and Gao Ling, eds. *Ha'erbin E-qiao shi* [History of the Russian emigrants in Harbin]. Ha'erbin: Heilongjiang renmin chubanshe, 2003.

Shi Yan and Sun Guangmei. "Zhongdong tielu guanliju de jigou shezhi jiqi xingzhi" [The establishment of the administrative divisions of the Chinese Eastern Railway]. *Beifang Weiwu* 1 (1997): 85–90.

Shirokogoroff, Sergei M. "What Is Shamanism?" *China Journal of Science and Arts* 3 (May 1924) and 4 (July 1924).

Shul'man, N.K., ed. *Amurskaia oblast'* [Amur Province]. Blagoveshchensk: Khabarovskoe knizhnoe izdatel'stvo, 1989.

Skachkov, P.E., and V.S. Myasnikov, eds. *Russko-Kitaiskie otnosheniia 1689–1916: Ofitsyal'nye dokumenty* [Russo-Chinese relations, 1689–1916: Official documents]. Moscow: Vostochnaia literatura, 1958.

Sladkovskii, Mikhail I. *Istoriia torgovo-ekonomicheskikh otnoshenii narodov Rossii s Kitaem* [The history of trade and economic relations between Russian and Chinese people]. Moscow: Nauka, 1974.

—. *The Long Road: Sino-Russian Economic Contacts from Ancient Times to 1917.* Moscow: Progress Publishers, 1981

Sliunin, N.V. *Sovremennoe polozhenie nashego Dal'nego Vostoka* [Current affairs of our Far East]. St. Petersburg: Tipografiia Ministerstva Finansov, 1908.

—. "Osnovnye cherty shamanizma nanaitsev i ultchei" [Main features of shamanism among the Nanai and the Ul'chi]. In *Antropologiia i istoricheskaia etnografiia Sibiri* [Anthropology and historical ethnography of Siberia], edited by V.A. Dremov, R.F. Its, and N.A. Tomilov, 141–48. Omsk: Omsk University, 1990.

Sokolov, N.A. "Pereselencheskoe dvizhenie v severnuiu Manchzhuriiu" [Settlement movement in Northern Manchuria]. *Vestnik Manchzhurii* 3 (1932): 55–60.

Soobshchenie Evropy s Dal'nim Vostokom [Europe's transport connection with the Far East]. Timetable: Winter 1912–13.

South Manchuria Railway Company, ed. *Man-Mō no taisei: Jinkō, kōchi oyobi nōsanbutsu yori mitaru* [General conditions of Manchuria: From the standpoint of population, arable land, and agricultural products]. Dalian: SMRC, 1919.

Spence, Jonathan. *In Search of Modern China.* New York: W.W. Norton, 1990.

Stakheev, Dmitrii I. *Za Baikalom i na Amure* [Beyond the Baikal Lake and along the Amur River]. St. Petersburg: Tip. K. Vul'fa, 1869.

Statisticheskie svedeniia o torgovle Rossii s Kitaem i po otdel'nym vostochno-aziatskim granitsam za 1901–1907 gg. [Statistical data about the trade between China and Russia and along selected East Asian borders from 1901 to 1907]. Moscow: Moskovskii birzhevyi komitet, circa 1908.

Starikov, G.F., and A.A. Stepanov. "Important Monument to Far Eastern Cartography." *Voprosy geografii Dal'nego Vostoka* 6 (1963): 292–300.

Steinberg, John H., Bruce W. Menning, David Schimmelpenninck van der Oye, David Wolff, and Shinji Yokote, eds. *The Russo-Japanese War in Global Perspective,* vol. 1. Leiden: Brill, 2005.

Stepanov, A.A. "Nekotorye voprosy istoprii Khabarovska" [Several questions about the history of Khabarovsk]. *Voprosy geografii Dal'nego Vostoka* 4 (1960): 328–50.

Stephan, John J. *The Russian Far East: A History.* Stanford: Stanford University Press, 1994.

—. "Sakhalin Island: Soviet Outpost in Northeast Asia." *Asian Survey* 10, 12 (1970): 1090–100.

Stolitsa, M.S. "Trudnye gody" [Difficult years], *Voennyi sbornik* 7 (July 1908): 69–88.

Studness, Charles M. "Economic Opportunity and Westward Migration of Canadians during the Late Nineteenth Century." *Canadian Journal of Economic and Political Science* 30, 4 (November 1964): 570–84.

Suleski, Ronald. *Civil Government in Warlord China: Tradition, Modernization, and Manchuria.* New York: Peter Lang, 2002.

—. *The Modernization of Manchuria: An Annotated Bibliography.* Hong Kong: Chinese University Press, 1995.

Sun Chunri. *Zhongguo chaoxianzu yimin shi* [The history of migration by China's ethnic Koreans]. Beijing: Zhonghua shuju, 2009.

Sunderland, Willard. *The Baron's Cloak: A History of the Russian Empire in War and Revolution.* Ithaca: Cornell University Press, 2014.

Tang, Peter S.H. *Russian and Soviet Policy in Manchuria and Outer Mongolia, 1911–1931.* Durham: Duke University Press, 1959.

Taskina, E.P. *Russkii Kharbin* [Russian Harbin]. Moscow: Moscow University, 1998.

Tong Dong. *Sha E yu Dongbei* [Tsarist Russia and the Northeast]. Changchun: Jilin wenhua chubanshe, 1985.

Tove, L.L., and D.V. Ivanov. *Otchet po statistiko-ekonomicheskomu i tekhnicheskomu issledovaniiu zolotopromyshlennosti Amurskogo-Primorskogo raiona* [The report on statistical, economic, and technical research about the gold mining industry in the Amur and Maritime regions], vol. 2, pt. 1: *Amurskaia oblast'*. St. Petersburg: Iakor', 1905.

Tsvetkov, Vasilii, ed. *General Diterikhs*. Moscow: Posev, 2004.

Turner, Frederick Jackson. *The Significance of the Frontier in American History*. New York: Henry Holt and Company, 1921.

Tuzhilin, A.V. *Sovremennyi Kitai* [Modern China]. St. Petersburg: Tipografiia imperatorskogo uchilishcha glukhonemykh, 1910.

Twitchett, Denis, and John K. Fairbank, eds. *The Cambridge History of China*, vol. 10: *Late Ch'ing, 1800–1911*, pt. 1. Cambridge: Cambridge University Press, 1978.

Ukhtomskii, E.E. *Puteshestivie gosudaria imperatora Nikolaia II na vostok (v 1890–1891)* [The tour of the Tsar Nicholas II to the East, 1890–1891]. Leipzig: F.A. Brokgauz, 1897.

Unterberger, Pavel F. *Priamurskii krai, 1906–1910* [Priamur Region, 1906–1910]. St. Petersburg: Tipografiia V.F. Kirshbauma, 1912.

Vavilov, S.I., ed. *Bol'shaia Sovetskaia entsiklopediia*, vol. 2 [The Great Soviet Encyclopedia, vol. 2]. Moscow: Bol'shaia Sovetskaia Entsiklopediia, 1950.

V., "Blagoveshchenskaia 'Utopiia'" [Blagoveshchensk "Utopia"] *Vestnik Evropy* 10 (1910): 231–41.

Van de Ven, Hans J. "Public Finance and the Rise of Warlordism." *Modern Asian Studies* 30, 4 (1996): 829–68.

Van Deusen, Kira. *The Flying Tiger: Women Shamans and Storytellers of the Amur*. Montreal and Kingston: McGill–Queen's University Press, 2001.

Vasilenko, N.A. "Kto stroil KVZhD: O chislennosti i natsyonal'nom sostave naseleniia KVZhD v 1897–1917" [Who built the CER: The size and national distribution of the population along the CER during 1897–1917]. *Rossiia i ATR* 2 (1995): 65–71.

Vasilevich, G.M. *Evenki: Istoriko-etnograficheskie ocherki (XVIII–nachalo XX vv.)* [The Evenks: Historical and ethnographic essays]. Leningrad: Nauka, 1969.

Vereshchagin, Alexander V. *Po Manchurii (1900–1901) Vospominaniia i rasskazy* [Across Manchuria (1900–1901) memoirs and short stories]. St. Petersburg: Sklad v knizhnykh magazinakh V.A. Berezovskogo, 1903.

Victoir, Laura, and Victor Zatsepine, eds. *Harbin to Hanoi: The Colonial Built Environment in Asia, 1840 to 1940*. Hong Kong: Hong Kong University Press, 2013.

Volnogorskii, P.R. *Velikii put'* [The great route]. Moscow: Izdanie Tikhomirova, 1904.

Voskresenskii, Aleksei D. *Diplomaticheskaia istoriia Russko-Kitaiskogo Sankt-Peterburgskogo dogovora 1881 g.* [Diplomatic history of the Sino-Russian St. Petersburg Treaty, 1881]. Moscow: Pamiatniki istoricheskoi mysli, 1995.

—. *Rossiia i Kitai: Teoriia i istoriia mezhgosudarstvennykh otnoshenii* [Russia and China: Theory and history of interstate relations]. Moscow: Moskovskii obshestvennyi nauchnyi fond, 1999.

Wang, Chin-Chun. "The Chinese Eastern Railway." *Annals of the American Academy of Political and Social Science* 122, 1 (November 1925): 57–69.

Wang, Gungwu. *The Chinese Overseas: From Earthbound China to the Quest for Autonomy*. Cambridge, MA: Harvard University Press, 2000.

Weber, David J. *The Mexican Frontier, 1821–1846: The American Southwest under Mexico*. Albuquerque: University of New Mexico Press, 1982.

Westwood, J.N. *Russia against Japan, 1905–1905*. New York: SUNY Press, 1986.

Witte, Sergei. *Vospominaniia* [Memoirs]. Berlin: Slovo, 1922.

Wolff, David. *To the Harbin Station: The Liberal Alternative in Russian Manchuria, 1898–1914*. Stanford: Stanford University Press, 1999.

Woodcock, George, and Ivan Avakumovic. *The Doukhobors*. Toronto: Oxford University Press, 1968.

Wu Lien-teh (G.L. Tuck) and Hulun Taotai. "First Report of the North Manchurian Plague Prevention Service." *Journal of Hygiene* 13, 3 (October 1913): 237–90.

Xin Peilin, Zhang Fengming, and Gao Xiaoyan, eds. *Heilongjiang kaifa shi* [Historical development of Heilongjiang Province]. Ha'erbin: Heilongjiang renmin chubanshe, 1999.

Xu Shichang. *Dongsansheng shenglue* [Brief administrative account of the Three Eastern Provinces]. 12 vols. Taipei: Weihai chubanshe, 1965. Originally published in 1911.

Xu Shuming. "Qing mo Jilin sheng Heilongjiang sheng de xinxing chengshi he gongshangye" [New towns and enterprises in Jilin and Heilongjiang provinces during the late Qing]. *Qingshi yanjiu* 8 (1997): 320–41.

Xue Xiantian. *Zhongdong tielu hulujun yu Dongbei bianjiang zhengju* [Chinese Eastern Railway patrol police and the political situation of the Northeastern borderland]. Beijing: Shehui kexue wenxian chubanshe, 1993.

Xue Xiantian and Zhou Xinmin, eds. *Zhong-E guanxi zhongwen wenxian mulu, 17–20 shiji* [Catalogue of Chinese documents on Sino-Russian relations, from the seventeenth to the twentieth century]. Chengdu: Sichuan renmin chubanshe, 2002.

Yakovlev, A.N. *Rossiya i SShA: Diplomaticheskie otnosheniia 1900–1917* [Russia and the United States: Diplomatic Relations, 1900–1917]. Moscow: Mezhdunarodnyi fond Demokratiia, 1999.

Yan Junguang. *Chaoxian zu* [The Korean nationality]. Beijing: Renmin chubanshe, 1996.

Yang Tianshi. *Cong dizhi zou xiang gonghe* [From monarchy to republic]. Beijing: Shehui kexueyuan wenxian chubanshe, 2002.

Yi Baozhong. "Lun Qingmo Dongbei diqu de shuitian kaifa" [Development of paddy fields in the Northeastern region in the late Qing dynasty]. *Jilin Daxue Shehui Kexue Xuebao* 1 (January 2002): 92–97.

Young, C. Walter. "Economic Factors in Manchurian Diplomacy." *Annals of the American Academy of Political and Social Science* 152 (November 1930): 293–307.

—. *The International Relations of Manchuria*. Chicago: University of Chicago Press, 1929.

Young, John. *The Research Activities of the South Manchuria Railway Company, 1907–1945: A History and Bibliography*. New York: East Asian Institute, Columbia University, 1966.

Young, Louise. *Japan's Total Empire: Manchuria and the Culture of Wartime Imperialism*. Berkeley: University of California Press, 1999.

Zagorul'ko, A.V. "Koreitsy na Rossiiskom Dal'nem Vostoke, 1863–1938 gg." [Koreans in the Russian Far East, 1863–1938]. In *Narody Sibiri* [People of Siberia], edited by Iu.B. Simchenko, 57–116. Moscow: Institut etnografii i antropologii im N.N. Miklukho-Maklaia, 1997.

Zatsepine, Victor. "An Uneasy Balancing Act: The Russian Émigré Community and Utopian Ideals of Manzhouguo." *Journal of Northeast Asian History* 10, 1 (Summer 2013): 131–53.

Zeng Pu. *Nie Hai Hua* [Flowers in the sea of sin]. Shanghai: Shanghai guji chubanshe, 1979. Originally published in 1905.

Zhang Fengming. *Zhongguo Dongbei yu Eguo (Sulian) jingji guanxi shi* [The history of economic relations between China's Northeast and Russia (Soviet Union)]. Beijing: Zhongguo shehui kexue chubanshe, 2003.

—. "19 shiji hou ban Heilongjiang diqu jinkuangye de xingqi he fazhan" [The rise and development of gold mining in Heilongjiang region during the late nineteenth century]. *Heilongjiang shehui kexue* 6 (2008): 140–42.

Zhang Zonghai. *Yuandong diqü shiji zhijiao de Zhong-E guanxi* [A century of change of Sino-Russian relations in the Far Eastern region]. Ha'erbin: Heilongjiang renmin chubanshe, 2000.

Zhao Songqiao. *Geography of China: Environment, Resources, Population, and Development.* New York: John Wiley and Sons, 1994.

Zhao Yuntian. "Qingmo bianjiang xinzheng yanjiu shuping" [Highlight study on the new policy towards borderlands in the late Qing dynasty] *Qingshi yanjiu* 3 (2002): 116–22.

Zhongguo gujin diming da cidian [Dictionary of China's ancient and modern place names]. Shanghai: Shouwu shuguan, 1933.

Zhongguo shehui kexueyuan jindai shi yanjiusuo [Institute of Modern History, Chinese Academy of Social Sciences], ed. *Sha E qin Hua shi* [History of the Tsarist Russia's aggression against China], 4 vols. Beijing: Renmin chubanshe, 1978–90.

Zhou Xifeng. "Jian shu Qingdai Nenjiang liuyu de Ewenke zu" [Brief account of the Ewenki people in the Nen River valley]. *Heilongjiang Minzu Congkan* 4 (2002): 77–81.

Zhu Daren. *Zhongguo dituce* [China atlas]. Beijing: Zhongguo ditu chubanshe, 2001.

Zolotarev, V.A., and I.A. Kozlov. *Russko-Iaponskaia voina, 1904–1905 gg. Bor'ba na more* [Russo-Japanese War, 1904–1905: Sea battles]. Moscow: Nauka, 1990.

Zolotarev, V.A., and Iu.F. Sokolov. *Tragediia na Dal'nem Vostoke* [The tragedy in the Far East], vol. 1. Moscow: Animi Fortitudo, 2004.

Index

Note: "(f)" after a page number indicates a figure; "(t)" after a page number indicates a table.

Contemporary Chinese Studies

Glen Peterson, *The Power of Words: Literacy and Revolution in South China, 1949-95*

Wing Chung Ng, *The Chinese in Vancouver, 1945-80: The Pursuit of Identity and Power*

Yijiang Ding, *Chinese Democracy after Tiananmen*

Diana Lary and Stephen MacKinnon, eds., *Scars of War: The Impact of Warfare on Modern China*

Eliza W.Y. Lee, ed., *Gender and Change in Hong Kong: Globalization, Postcolonialism, and Chinese Patriarchy*

Christopher A. Reed, *Gutenberg in Shanghai: Chinese Print Capitalism, 1876-1937*

James A. Flath, *The Cult of Happiness: Nianhua, Art, and History in Rural North China*

Erika E.S. Evasdottir, *Obedient Autonomy: Chinese Intellectuals and the Achievement of Orderly Life*

Hsiao-ting Lin, *Tibet and Nationalist China's Frontier: Intrigues and Ethnopolitics, 1928-49*

Xiaoping Cong, *Teachers' Schools and the Making of the Modern Chinese Nation-State, 1897-1937*

Diana Lary, ed., *The Chinese State at the Borders*

Norman Smith, *Resisting Manchukuo: Chinese Women Writers and the Japanese Occupation*

Hasan H. Karrar, *The New Silk Road Diplomacy: China's Central Asian Foreign Policy since the Cold War*

Richard King, ed., *Art in Turmoil: The Chinese Cultural Revolution, 1966-76*

Blaine R. Chiasson, *Administering the Colonizer: Manchuria's Russians under Chinese Rule, 1918-29*

Emily M. Hill, *Smokeless Sugar: The Death of a Provincial Bureaucrat and the Construction of China's National Economy*

Kimberley Ens Manning and Felix Wemheuer, eds., *Eating Bitterness: New Perspectives on China's Great Leap Forward and Famine*

Helen M. Schneider, *Keeping the Nation's House: Domestic Management and the Making of Modern China*

James A. Flath and Norman Smith, eds., *Beyond Suffering: Recounting War in Modern China*

Elizabeth R. VanderVen, *A School in Every Village: Educational Reform in a Northeast China County, 1904-31*

Norman Smith, *Intoxicating Manchuria: Alcohol, Opium, and Culture in China's Northeast*

Juan Wang, *Merry Laughter and Angry Curses: The Shanghai Tabloid Press, 1897-1911*

Richard King, *Milestones on a Golden Road: Writing for Chinese Socialism, 1945-80*

David Faure and Ho Ts'ui-P'ing, eds., *Chieftains into Ancestors: Imperial Expansion and Indigenous Society in Southwest China*

Yunxiang Gao, *Sporting Gender: Women Athletes and Celebrity-Making during China's National Crisis, 1931-45*

Peipei Qiu, with Su Zhiliang and Chen Lifei, *Chinese Comfort Women: Testimonies from Imperial Japan's Sex Slaves*

Julia Kuehn, Kam Louie, and David M. Pomfret, eds., *Diasporic Chineseness after the Rise of China: Communities and Cultural Production*

Bridie Andrews, *The Making of Modern Chinese Medicine, 1850-1960*

Kelvin E.Y. Low, *Remembering the Samsui Women: Migration and Social Memory in Singapore and China*

Jiayan Zhang, *Coping with Calamity: Environmental Change and Peasant Response in Central China, 1736-1949*

Alison R. Marshall, *Cultivating Connections: The Making of Chinese Prairie Canada*

Ruoyun Bai, *Staging Corruption: Chinese Television and Politics*

Christopher G. Rea and Nicolai Volland, *The Business of Culture: Cultural Entrepreneurs in China and Southeast Asia, 1900-65*

Eric Hyer, *The Pragmatic Dragon: China's Grand Strategy and Boundary Settlements*

Ning Wang, *Banished to the Great Northern Wilderness: Political Exile and Re-education in Mao's China*

Norman Smith, *Empire and Environment in the Making of Manchuria*